You Must Die Once

Gantsara: Alone across Mongolia

Robinson's fearless nature and gritty resolve to make the journey, even though the odds are stacked against him, make his book a compelling page-turner . . . *Gantsara* is an entertaining and revealing travel book about a country that is perhaps unfamiliar to most. It is certainly the best book I have read in this genre in recent years.

Nelson Mail

In an era when most travel writing is by journalists on junkets, with even the adventure laid on, an account of a true odyssey is a rare treat . . . Robinson takes the cake with his story of trail-blazing across Mongolia on horseback.

Air New Zealand

Wow. Now this is an adventure . . . It is a simple, straightforward, unpretentious account of an extraordinary journey . . .

New Zealand Herald

This is an outstanding documentary journey, beautifully written, I totally recommend it.

Hawkes Bay Today

YOU MUST DIE ONCE

TIBET, A JOURNEY TO THE CENTRE OF THE UNIVERSE

IAN D. ROBINSON

HarperCollins*Publishers*

A catalogue record for this book is available
from the National Library of New Zealand

First published 2006

HarperCollins*Publishers (New Zealand) Limited*
P.O. Box 1, Auckland

Copyright © Ian D. Robinson 2006

Ian D. Robinson asserts the moral right to be identified
as the author of this work.

ISBN 1 86950 546 8

Cover design by Stuart Horton-Stephens
Cover image: Ian Robinson with a resident monk,
on arrival at Seka Gompa.
Photographs by Ian D. Robinson
Typesetting by Springfield West

Printed by Griffin Press, Australia, on 79 gsm Bulky Paperback

Author's note: Some of the names of people mentioned in this book
have been changed to protect their identities.

On any great journey, so the Tibetans say, you must die once before you reach your destination.

Dedicated to the memory of
Khensur Thabkye Rinpoche.
Please return swiftly.

And for Y.M.
(Your Precious Self)

My deepest thanks to the people of Tibet.

The Journey

It may be long, I will keep going.

There may be danger, I will be brave.

There may be storms, I will find shelter.

There may be hunger, I will be given food.

There may be rivers, I will cross them.

There may be mountains, I will find a way through.

There may be those to stop me, I will elude them.

There may be great fear, I will ride with it.

There may be loneliness, I will think of you.

There will be a destination, I will reach it.

I will have a home, I will return to it.

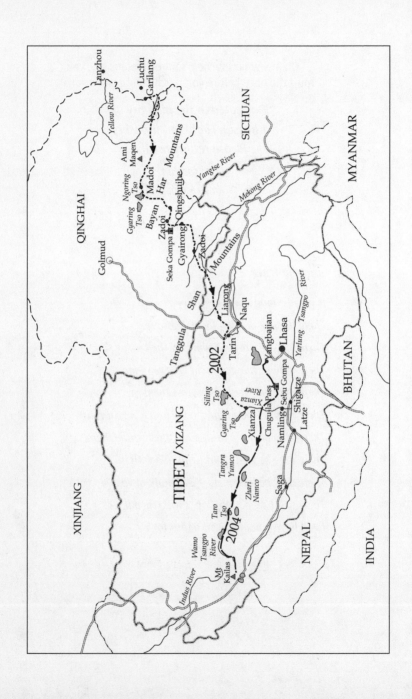

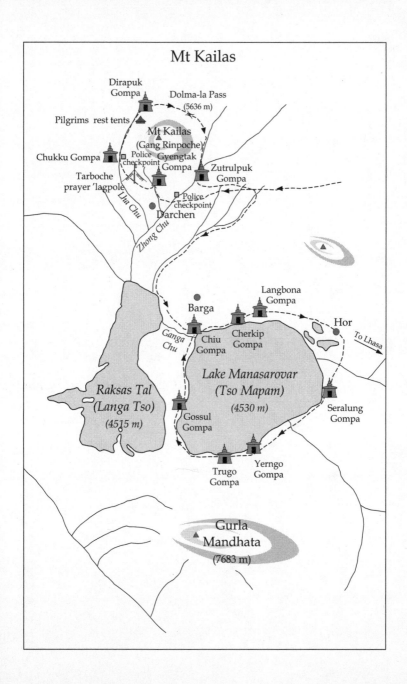

Part One

Chapter One

'No, Mr Robinson, you cannot choose between paying the fine and going to jail!'

'I'm just saying I don't mind, lock me up if you want.'

'If we do we must notify your embassy in Beijing, who will inform your government in New Zealand, who must then inform your family.'

I thought of my poor mother getting a call from someone in Foreign Affairs telling her I'd been thrown in a dungeon in darkest Tibet. I couldn't let that happen. 'You don't have to inform anyone, I don't mind.'

'But that is an agreement my country has with yours and . . .'

I couldn't be bothered listening as the Tibetan policeman reminded me of my crimes. I looked out the window and across a courtyard lined with white jeeps. All the buildings were modern and Chinese, but beyond the walls I could see multicoloured prayer flags fluttering under the eaves of traditional villas in the narrow streets of Lhasa.

Months before I'd watched similar flags flutter on the other side of the world. I'd sat in my car across from the house I'd rented with a girlfriend. For a few happy months we'd shared our lives and my bed, but it was too small to fit her, me and my self-centred ego. As my sense of self grew larger she was slowly pushed to the edge until one morning she left me. I still hadn't really gotten over her. I'd avoided driving past the house for two years, knowing I'd be reminded of how I'd thrown it all away.

That day, as I'd listened to our favourite song on my car stereo, I knew it was time to move on. She was now my past, and like a signpost the Tibetan prayer flags hanging in the porch were pointing me towards the future, towards Tibet, towards a journey that would take me longer to complete than I ever dreamed. A journey on which I hoped and prayed, I would die once.

As the bus pulled into the main street of Luchu, a tiny Tibetan town on the frontier with China, a young monk in crimson robes stared at me through the window. When the bus passed him he leapt up and chased it along the street and when it came to a halt he stood waving to me like a long-lost friend. I'd never seen him before, or the huge rough-looking Tibetan villager with him, but they'd been waiting for me for two days.

It was March, 2002 — I'd flown from Hong Kong to the Chinese city of Lanzhou, then taken a bus to Luchu. The monk, Jigme, and the villager,

Dhondup, were brothers. I'd taken Buddhist teachings from their lama uncle, Khensur Thabkye Rinpoche, at a Buddhist centre in New Zealand until his passing two years earlier. Through a friend we'd made shaky arrangements for them to help me get started on my journey. It was a great relief to find them; Jigme could speak a bit of English and Dhondup could help arrange anything I needed.

After bowls of *tukpa* (a meaty noodle soup) in a little Chinese restaurant, we checked into one room in a hotel. The next day we were picked up by a driver in a tiny van and taken through heavily falling snow to the village of Garilang, where Jigme was a monk at the small monastery. I stayed in Jigme's family home, a three-room Tibetan mud-brick house he shared with his ancient mother and even older aunt. I asked him how old the ladies were, but he wasn't sure — I couldn't guess, but they looked to be about two hundred and fifty years old. They were delightful, cackling at my attempts to speak the few words of Tibetan I knew, constantly preparing food for me and stoking up the stove fuelled with dry yak dung. Their faces were almost black and their wrinkles told of a hard life, their hands so rough from constant work I sometimes saw them pick up red-hot embers with their bare fingers.

That evening I sat with Dhondup and Jigme looking at my maps under a dim light bulb, talking about my plans. I had set myself what must have looked to them to be an impossible task. Now that I was actually in Tibet, with a freezing wind howling outside, I was beginning to realise the enormity of what I was going to attempt.

My goal was Kailas (Gang Rinpoche in Tibetan), a mountain in the far west near the Nepalese border. I planned to travel alone by horse more than three thousand kilometres across the Tibetan plateau. Spring was just beginning, though it was bitterly cold, with a constant wind. To reach Kailas I would have to cross some of the toughest terrain on the planet: mountain ranges, deserts, frozen wastes, from waterless places to some of Asia's largest lakes and rivers. I would have to deal with altitude — rarefied air at heights of over four thousand metres — severe cold, snowstorms and blizzards, lack of food, extreme isolation and loneliness, and the Chinese authorities.

Most of Tibet is closed to foreign travellers — visiting all but a few tourist spots is illegal without special permission and I knew that if I asked to ride alone across the vast wastes on the maps before me I would be refused. Instead, I worked on the principle that if you don't ask no one can say no. I'd have to avoid the police and if I was caught I'd have to accept whatever punishment they dealt me.

There was one thing in my favour: I'd done this kind of thing before. In 1992 I was one of the first individual tourists given a visa to Outer Mongolia, where I spent seven months, four of them riding alone across the steppe on Mongol ponies, covering nearly three thousand kilometres. I'd also been to Tibet in 1990, spending six weeks on the plateau as part of a six-month backpacking journey through China, Tibet, Nepal and India. I'd spent a week roaming the grasslands on horseback before hitchhiking to Lhasa and I'd been arrested for being in a 'closed' area after leaving the city but escaped with another traveller and made it to Kathmandu. If anyone knew what they were doing it was me, but Jigme and Dhondup looked at me and shook their heads.

'Why you don't go by jeep?' Jigme asked.

'I want to travel like a Tibetan in the old days.'

'But this is very difficult, very far, very cold, no one in my village ever been to Gang Rinpoche.'

'Yes, but difficult is better for me, like *ne-kor*, a pilgrimage.' He translated this to Dhondup, who ran his fingers over the map near Garilang.

'My brother says there is another mountain, not so far. This mountain very good for *ne-kor*. Why don't you go there? We can come with you.'

'No, I want to go to Gang Rinpoche and I must go alone.'

The Tibetans nodded gravely, sensing it was useless trying to dissuade me. 'Don't worry, Ian, *kali, kali*, slowly, slowly, we will help you.'

Mt Kailas, Gang Rinpoche, 'The Precious Snow' — to Tibetan Buddhists, Hindu, Jains and Asian Shamans alike — is the home of the gods, the centre of the universe, the most sacred place in the cosmos. In Tibetan Lamaist mythology it's where the great Tantric yogi Milarepa defeated the masters of Bon, a pre-Buddhist shamanist religion, to secure the place of Buddhism in Tibet. One circuit of the mountain is said to wash away the sins of a lifetime, while a hundred and eight circuits ensure rebirth in Nirvana.

To early European explorers and geographers it held the secrets of the source of four of Asia's greatest rivers; the Indus, Karnali, Brahmaputra and Sutlej all spring from the mountain's slopes. Two of the world's highest lakes, Manasarovar and Raksas Tal, lie below the peak and are also holy places of pilgrimage. The region is one of the world's most remote. Few Tibetans make the arduous journey; even these days it's considered distant in the extreme, and to a Westerner must seem like the end of the earth.

But this is where I'd decided to go, hoping the journey would be more than a physical one. I prayed I would find clearer the Buddhist path on which I'd recently taken my first faltering, somewhat sceptical and unsteady step. I hoped I would be able to leave part of me behind in the frozen wastes — the part of myself I didn't like, the self-centred, selfish, lying, cheating, clinging me. As Jigme's uncle had skilfully tried to show me, this was the source of my unhappiness. This part of me was to blame for everything that was wrong in my life; it was because of this aspect of myself that I'd lost the best girl I'd ever known, and the reason I couldn't be content with another. If I could leave this part behind — lose him, outride him, banish him — I could find some peace.

Late in the evening after Dhondup left I stood in the courtyard peeing against the wall. The moon, not even half-full, was as bright as a full moon at home. I looked up and felt the first pangs of homesickness. It had been a while since I'd been on the road and I knew I'd be happy to go home when this trip was over, when the wanderlust in me had hopefully burnt out, but I felt I had to pay my dues. To have a home is a privilege and I wanted to earn the right to make one.

I enjoyed a few days with Jigme and Dhondup, with most of the time spent going from one house to the next. I was treated as an honoured guest — large meals were laid out and my bowl and teacup constantly topped up. I received a stream of visitors in traditional long cloaks or *chuba*, lined with lambskin and often trimmed with leopard fur, the women clinking with great lumps of amber, turquoise and coral in their hair or around their necks. Sometimes I was offered *khata*, a ceremonial white silk scarf they would lay across both hands and drape around my neck as a blessing and a sign of respect. I always felt humbled to receive this simple gift, promising to leave the scarves at Gang Rinpoche as an offering on behalf of those who had given them.

Usually in the late afternoon Jigme would say: 'Ian, let's go to meander!' He'd learnt to speak English in India, when he'd made the long, dangerous journey through the Himalayas to slip over the border. When he returned, after spending time in the monasteries re-established by the Tibetan refugee communities, he'd been arrested and spent several months in a Chinese prison.

This was my favourite part of the day, walking in silence in the hills. The wind was freezing and we could see snow-covered hills stretching away to the west. We would circ-ambulate the local temple, joined by villagers with *mala* (Buddhist rosaries) in their hands. When they saw me they would stop to ask Jigme who I was and what I was doing. When he told them, they wished me luck but shook their heads in astonishment. 'They say you are great, going to Gang Rinpoche by horse!' Jigme told me, but I wondered if 'great' was a polite translation of stupid, crazy or foolish. It would be a lifelong dream for these devout Buddhists to make the pilgrimage, but it was too far, too difficult and too expensive. I resolved to make my journey on their behalf, carrying their prayers and wishes, and if I made it to the mountain I would dedicate the merit to all those who rode with me in spirit.

At times either Jigme or Dhondup would disappear on Dhondup's motorbike, asking about horses, and one evening Jigme came back very late to say he'd found someone with two to sell. He told me the horses were of medium quality, both he and Dhondup warning that very good horses would make me a target for thieves.

In the morning I said goodbye to the old women, who pressed their hands together in prayer for my safety and success. The minivan arrived and we set off through the hills. On the way we stopped at Garser Monastery, which had been Khensur Thabkye Rinpoche's home before he'd fled to India following the Chinese invasion. There, refugee monks re-established the great monastic universities of Tibet and kept alive the dharma, the teachings of Buddha and the great Indian and Tibetan masters who followed him. When he fled on foot through the mountains with a group of monks he carried a heavy Buddhist text instead of food and clothing. When the other monks criticised his choice he replied: 'Without the dharma, even if we survive, we have nothing.'

Khensur Thabkye Rinpoche was one of twelve children, nine of whom died in infancy. As the first-born son he was expected to care for his parents in their old age; however, from the time he was young he wanted to join a monastery. His father refused, but one night the boy stole a horse and rode to the local temple and his parents gave in and let him take the crimson robes of a monk. When the Chinese invaded, dozens of his family were killed, thirty-seven in a single day when the Red Army attacked their nomad camp.

He became abbot of his monastery in India. *Rinpoche* means *precious* and he had been a precious teacher, some say a *living Buddha* or *enlightened one* — he had touched my life, as he had many others, and changed it for the better.

He lived in New Zealand for twelve years and founded his own centre, where I'd met him. On my first visit to Tibet I'd taken an interest in the Tibetan faith. Not too seriously, though, spending more time in bars than listening to teachings, and more energy in the pursuit of women than in transforming my mind. Despite Rinpoche's efforts I'd constantly turned away from the teachings, running back to what I knew best — drink and sex — to find happiness, when I knew those things only led me into more frustration and despair. Like a man who's sick but refuses medicine prescribed to him by the best doctor, I drank poison instead.

Rinpoche passed away in 1999 on a visit to Tibet — he had been reunited with family, visited his old monastery and met his own teachers, and then departed this life for the next. I'd been shocked by his death; for some reason I'd taken it for granted he'd always be waiting in the Buddhist centre whenever I bothered to turn up. Suddenly he was gone and that illusion of permanence was shattered — even in death he was teaching me. Before I left New Zealand I'd been given a few grams of his ashes — if I reached the holy mountain I would sprinkle them at sacred sites. It sounded very romantic, carrying the ashes of a great lama across the barren wastes to a heavenly peak on a legendary epic, but as I was soon to find out the reality would be no fairy tale.

By afternoon we were back in Luchu. We spent the rest of the day jostling with villagers and sheepskin-clad nomads in the market. Dhondup found some gear for the horses — a saddle and a wooden packsaddle, bridles, hobbles and ropes. I'd brought my own canvas saddlebags and in the market I bought a long Tibetan knife and a *chuba*. In the evening I sorted my gear, trying to convince Dhondup and Jigme that I knew what I was doing. They were still deeply concerned: about the weather (it was snowing again), about the Chinese police, about thieves, about the horses, about my lack of Tibetan. Dhondup even turned up with fifty packets of instant noodles!

After dinner I wrote some last letters as Jigme turned on the TV, flicking through broadcasts from China, propaganda movies and stupid game shows. During the commercial breaks there were ads for cosmetics and underwear; perfect Chinese girls moistened their soft lips and flitted across the screen in push-up bras. I looked out into the gloom of the filthy street, pigs grunting through garbage in the gutters. *What am I doing? I could be in Hong Kong drinking a martini in a bar with a girl just like that!* As Jigme stared at the winking girl on the screen, I wondered what was going on in his monk's mind. Did he see her appearance as an illusion? Did he see beneath her perfectly smooth skin to the flesh and blood beneath? Did this cure him of any attachment? Or was he like me, slipping her sweet dark eyes back into her pretty head, her seductive lips back where they're meant to be, her warm tongue in her cute little mouth. *Oh God, it's hard to let go!*

I didn't sleep well. The hotel halls were noisy with truck drivers yelling at each other and I couldn't stop thinking of the journey. Part of me couldn't wait to feel the rawhide reins in my hands, but the other part knew this was going to be tough.

The taxi van arrived at nine thirty and we headed southwest through the hills and across grasslands. After about fifty kilometres we stopped in the middle of nowhere at the top of a low pass where a young Tibetan waited with two horses. The horses were black geldings, quiet, in reasonable condition and good enough to get me started — my first Tibetan ponies. I would ride the better of the two and use the other as a packhorse to carry my saddlebags, two sacks of straw and half a sack of grain, which Dhondup insisted I take as there wouldn't be enough grazing for the horses. I didn't like the idea of such an unwieldy load but there wasn't much grass about yet. I gave Dhondup six thousand Chinese yuan to cover the horses, all the riding gear, the cost of the minivan, and a bit extra for all their trouble.

I was ready. I put on the *chuba*, the great heavy cloak difficult to wear, with the hem almost reaching the ground and long sleeves down to my knees. Dhondup and Jigme presented me with *khata* and I gave Jigme my backpack. I'd had it for fifteen years and it had taken me round the world. I couldn't take it with me, but I was attached to it like an old friend. I suddenly thought I could get him to post it back home for me. *Let it go, Ian!*

It was time to go. *'Tujachay Jigme, tujachay Dhondup.* Thank you so much for helping me.'

'Oh Ian, you are welcome, please be careful, I wish you will be happy; Gang Rinpoche is very far, but every day I will pray for you to go safely. *Kali, kali*, go slowly, and go well.'

We shook hands and I climbed into the saddle, suddenly remembering I'd hardly been on a horse since Mongolia, ten years before. Jigme reached into the folds of his robes and took out a pile of paper 'wind horses', prayers printed on thin pieces of coloured paper. He threw them into the air, *'Lah so so so so so so!* Good luck, Ian! Good luck!'

The papers swirled above my head and were whipped away, the unseen element of the wind activating the prayers and blessing me and my horses. I waved goodbye and turned the horses west, towards the Tibetan plateau, towards adventure, towards the greatest challenge of my life, towards the sacred mountain — Gang Rinpoche.

Chapter Two

I set off slowly down the pass into a wide valley. It wasn't long before I had to stop and fix the packsaddle, which started to slip, weighed down by the sack of grain. We travelled on a wide 'road' made of dozens of animal tracks that eventually followed a small river. The rest of the grassland was fenced. When I'd ridden here in 1990 fences were almost unheard of, the entire grassland open all the way to Lhasa. In an effort to control the semi-nomadic Tibetans and prevent squabbles over grazing, the Chinese authorities had allocated set pastures to each family. It was like taming the Wild West.

By three in the afternoon I reached the other side of the valley. Looking back I could almost see where I'd said goodbye to Jigme and Dhondup, but decided I'd gone far enough for day one anyway and stopped below some hills. I unloaded the horses and set them out to graze, tethering them on long ropes with short iron stakes and placing hobbles on their ankles. I filled their nosebags with grain and gave them a handful of straw. With difficulty I set up my lightweight hiker's tent and scavenged wood for a fire. There was no significant vegetation in the valley but I found a few sticks at an old nomad campsite, split them with my knife and soon had a small fire. I had no appetite — with all the heavy meals I'd eaten in the last few days I was glad to give my stomach a rest.

With darkness snow began to fall and I crawled inside the tent and unrolled my sleeping bag. In the day's last gloom I wrote my diary and recited a short prayer, taking refuge in the Buddhas and their teachings, asking them to protect all living beings, to guide us from suffering and lead us to happiness. The snow was getting heavier, large flakes shishing down the sides of the fly and collecting at the bottom. At the end of the prayer I added: *Please let me still be in possession of two live horses tomorrow!*

I slid into the down bag, spread the *chuba* over it as an extra blanket and pulled the hood over my head.

By morning the tent was half-buried. When I unzipped the door a bank of snow fell inside and I had to dig my way out. It was a baptism of ice — a tough way to start the trip. To my relief the horses were still there, grazing under blankets of frozen snow. I pulled on my boots and crawled outside. Low cloud hung in the valley; it was completely white, still and silent except for the gasp of my breath in the cold. I felt awful, nauseous and exhausted as I started to pack my gear. Altitude sickness. Every action took enormous effort — walking across to get the horses drained me, it took over an hour to pack up and load the horses, and by the time I heaved the sack of grain into place I was completely shattered.

An old Tibetan and his son wandered over and offered me tea at their home a few hundred yards away. Nothing sounded more inviting and we trudged through the snow leading the horses. Inside their simple mud-brick home I sat by the fire and was given bowls of Chinese tea. They served me lumps of bread but I could hardly eat, the thought of food making me feel sick. I could barely spare the effort to talk and sat there gasping for breath as if I'd just run a marathon. The Tibetans exchanged worried glances.

'*Kan an dro?*' the old man asked, where are you going?

'Gang Rinpoche, I'm doing *ne-kor*, a pilgrimage,' I told him. '*Nga nang-pa yin.*' I'm Buddhist, I added and held up my *mala*.

'Gang Rinpoche! *Shay-ta ta-ringpo!*' It's very far, he told me.

'*Rey, hako.*' Yes, I know.

After a few minutes I got up to leave. '*Ma rey, ma rey.*' No, no, he said and gestured for me to stay put. It was tempting to spend the day sitting by the fire drinking tea, but I had to get moving. I would have to learn to cope with the snow, the cold and the thin air. There was no way I could avoid them and hiding by the fire every time it snowed wasn't going to get me far.

I set off into the hills and found that, despite the deep snow, the horses went well, walking strongly. I rode high up a steep, wide slope, the trail hidden beneath the snow, but it was as if my horses knew the way. At the top of the pass I got off and walked them through the hills, the weather swinging from cold falling snow one minute to warm sunshine the next. Walking warmed me up, but it was a struggle to keep going with the bulky *chuba* weighing me down. In the afternoon the hills fell behind and the trail met up with a vehicle track we followed for the rest of the day.

In the early evening I found a family in the next valley. As I rode up barking dogs brought a young man, his wife and their small boy out to greet me. I was taken inside to meet an ancient grandmother and a tiny baby, and given tea by the fire. The family stared at me with bewildered grins. They'd probably never been face to face with a Westerner and I tried to communicate but my Tibetan was hopeless and my Chinese even worse. I was prepared for this and I took out some photos from home. Pictures of my family, which I could describe to them: '*Ama, phapa, bingya bu, bingya bumo.*' This is my mother, my father, brothers, sister, etc. They crowded round the tiny album.

'*Nyu Ziyland.*' I showed them a photo of myself standing up to my knees in water at the beach in New Zealand. These people had never seen the sea and probably thought it was a large lake or river. '*Gyam-tsho,*' I told them, this is

18

the sea. I also had a small world map laminated in plastic. On it I had circled the Tibetan plateau. '*Po*,' I said and pointed to the region, then pointed to the fascinated family, this is where you're from. They nodded.

I pointed to mainland China, '*Gyanak*.' Then India. '*Gyagar*. The Dalai Lama's here.'

'Aa! Dalai Lama! Gyelwa Rinpoche!' I pointed to the two small islands at the bottom of the world. '*Nyu Ziyland*.' And tracing my finger around the coast I repeated, '*Gyam-tsho*.' It's in the sea, it's an island.

They would probably never really comprehend where my home was and how far I was from it but despite the impossible differences between my world and theirs they could relate to the photos. I had a family somewhere, a mother far away and probably missing me. I also had a photo of Khensur Thabkye Rinpoche. When they came to his picture, although they would never have heard of him, the man removed his hat and touched the photo to the top of his head as a blessing, then passed it round the rest of the family, even touching it to the baby's forehead.

I put my horses out for the night on the hillside. There was little grass but I gave them nosebags and fed out more of the straw. Back inside I was given a place to sleep next to the tin stove. They offered me bread but I couldn't touch it; I'd hardly eaten all day and still felt nauseous. I unrolled my sleeping bag, said my prayers and crawled inside. It was only the second day of the ride and I could already feel it was a very long way to Gang Rinpoche.

The next morning was beautiful, clear skies sparkled sunlight on the snow as I brought the horses in and loaded them up. I still didn't feel like eating, but the old grandmother gave me a bowl of delicious warm goat's milk. I set off down the valley following a stream that led into a larger valley with a stony road. The valley was quiet and empty but a sudden speck of movement told me I wasn't alone. I looked up to see a large grey wolf moving up the slope. I watched it for a few minutes — it had seen me and would stop and look back every few metres, but didn't seem too bothered. The silent apparition stopped at the top of the ridge and looked at me one more time before it vanished.

As the day wore on the road became busier; occasionally heavy trucks roared past, spooking the horses. A couple of jeeps went by; I was nervous knowing they could be driven by Chinese police. However, no one seemed to take much notice of a lone rider. I'd tied a bandana around my face and pulled the wide collar of the *chuba* up as far as I could, hoping to blend in.

I carried on into the afternoon as the valley opened into a small plain. There was no one living this far up but as I neared the top a Chinese man came running across from the road, shouting and waving a small flag. I had no idea who he was or what he wanted but I stopped the horses and he babbled something to me and pointed up the road. I felt the shockwave before I heard the blast. BOOM! He was part of a road construction team and was trying to warn me they were using dynamite to clear rocks. After that I crossed to the other side of the plain and rode higher on an animal trail. I heard the blasts behind me all afternoon; it sounded as if they were trying to blow up the whole mountain.

I met the road again as it neared the top of the valley. A telegraph wire ran alongside, just two wires on slender poles; hung on the poles at regular intervals were signs warning the locals what would happen if they interfered with the wires. One sign had a picture of a man dressed in a *chuba* rolling up a coil of stolen wire. Behind him was a Chinese policeman with his foot raised about to kick the thief with a heavy boot. Another showed a Tibetan taking pot-shots at small birds perched on the wire, something they would never do — because of their Buddhist beliefs hunting isn't common and they certainly wouldn't bother shooting anything too small to eat. This time the policeman had drawn his pistol and was about to shoot the hapless offender. Harsh punishment for damaging a piece of wire.

The afternoon turned cold, the skies clouded over and snow fell in light flurries, as a freezing wind blew up the valley. Late in the afternoon we reached the pass marked with a large pile of stones known as a *lhabtsi;* in the centre was a post with ropes running off it which were hung with hundreds of prayer flags. The small cotton sheets with prayers printed on them were whipped back and forth by the wind and looked like old washing, but every time they snapped in the breeze the prayers they held were released across the land, blessing it. Wind horses covered the ground.

I sat on the top of the pass for a while as the horses rested and grazed. The view looking west was immense, a vast open valley spread out before me. In its centre flowed the Yellow River, one of China's greatest waterways, and not far below in the distance I could see a jumble of buildings that marked the tiny town of Maqu. I took out my map, an American military aerial navigation chart, and checked my compass. Both the river and the town were marked so I could tell exactly where I was.

By evening I'd reached the valley floor and stopped on the open grassland for the night. There was reasonable grass for the horses and I put my tent up in the wind that howled across the plain. The effort blew away my last ounce of energy. Just as it got dark I crawled inside my sleeping bag.

I felt much better in the morning; the valley was lower than the area I'd ridden through in the past two days and the air must have been slightly thicker. I set off towards the river, giving Maqu a wide berth. I was nervous about the authorities.

In the afternoon I came to a house near the river and was greeted by a pack of ten dogs. Tibetan mastiffs are vicious and I was always happy to be mounted when I approached a house. If they weren't tied up they'd come tearing out and attack the horses, trying to bite their flanks and taking chunks of hair out of their tails. I had to wait for the family to chase the dogs off before daring to climb out of the saddle.

'*Demo,*' I said, using a local Amdo greeting. There was no response from the old man. '*Demo,*' I tried again. '*Nga nang-pa yin,*' I'm a Buddhist, hoping to break the ice.

'Aa?'

'*Nang-pa yin*, I'm doing *ne-kor.*'

We stood there staring at each other. I was hoping to be invited in and given tea, but it seemed I was going to have to ask. 'Have you got any *cha*?' I held an invisible bowl up to my mouth.

'Aa! *Cha tung, cha tung*!' Drink tea, drink tea, he understood and I was ushered inside.

The family's mud-brick home consisted of two rooms in a dirt yard with an entrance passage separating them in the middle. The room on the right was a storeroom filled with sacks of grain, farm implements and tools; to the left, behind a heavy curtain greasy with fat, was the main room where the family lived. The floor was hard-packed earth, and in the centre was a tin stove with a pipe going through the ceiling. There was a raised sleeping platform on one side and a couple of old chairs. On a high shelf was a small altar with a couple of butter lamps, a simple image of Buddha and an old photo of the Dalai Lama.

I sat on the edge of the sleeping platform as the old man's wife handed me a bowl of Chinese tea. I blew the leaves floating on the top to the opposite side of the bowl and drank; it was good to taste something hot for the first time in nearly two days. I showed the old man my photos and gave him the commentary that went with it, but then my Tibetan language skills pretty much ran out. My host was curious as to who I was and what I was doing, but I couldn't understand most of his questions.

'*Tsampa sa*?' he asked, do you want to eat *tsampa*?

Tibet wouldn't be Tibet without *tsampa*, or roasted barley flour. This basic dish is the staple diet and I was to become very, very familiar with it in the weeks to come. At times I would go for days and not eat anything else. Barley grain is roasted in a pan filled with black sand. First the sand is heated on the fire and then the grain is mixed with it until it roasts. The sand is sifted off and the grain ground into flour — *tsampa*. The old man placed an ancient wooden box beside me; inside it was divided into two compartments, one containing *tsampa* and the other holding *chura*, crumbled lumps of dry cheese. I served the *tsampa* into my bowl with a large spoon and then added a small amount of *chura*, and the old woman added a dob of butter she scraped from a great lump sitting on the floor wrapped in a bag made from a yak hide. The butter was very 'ripe' and had probably been made the previous summer. She poured a little more tea in my bowl and I let the butter melt.

Now came the tricky part. Using my hand I had to mix the *tsampa* into a ball-like dough. However, the bowl was small and the Tibetans, to be generous and hospitable, always fill the bowl to the brim. To me it seemed to defy the laws of physics how anyone could mix *tsampa* without spilling half the flour over the side. To the Tibetans it's as easy as using a knife and fork; in a few moments they would have a moist ball of dough in their hand and a perfectly clean bowl. However, they'd mastered the technique over a lifetime and I hadn't — soon the floor around me was dotted with bits of *tsampa*, my hands were covered in a gooey mess and later I found lumps of the stuff up the sleeves of my *chuba*. It was rather embarrassing until the old man handed me an aluminium spoon. I stirred the mess into something like dry porridge and ate it as it was, not very appetising but welcome all the same.

I set off again and by mid-afternoon I'd reached the river. A great muddy brown flow between high walls, the river wound its way from Tibet across China to the sea. The area was very dry and sandy; huge dunes had been blown up in places and the wind howled across the plain, sending occasional clouds of dust skywards in its wake. I led the nervous horses across the river on a long bridge, then carried on down the other side, heading northwest. In the evening I camped alone above the river in a lovely spot where nomads would camp after the rains brought the dry brown grass back to life. I found a few sticks and managed to make a small fire.

My camp had been spotted and I was soon visited by five Tibetans mounted on yaks, an advance party bringing their animals to the river flats to graze before the main summer camp arrived in a few weeks. Yaks are wonderful beasts and as much part of the landscape of Tibet as the mountains and rivers. With their massive curved horns, the great shaggy creatures remind me of American buffalo; they don't moo like cows but constantly grunt to each other as they graze. The Tibetan *drokpa*, or herdsmen, rely on them for milk, meat and their woolly hair, which can be clipped and woven into ropes and heavy cloth to make tents.

They can also be ridden. The five men galloped into my camp on their black yaks saddled like horses — the animals are powerful and difficult to control even with a wooden ring through the nose — and wheeled about for several minutes until the animals calmed down enough for them to jump to the ground. The men all wore sheepskin *chubas* and had long knives stuck in sashes around their waists like the bandits and brigands of not so long ago. They looked wild and rough, with shaggy hair like their yaks. The eldest, who seemed to be their leader, strode up to me, removing his hat and extending his hand, his wide grin showing teeth capped with gold. The others lined up to copy him and after the handshaking ceremony we sat down by my tiny fire.

Again I took out my photos, followed by the map, then showed them my compass. They were fascinated by everything I had, examining my tent as if it had come from outer space, feeling the nylon fabric in their fingers, trying to work out how it went up. Then they wanted to see my camera and binoculars, my pocket knife, water bottle, sleeping bag, flashlight, cooking pot, watch, hat and on it went, as if I was a travelling museum filled with intriguing exhibits. The men were polite and never asked me to give them anything and usually looked without touching, so I wasn't worried about theft, but being under the microscope became tiring. They would probably have been happy to sit there all night, but I'd had enough. It was getting dark, the wind had finally died and evening was the perfect time to stare into the embers of the fire and relax.

As politely as I could I explained I was going to finish my tea and go to sleep and I gestured that perhaps it was time for them to leave. We shook hands and they wished me a safe journey before leaping back onto their yaks. They lined up for me to take a photo then turned their beasts towards their camp and galloped off in a thunder of hooves, singing at the tops of their lungs.

I poured myself a last mug of strong black tea from my little cooking pot; there was just enough hot water left to wash my hands. I hadn't really washed them since I'd set out from Luchu; it felt so good to soak my fingers in the warm soapy water and I realised what a simple luxury hot water is, something I'd always taken for granted. The sky was clear and a billion stars shone, so bright and vivid they almost looked unreal, but with the sun gone it was freezing and at nine o'clock I crawled into my sleeping bag and wrote my diary. It was Saturday night and I was already in bed. I wondered what was happening in Hong Kong and Shanghai.

The next day I carried on downriver, riding all day and only taking a couple of short breaks. I estimated I was travelling about twenty-five to thirty kilometres each day. By this time I was getting used to long hours in the saddle; my back, bum and legs would still ache, but occasionally I would get off and walk, leading the horses. The horses were quiet and well behaved, but they were starting to tire and I was hoping to find a place to take a day off and rest them.

That night I stayed with a family at the base of some hills. Finally I had my appetite back and I was starving, having hardly eaten anything since I'd left Luchu, five days earlier. Luckily I was offered more than *tsampa*. A young daughter kneaded white flour into dough and rolled it out on a board before cutting it into wide noodles. She took down a dried leg of mutton hanging from the ceiling and cut off lumps into a large pan of boiling water. Taking some china bowls from a shelf she wiped them 'clean' with a greasy rag. She then 'washed' several pairs of chopsticks by throwing them on the wooden floor, filthy from everyone's boots after they'd walked through the cattle yards outside, and poured hot water on them. In all the Tibetan houses I visited everything was filthy, the people were filthy, their clothes were filthy, their hands were filthy, the eating utensils were dirty — everything was covered in grease from butter and fatty meat. They made an attempt to be clean and occasionally I saw them wash their hands. Their homes were tidy, the dirt floors were swept and things put away neatly, but there was never a time when anything was actually what I'd call clean.

For a moment I worried about hygiene but realised it was pointless; I was becoming filthy too, and if I refused food unless it was served in perfectly clean bowls I'd starve to death. Besides, tonight I was so hungry my stomach was crying out for anything, hygienic or not. I was given two steaming bowls of meaty *tukpa*, which I gobbled down, much to the amusement of the family. I could feel the nutrition from the food flowing into my body like a drug.

The next day I was given another bowl of *tukpa* before setting off. I was told there was a *gompa*, or monastery, in the next valley, so I made a slight detour and rode through a small village watched by curious locals. I tied my horses in a tiny dirt yard and walked up to the main temple, a huge and imposing structure of high whitewashed stone walls topped with ochre parapets. Immense pillars made from whole trees supported a great balcony at the entrance where magnificent red medieval doors were propped open and a huge heavy curtain hung in the doorway.

A couple of junior monks in crimson robes stared at me as I stood outside. I took off my hat and gestured to them, asking if it was all right to go inside. They looked at each other uncertainly and nodded, open-mouthed and wide-eyed. I made prostrations on the floor in front of the curtain, touching my hands, knees and forehead to the floor three times. The monks seemed surprised to see I looked as if I knew what I was doing, although my appearance was completely alien. I pulled off my boots and left them by the door along with hundreds of others. One of the monks pulled the curtain aside and I stepped over the threshold.

Morning prayers were in progress and the eyes of two hundred monks and lamas turned to look at me. They didn't stop their low guttural chanting and the air inside the dark temple was electric. The hairs on my arms and the back of my neck stood up and I almost felt afraid, not really knowing if I should be there. I bowed deeply to an elderly lama, probably the abbot, who was seated on a high throne at the back of the great room, who didn't move or acknowledge he had seen me.

I crept further inside, moving around the temple clockwise behind the monks seated on low benches. The walls were lined with gilt statues of Buddhas, gods, saints and demon protectors. I touched my forehead to the base of each one to receive their blessing and also to try to look respectful and humble. At the rear of the room was a figure of Buddha Shakyamuni, some ten metres high; his half-closed compassionate eyes looked down and he smiled, reassuring me. I continued on past cabinets reaching from the floor to ceiling, filled with thousands of small images and sacred texts wrapped in colourful cloth. Back at the door I turned and bowed to the abbot again; this time he smiled and nodded. I looked round at all the monks and two hundred faces burst into friendly grins. Suddenly I was outside in the bright sunlight, my mind buzzing, the electricity created by the monks' chanting still with me. I felt stunned, as if what I'd just seen had been a dream. I walked back through the village towards my horses. The prayers must have ended and dozens of young monks burst out of the temple, eager to get a closer look at the stranger. They raced down the alleys and I was carried along in a flow of laughing, shouting crimson.

That night I stayed in the home of an old couple; however, there were no bowls of *tukpa*. The people were poor and seemed to have nothing to spare. I was given mouldy bread and bowls of tea so weak I'm sure it was just hot water. In the morning I carried on up the valley, still following the Yellow River. The plain seemed to go on for ever, the horses were tired and progress so slow it felt as if we weren't moving. The skies clouded over and the wind screamed. I pulled the *chuba* up around my face and hunched over the saddle in a hopeless attempt to keep warm. I hadn't eaten anything substantial since the day before and the lack of food doubled the effect of the cold. Late in the afternoon I found a family living in a kind of half-tent, half-house. I tied the horses outside and went inside, where I was given tea. I was exhausted, cold and hungry, but when I asked if I could stay the night the father shrugged and looked away. When I asked again he shook his head and bluntly said, '*Ma rey.*'

I stood up and left, but was too tired to go far, riding another kilometre and camping at the first decent spot I could find. There was little grass for my poor horses and I'd run out of grain. I went hungry; there was no way I could light a fire in the wind and besides there was nothing to burn.

It was a freezing night and I hardly slept; breakfast was a mouthful of cold water. It was the eighth day without a break and I was desperate to find somewhere to take a day off. I stopped at a little house at about midday and was met by two nice women and a little old man, who gave me tea and *tsampa*. I was grateful, but my body was crying out for protein. I'm not a great meat eater but it was all I could think of then. In the corner of the single room the family had a little shrine to the Buddhas and local deities. Before leaving New Zealand I had copied dozens of Dalai Lama photos. In Tibet it was illegal to have more than one photo of His Holiness, and I could be done for 'supply', but there was no baggage search coming over the border from Hong Kong. I slipped one from between the pages of my notebook and handed it to one of the women.

'Aa! Gyelwa Rinpoche!' they exclaimed, touching the photo to the tops of their heads and then handing it back, thinking I had just given them the picture to look at. When I indicated they could keep it they were overcome. Both women burst into tears. I was moved — it had cost me nothing to give them this simple gift but it meant so much to them and brought them such happiness. I was tired, hungry and cold. Tibet was proving to be a brutal and unforgiving land, yet I was suddenly faced with such warmth and gratitude, some of the tension I'd been carrying inside me snapped. I put my head in my hands as I realised how incredibly fortunate I was to be there.

Tenzin Gyatso, the 14th Dalai Lama, fled the Chinese invasion of Tibet in 1959 and has lived in exile in India ever since. The Chinese authorities have long tried to erase his image from the minds of Tibetans, a task that seems to me like trying to stop the wind from blowing — it might be easier to erase the mountains. He is still revered as the human incarnation of Chenrezig, the goddess of compassion. For nearly fifty years his importance has been suppressed but it will take a thousand more before he is forgotten.

The two women bowed to me over and over, almost touching their heads to my feet and the old man clasped his hands together in prayer as if I was holy. I was embarrassed and begged them to stop. The photo was placed in the middle of their shrine and the whole family made prostrations towards it; the younger of the two women kept repeating his name: 'Gyelwa Rinpoche, Gyelwa Rinpoche!' over and over as she cried. A minute later there was a great feed of yak meat frying away on the stove! The old man invited me to stay the rest of the day; we went outside and unloaded the horses and he filled their nosebags with wheat before we set them out to graze.

That night I slept well in the warm little house, with a full stomach. In the morning I was given a bowl of *tukpa* for breakfast, but before I could even think of setting off it began snowing heavily. It seemed like a good opportunity to take a day off and when I asked the old man if I could stay he insisted that I did. It snowed on and off all day and I was glad to spend most of it by the fire with the old man. He sat on one side of the sleeping platform watching me make adjustments and repairs to my tack while he spun a prayer wheel in his hand with an orphan goat at his side. Every now and then the animal would stand up and drop on the old man's bedding, but he didn't seem concerned and brushed the droppings onto the floor.

The house had a flat roof and in the afternoon I helped one of the women sweep off the snow; if left it would seep into the roof when it melted. I offered to help when she made fresh fried bread, but she seemed ashamed to let a man help her in the kitchen. My offer was a bit selfish — the bread was delicious and I was constantly hungry.

The snow continued outside in a howling wind, but inside it was warm and quiet. The old man spun his prayer wheel and mumbled mantras while the woman spun yak hair into thick thread on a little wooden spindle. With my back leaning against the wall and my feet by the fire I read a book I'd brought with me by the Dalai Lama, also sneaked over the border hidden in my pack. Since I was travelling across the land of the dharma I thought I should do something to increase my understanding. The book was based on the *lojong*, or mind training/thought transformation teachings handed down from the great Indian master Atisha to his Tibetan disciples.

The object of these teachings and the goal they aspire to is to develop the 'awakening mind', the desire to attain enlightenment for the sake of others. Through these teachings we learn that our experiences are just projections of our minds. I might look at a seafood salad and think it's delicious, whereas my elderly Tibetan host, who has probably never eaten fish, would be disgusted, thinking it's food fit for animals or beggars. Similarly, if I were told I'd have to live the rest of my life in this tiny house on the freezing snow-swept plain I'd find it unbearable; however, if he were told the same he'd probably be overjoyed, not wishing to be anywhere else.

The seafood salad and the tiny house appear the same to our eyes, but our minds see them completely differently; the question is: who is right and who is wrong? Both and neither. The problem is that I see these things as relating to me, the all important me, the me who wants this but doesn't want that, the me who likes and dislikes, the me who is always me, me me!

The idea in the teachings is that if I could train my mind to see in an unbiased way, neither good nor bad, if I could teach myself to recognise that all these things are illusions projected by my mind, then I wouldn't feel unhappy when I encountered something I didn't like, nor would I be overly excited when something good happened. I wouldn't have enemies, I wouldn't be attached to young women, I wouldn't mind the snow or slow horses, I wouldn't be concerned if I had something or if someone else received it instead. I could stop thinking about me and think about others, I could subdue my own mind and eventually escape from the cycle of life, death, rebirth and suffering. I could be free and I could help others to become free. Well, that's the idea, anyway. I just hoped it would stop snowing by morning. I didn't want to feel cold and right then I wanted some more tea and another chunk of that lovely fresh bread.

Over the next few days I left the Yellow River valley behind and climbed into the Maqen Gangri mountains. The range contains a six thousand, two hundred and eighty-two-metre peak the locals call Ami Maqen. As I climbed higher into rocky valleys on rough stone trails the scenery became more exciting and dramatic. At night I camped surrounded by massive peaks next to rushing mountain rivers, during the day every turn brought a new view and every pass I crossed was marked by prayer flags. And every time I topped a pass and started down the other side I felt I was putting a barrier behind me, as if I was trying to stop something following me.

The exciting scenery had its price, as the weather turned bitterly cold. The skies were clear but a fierce wind screamed constantly, finding its way through my thick layers and freezing me to the core. When I woke in the mornings the river I had drawn water from the previous night would be frozen solid and silent, my water bottle inside the tent would be frozen and the inside of the tent and my sleeping bag covered in sheets of frost. It was much too cold to wash my hands or face in the river, or even brush my teeth. Anything that got wet, including my fingers, would freeze in an instant in the wind.

At night I'd hardly sleep; it was too cold. I'd lie curled in my sleeping bag with all my clothes on and the *chuba* on top. My sleeping bag was a four-season down bag, but even with the hood over my head and the drawstring pulled closed so I only had a tiny hole to breathe through, I'd freeze. By morning the woollen hat I wore to sleep had slipped over my face, I'd open my eyes, see nothing but pitch black and think it was still the middle of the night. I'd spend ages trying to force myself out of the relative warmth of the tent to spend another day being blasted by freezing wind.

With every breath, I was also tested by the altitude. I was now much higher than I'd been in the river valley, at least four thousand metres at times, and in the thin air every small task took on huge proportions. Packing up my tent and loading the horses seemed to take a massive effort; putting on the bulky *chuba*, which I now wore all the time, would leave me gasping for breath. Lifting the saddlebags, which probably weighed less than twenty kilograms, onto the packhorse's back left me so short of breath I'd have to lean against the animal and rest for a full minute to recover. Worst of all, parts of the trail were too steep to ride and I'd have to walk leading the horses and it could take an hour to cover a few hundred metres. I'd count my steps to fifty and then stop for a couple of minutes to breathe, before counting another fifty, then another, on and on until we'd reach the pass where I'd usually collapse in an exhausted heap. The combined cold and altitude had a debilitating effect, as if I'd been struck down by a severe illness.

It was now two weeks since I'd said goodbye to Jigme and Dhondup and the horse I'd been riding was exhausted, with an open running sore on his back where the saddle had rubbed him raw. During the day I'd tried to find another horse to replace him, but there were not many people living in the mountains and very few horses. I asked everyone I met if they could sell me another mount, but no one could. I hated riding him knowing he must be in pain, and walked as much as I could, but as we headed into another pass, the highest so far, I had to get on and ride. There was no way I could walk. I hadn't eaten anything that day and very little the day before; I was weak and cold, and I was frightened.

As the afternoon wore on we climbed higher into the pass on a rough road that looked as if it was never used. I'd passed the last house in the morning; this part of the valley was too high and too cold for anyone to live. Apart from my poor horses I was completely alone. The only sound was that of the horses' steps and the whistle of the wind. On and on we went. Every time we topped a rise I was sure it must be the top of the pass, but instead I'd see the road continuing on ahead. The skies clouded over and darkened and snow fell on and off. It was getting late and I was terrified I wouldn't make it across and have to spend the night in the pass. With the cold and the altitude I knew that would be extremely dangerous. I needed to spend the night at a lower level, which meant I either had to cross the pass or turn back.

With the heightened altitude my senses seemed sharper and more intense, my emotions swinging wildly and so close to the surface I could feel them coming out through my skin. One moment I would be shaking with fear and praying: *All Buddhas and holy beings, please protect me and my horses, please bestow your blessings on our bodies and minds!* The next I'd be defiant, even angry: *Come on, Ian! You can do it! Kick this bastard mountain in the arse!*

I thought of Edmund Hillary and Sherpa Tenzin as they neared the top of Everest; they must have been terrified but somehow they found the courage to take one step after another. Of course, my mountain was a dwarf compared to theirs, but to me it seemed just as much of a 'bastard' to be 'knocked off'. I remembered the Tibetan saying: *You must die once.* I still wasn't sure what it meant, but it almost felt as if I was dying now.

Finally, just as the sun touched the mountain peaks on the horizon, we reached the top. Frozen prayer flags flapped stiffly in the wind and we struggled through knee-deep snow on to the other side. Far below I could see the brown grass of the valley floor, while all around white peaks stretched into the distance. The view was breathtaking — literally — but there was no time to enjoy it. I tugged on the lead rope of my poor cold, tired horses and set off down the trail.

In the last twilight I pitched my tent on the frozen ground of the valley floor. I had hoped to find a family to stay with, but no one lived this high. The grazing was good and I unloaded the horses and put them out for the night. The saddle blankets on the riding horse were stuck to his back where the wound had bled. I felt awful for him, I felt selfish; was it right for me to be causing these poor animals to suffer just so I could achieve my own goals? Certainly I would have to find a new mount the next day.

After another freezing night I continued down the valley, the priority of finding something to eat second only to that of finding a new horse. I followed the river as it ran between the hills and at every bend I expected to find a family in a warm house where I could escape the wind and get some tea and something to eat. However, the valley was empty and I didn't find anyone until I reached the bottom in the afternoon. I rounded a bend and found a small village, a few 'streets' of little houses and a small temple.

As I approached, desperate for shelter and food, I found a small black and white bird flapping on the ground. It was dying and my first instinct was to leave it there, but then I thought that perhaps it was more than just a dying bird, perhaps someone was trying to test me. After all, the Buddhas are said to be able to manifest themselves anywhere and in any form; what if this was one of them, flapping on the ground in front of me and I just walked by and left the poor creature to die? I picked up the bird and slipped it inside the folds of my *chuba*. When I checked it a minute later it was dead.

On the edge of the village I met a group of young monks. We tied my horses to a post and they took me inside for tea and *tsampa*. At last, something warm to eat! I told the monks I needed to buy another horse, but they had none to sell and after a few minutes I walked out to the small temple. It was locked but I buried the bird under a pile of stones and said a simple prayer, asking the Buddhas to guide it towards a happy rebirth.

On the way back to the village to get my horses I met two young Tibetan guys who took me to an abandoned house on the edge of the village. They were laughing and pointing at something inside and gesturing for me to go in. I took off my hat and stepped through the doorway. The single room seemed empty, but as my eyes adjusted to the gloom I could make out a pitiful figure in the corner.

A woman lay on a cot with a bowl of embers beneath her trying to stay warm. She was obviously very ill and I had a clear impression she was dying. It was a shocking scene; she was dying alone with no one to help her, while the two men stood in the doorway laughing. When the woman saw me she started mumbling something incoherent and reached out her arms, begging for help. I felt helpless, there was nothing I could do. I have no medical knowledge, I had a few simple medicines but I had no idea what was wrong with her and I worried that if I gave her something it could make her worse. I gave her some money, I thought that at least she might be able to buy some food. On the ledge of the glassless window was a bag with a few mouldy pieces of bread and a jar of cold tea, but that was all.

Was this another test? If it was, there was nothing I could do to pass it. I turned and walked towards the door angry, furious that this poor woman should have to die this way. She was in a village, there were Buddhist monks here! Why was no one helping her? The two idiots moved out of my way. I pointed to the woman: 'Why don't you help her?' They just shook their stupid heads and giggled. I shook my fist in their faces; it was taking all my patience for me not to thump them, and I knew it was just my own feelings of helplessness and a desire to take it out on someone. I walked off and when they tried to follow me I turned and sent them away: 'Fuck off!'

Tibet is now part of China, for right or for wrong, and the Chinese government make a great show of how they have improved the quality of life for the average Tibetan, but I saw little evidence of it. Where was a doctor to treat this woman? Why was there no medicine for her? There was a Chinese settlement nearby; why had no one come to help her? Why hadn't the people in the village gone to get help? Where were the benefits the Chinese occupation had brought? On the Tibetan plateau there was no electricity except for small solar panels that created enough power to run a single light bulb at night. The people bought these themselves if they could afford it. There was no running water — even in the towns people still had to trek out to the river with pails and barrels. There were no telephones. There was education for the children, who were sent to school where they learned

Chinese and were politically indoctrinated; it was hardly an improvement, and they were being encouraged not to study the dharma.

The only improvement I saw was roading. In the mountains I often passed Chinese construction crews cutting away at the hillsides with picks and shovels to make new roads, to link isolated communities with larger centres. But who does this benefit? The Tibetans? Or the Chinese, who could then move more settlers into these remote regions? By doing this the Chinese dragon quietly sinks her claws deeper into the back of the Tibetan yak, which is slowly bleeding to death.

I took my horses and set off walking west. I hadn't gone far when a couple of men came after me on an old motorbike. Word that I was looking for a new horse had spread through the village and the men had one to sell. One of them told me the horse was at his home somewhere over the hills and asked me to stay in the village overnight and he'd bring it the next day. I didn't want to stay there, so I told him I'd go with him to his home.

It was getting late, usually about the time I'd stop for the night, when we started into the hills. I rode until it got too steep and the Tibetan led my packhorse. Before long I was having to stop and gasp for breath every few minutes while the Tibetan laughed. The sun set just as we got to the top; we stopped and looked out across the vast landscape with Ami Maqen rising in the centre of the dark blue sky. The man was in a hurry to get going and we carried on down the other side into the darkness. In the bottom of the narrow valley we headed towards a small house which I thought must be his home; however, as we got closer he called a greeting to his neighbour and we carried on. To my horror we still had another pass to cross. We didn't arrive until nine o'clock; I was exhausted. We left the horses in the yard with an armload of straw each and went inside.

His wife was shocked to see her husband turn up with someone as strange as me and his two little kids stared in disbelief at the white-skinned, blue-eyed monster! They were filthy and constantly wriggling in their clothes, which must have been infested with lice. I just prayed they wouldn't crawl into mine during the night. I was given tea, a bowl of rice with butter and yak bones before I unrolled my sleeping bag on a bench on one side of the small room. The candles were blown out and I closed my eyes and thought of the poor woman I had met earlier. This land was harsh and it could be cruel; perhaps the Tibetans in the village had known it was her time to die, perhaps her good karma had run out and there was nothing they could do. Before I slept I said a simple prayer for her, asking the Buddhas to protect her, at least to let her pass peacefully. I knew I would carry the image of her to Gang Rinpoche, and probably for the rest of my life.

Chapter Three

In the morning I bought a new horse from my host, in exchange for my riding horse and two thousand six hundred yuan. It was a small grey gelding, really just a pony, but in good condition. I named the horses Ridey and Packy. Ridey was the riding horse, Packy was the packhorse — not very imaginative, but names all the same. We set off down the valley. Very quickly the mountains fell behind and I was riding through desert country; the ground was bare, with almost no grass and we wound our way through massive shifting sand dunes.

The only life I saw was dozens of tiny lizards and herds of wild *khang* (Tibetan ass) and gazelles. At first I was excited to see these skittish animals, but as the day wore on I became hungry and cold and began to resent them. They were shy of humans so wherever they were I wouldn't find people — there'd be nothing to eat and no shelter from the freezing wind.

In the afternoon we came to a large river. People were camped on the other side, in black yak-hair tents, but the river was too deep and fast to cross. I rode further north and came to a field of frozen snow — a solid sheet a hundred metres across. There was probably a marsh underneath or a shallow river inlet. The horses should have been able to cross, but Ridey refused to set one foot on it. I nudged him in the ribs: 'C'mon Ridey, *chu!* Move!'

He wouldn't budge. I got off and tried to lead him across, taking Packy in front so he could follow, but he dug his heels in and wouldn't take a step. There was nothing I could do but get back on and ride around the snowfield, kilometres out of our way.

The land was open and barren, the sun bright and the skies clear, but with nothing to stop it the cruel wind blew unchecked, though I kept scanning ahead, hoping to find a house. Eventually I saw one but was disappointed to find it empty, waiting for the summer, when the rains increased the grazing enough for the nomads' herds. I was so cold I lay in a hollow in the ground for a while with my hat over my face. Sometimes, just for a few seconds, the wind would die and I felt how warm it would be if it wasn't blowing, then it would scream again. Tibet was playing a cruel joke on me.

Late in the afternoon I left the sands behind and came into an area of sparse grasslands with enough grazing to support a few families. I stopped for tea with some nice old ladies before riding on into the evening when I camped alone in some low hills. That night I checked my maps. I wanted to keep heading northwest across the grasslands to reach two huge lakes, Gyaring Tso and Ngoring Tso, still several days away.

Over the next few days I carried on towards the lakes. One morning I woke to heavy snow, unzipping the door to find visibility almost down to zero. I decided to take a day off; the horses needed to be rested. I let them off to graze and spent all morning in the tent, brewing tea by warming a cup of water over candles and making a few adjustments and repairs to my gear. When I'd stopped the night before I'd seen an encampment of Chinese in white canvas tents about a kilometre away — at first I thought they might have been military, but when I looked through my binoculars I could see they were all in plain, drab clothes and there were women. I had no idea what they were doing and thought it better to keep away; however, as snow continued to fall throughout the day hunger and boredom drove me out.

In the afternoon I walked across to their camp. There were about twenty people, Tibetans and Chinese, staying on the grasslands while they searched for some kind of tiny seed, which I guess was used in herbal medicine. Because of the snow there was no work and half the people were crowded around a stove in the cook tent, where I was welcomed and given Chinese tea and steamed buns. Word went out that a foreigner had turned up out of nowhere and soon the rest of the group had crowded into the tent.

They were all poor, probably uneducated workers, and fascinated by my photos and anything else I could show them. I felt sorry for them, especially the Chinese; at least the Tibetans were at home, but the Chinese workers may have been brought in from other areas. The weather conditions even on a 'good' day were miserable and their flimsy canvas tents were no protection from the cold. They could spend weeks searching for the seeds and all for probably a few dollars pay. However, they seemed to accept their lot and were a lively, jovial bunch.

There was one rather cute Chinese girl — she probably hadn't had a bath in days but she had beautiful dark eyes and seemed intrigued by my pale blue ones. The other youngsters nudged her in the ribs and whispered to her. She blushed and giggled but didn't stop flirting. It had been weeks since that kind of thing had crossed my mind. Now I was reminded of what I was missing, what I might be doing on this freezing bleak day if I was anywhere else. Young women like this may have been out of my sight for the last few weeks, but the imprints they had long since made on my mind were still very much there.

Before too long the crush of people in the tent became too much and I started to feel claustrophobic. I stood up to leave and the work party's leader gave me some steamed buns to take with me. Everyone came outside to say goodbye and before I left I found a coin I'd brought from home and gave it to the girl. She thanked me in Chinese, giggled and fluttered her eyes. I took her little fingers in mine and kissed the back of her hand as the rest of the camp roared with laughter.

As I walked back a blizzard blew in again and I could hardly see a thing. I was worried I'd get lost but as I stumbled on, the forms of my horses slowly became clearer. I tethered them closer to the tent for the night and gave them half a steamed bun each.

As it got dark Tibet finally ran out of breath and the wind died. It was silent except for the distant howling of wolves. I lay in my sleeping bag reading, my feet like blocks of ice even inside two pairs of thick socks, and my breath forming in clouds in front of my face. In my book the Dalai Lama talked about how difficult circumstances could stimulate and enhance my spiritual practice. When I suffer it helps me to see how unsatisfactory my life is, to see how material comforts, money, a good job and lovely young women can never really make me happy. If I am surrounded by attractive possessions and attractive people it's easy for me to fool myself that I'm doing all right, that all this nice stuff is OK, it's all I need.

I'm distracted from doing the kind of things that will really help me find happiness, things like listening to Khensur Thabkye Rinpoche's teachings. I'm too busy, I have to work, I'm thinking about a new car, I have a date tonight. But before long new cars get old, the more money I have the more I want, and I want a better job, a more beautiful girlfriend. What happened to my happiness? What if I had chosen to spend this time and all this money in Shanghai or Hong Kong? What would I be doing now? Reading a book by the Dalai Lama or sitting in a hotel bar with someone with dark eyes? And when I'm old, which one is going to be of more benefit to me? It seemed painfully obvious, but still I thought about the cute girl at the Chinese camp. She was probably in bed now. I wondered if she was thinking of me?

As I continued towards the lakes the grasslands slowly turned to desert, the ground became drier, the wind stronger and colder. One night I camped alone in a little gorge in the sandy hills where there was a strip of grass beside a frozen stream. On an eroded bank I found enough grass roots woody enough to burn and made a fire. An hour later I was still trying to get the water to boil to cook some instant noodles. I was hungry, cold and exhausted and almost in tears as I cursed at the fire and screamed at the wind that kept blowing it out. Once again, what should have been a simple task was taking a huge amount of effort and energy. On the cliff above my lonely little camp two eagles screeched from their nest on the cliff face.

In the morning I checked the maps; they didn't make much sense and I wasn't really sure where I was. I'd tried asking directions to the lakes, but no one seemed to understand me. I think the names of places, rivers and lakes on my maps were official names and the locals simply called the features something else — and my Tibetan was nowhere near good enough to question them.

Before long I came to another large river, too deep and dangerous to cross. I followed it all day, hoping it was going to turn to the west so I could ride around it, but by afternoon I was heading southeast, opposite to the way I wanted to go. The horses were dreary and tired as they struggled over the sandy ground; progress was slow and the wind was crushing my spirit like a curse. It was the coldest day yet; there were no people, no shelter from the wind, nothing to eat or drink, nothing to give me comfort.

By late afternoon I was in despair. I would have been encouraged if I was making some progress but instead I was losing ground as I found myself riding in the wrong direction. This was the most inhospitable, wretched, joyless, unkind place I'd ever seen. The cold was killing me, I hated Tibet, and I felt as if Tibet hated me too, as if she wanted to destroy me. How could the dharma have thrived in such an uncompassionate land? At that moment I would have done anything to get out of there. Eventually I dragged myself back up in the saddle. The day was a write-off and best put down to experience. I headed back through the hills to the campsite I'd left that morning. I'd achieved nothing. The eagles wheeled above the cliff as I led the horses into the gorge, their screeches now sounding like laughter.

A couple of days later I was camped in the hills a few kilometres from the tiny town of Madoi. It was good to know where I was and that night I wrote a letter home. I'd brought some pre-stamped envelopes and hoped to find someone to post one for me. It was hard to write more than a few lines. How could I possibly explain on one sheet of paper what I was going through?

In the morning I rode out of the hills and met up with a road leading to Madoi. I hadn't gone far when I found a small village — actually more of a large truck stop, just two rows of small buildings on either side of the road. I watched the street from a distance with my binoculars as trucks came and went and the occasional bus groaned by. I was dying to ride down, drawn to the rundown buildings as if they were some kind of fabled city. I knew there would be little shops and noodle houses. I could stock up on 'goodies', I could buy a hot meal. I wanted to spend money, sit on a chair inside a building and pay for food. I realised I was desperate to do something 'normal' but fear of the authorities held me back. Although it was just a cluster of shacks, there could be police.

I walked my horses to the end of the village, where I could see the road between two old buildings. I stood there for several minutes arguing with myself. *It's not worth it, Ian. Just get on and ride. But then again, the place is tiny, there probably aren't any cops, think of the food!*

Before long I was noticed and a young Tibetan wandered out. I pointed further west past the town and asked him, *'Madoi?'*

'Rey.' He nodded.

'Madoi, dra khang yawrey?' Is there a post office there?

'Rey, rey.'

I took the envelope from the folds of my *chuba*, indicating that I wanted him to post it for me. He seemed to understand. I asked him another question. *'Sa khang yawrey?'* and pointed to the buildings. Is there a restaurant here? He nodded and went on his way.

It was too much to resist. I'd have to take my chances with the law. I hadn't eaten a hot meal in days and I was ravenous. I crossed the street at one end of town and skirted behind the buildings, led my horses halfway along the row of shacks and tied them in an abandoned yard. No one saw me and I made my way through the yards, taking careful note of which way I'd come in case I had to make a fast getaway. I squeezed through two padlocked gates and found myself standing in the middle of the street.

A few locals turned to see me, surprised but friendly: a mechanic working under the hood of an old truck; a young Chinese man peeling a flat tyre off its rim. I looked up and down the street but couldn't see anything that looked like a police station. To my left was a brick building with a sign above its door showing a steaming bowl heaped with food and a pair of chopsticks. A restaurant!

I pushed aside the curtain and stepped through the door. At first the two Chinese staff looked startled to see me. I didn't blame them; on the wall was a small mirror and I caught my reflection for the first time in weeks. With the *chuba* and the long knife on my belt, a black scarf tied around my head and three weeks' growth on my face I looked like Genghis Khan. One of them rushed to pull up a chair and wiped down a little wooden table. I was surely their first Western guest and perhaps they imagined I was the start of a lucrative wave of tourism about to hit their tiny village. I took a seat, feeling as if I was in a Wild West saloon. One of the men brought me a basin of hot water and a bar of soap and I washed my hands for the first time in days. The chef came out with samples of different ingredients in his hands and I pointed to what I wanted and before long two dishes of fried rice with beef, onions and ginger were placed in front of me. I dived in and stuffed myself.

By now the restaurant was full of curious onlookers trying to fathom where the stranger had suddenly appeared from. No one had seen me get off a bus, so how had I got there?

'Nga ta nyi yawrey,' I told them, I have two horses.

'Gyagar?' one of the men asked. Are you from India?

Obviously they had no idea what Indians look like, but knowing I wasn't Chinese they must have wondered where else I could have come from by horse. Once again my photos and little world map came in handy.

After lunch I went outside with my crowd of helpers and checked out a couple of little *tsong khang*, shops where I stocked up on toilet paper, candles, a bottle of Pepsi, some Chinese biscuits and a tin of oily corned beef. I didn't forget Ridey and Packy and also purchased a bag of grain.

I set off again feeling great. There had been no sign of cops and I'd had a huge meal. In the afternoon I crossed a large river and rode high into some hills, where I camped. That night I looked at the maps and worked out that Ngoring Tso couldn't be more than twenty kilometres away and I should reach it the next day. I sat outside as it got dark, drinking my Pepsi and munching my way through the biscuits as my horses chomped on their nosebags. I was still buzzing from the day's events when I suddenly realised there was another reason I was feeling so good: it wasn't cold! The sun had shone all day and the wind had died; it had actually been relatively warm. It was amazing what a difference it made. It was likely the better weather wouldn't last but I would enjoy it while it did; my whole mood was a complete contrast to that of a few days ago and I felt blessed. Even the horses seemed happy.

In the morning I crossed a wide valley before climbing into the hills again where finally Ngoring Tso came into view. The entire lake was completely frozen, one vast expanse of solid ice. An hour later I stood on the silent shore squinting at the glaring sheet of white ice. The lake must be at least thirty kilometres wide from north to south and although I didn't dare set foot on it, I think I could have walked all the way across. I was still in a great mood from the day before and felt elated at reaching my first real destination.

I spent two nights in the hills near the lake with a *drokpa* family who had made their summer camp in two black yak-hair tents. The wide, low dwellings were spacious and roomy and looked like those of the Bedouin in the Middle East. The family probably had a house somewhere not too far away, but in summer they would round up their animals and move to other areas to graze their stock. This family had arrived with all their belongings loaded onto yaks; they had about fifty along with a hundred or so sheep and goats. After they set up camp they returned to the lake with one yak to cut great blocks of ice for drinking water. There was a brackish pond near the lake where their stock and my horses could be watered, but other than the frozen lake there was no other source of water.

It was warm during the day and the horses grazed and rested while I lazed around my tent. In the afternoon I wandered over to my neighbours and a rough, long-haired grandfather invited me in and gave me tea and *tsampa*. One of his sons was a monk who had been released from his monastery to help his family over the busy summer, another of his sons had recently become a father. In the evening his wife fed the infant and put him to bed. She opened a large bag made from yak-hair felt and poured a basin of warm ash from the fire inside; on top of this she placed a matted pad of sheep's wool that I guessed would soak up any leaks during the night like a nappy; then she sat the child inside in a cross-legged position and finally wrapped the whole thing up in a snug bundle with only the baby's head poking out.

Over the next few days I rode southwest across empty plains and into the Bayan Har mountains. The grazing was better but the weather turned cold again. It snowed most nights and the cruel wind returned. One night I camped alone high in the mountains and woke in the morning to find a pair of wolves watching me from on high. That night I thought it might be better to stay with someone and was lucky to be hosted by a family in a yak-hair tent. The woman cooked me a delicious meal of meat and rice before she herded the yaks back into camp for the night and tethered them to the ground with long rope lines held in place with wooden stakes. She had almost finished the job and had just gone to catch a couple of stragglers when I decided this would be a good chance to get a close-up photo of one of these great grey animals with massive horns. I took out my camera and stepped closer. Unfortunately, the flash was on automatic and the yak bolted, ripping the tether line from the ground and setting half the herd into a stampede! *Oh shit!*

The poor woman stood there looking at me with her hands on her hips, shaking her head.

'*Gawn da, gawn da!*' I said over and over, I'm sorry, and offered to help her recapture the animals, which were now milling about on the edge of the camp. She waved her hands and pointed towards the tent saying something like: 'Just go back inside, you idiot!'

It wasn't long before the animals were resettled for the night and the woman could see the funny side of things. She laughed and shook her finger at me as she handed me another bowl of tea.

A couple of days later I found myself on a ridge overlooking the little Chinese settlement of Qingshuihe. Again I scanned the only street with my binoculars but couldn't see any police so, feeling confident after my last successful trip into town, I decided to take a closer look. I tied my horses behind the buildings, cut through a truck yard and emerged in the middle of the main street, right next to the police station. *Oh shit!*

I decided to carry on and was soon enjoying another great meal in a little Chinese restaurant. After a few minutes the door opened and a Chinese police officer walked in. My heart jumped out of my mouth and onto the dish in front of me. The officer didn't even look at me; he walked across the room, took a seat at another table and ordered some lunch. I picked up my heart with my chopsticks and slipped it back inside.

As I finished my meal the officer still hadn't glanced in my direction so I paid for my lunch and went out into the street. I walked up and down, stocking up on supplies in the little shops all the while followed by a crowd of onlookers who became an unruly crush as they all tried to squeeze through the doors into the shops behind me.

In the group were some proud-looking men in long *chubas*, metre-long swords stuck in their belts and their long hair tied on top of their heads in red tassels. They were Khampas. I was in the northern reaches of the Tibetan region of Kham, renowned for its bandits and fighters — these were the men who put up the main resistance to the Chinese invasion, fighting on horseback with swords and a few old guns before they were crushed by the Red Army.

A day later another massive mountain pass loomed before me under grey, threatening skies. I slowly climbed higher all day; it was cold and snowed on and off but the wind wasn't so desperate. Soon I passed the last houses — the barren mountains were silent and empty except for the occasional eagle. They would sit on rocks or crags watching me and my horses get closer, before gracefully spreading their great wings to lift off effortlessly.

Again thoughts built up inside me as we climbed. I wasn't afraid this time; I had become used to reading the conditions and the landscape ahead and I felt confident of crossing the pass. The mountains towered over me and I felt like a speck, so totally insignificant, nothing more than a single atom. Every few minutes emotions welled up inside, then I'd relax and feel a great calm, as if something had been lifted off me, as if I'd been relieved of a burden I didn't know I'd been carrying.

Late in the afternoon the top of the pass, marked by prayer flags, came into view. I knew the skies would hold out long enough for me to get across to the other side, there was no need to worry, no need to push the horses. A wave of happiness rushed up inside and I lifted up my arms, feeling as if I wanted to offer something to the mountain, but I had nothing to give, except myself. The pass was only a few hundred metres away, but I felt as if I wasn't ready to reach it. Once we started down the other side I knew I would feel differently and I wanted these emotions to continue. Something inside me was coming closer to the surface, something that wanted to come out, something I wanted to get rid of. I closed my eyes and let the reins fall slack, letting my horse walk on, feeling each step take me higher. With every hoof-beat I felt myself open, I felt a need to let myself go, let everything fall away. If I could let the illusion of who I am collapse and turn to dust, just give up trying to hold on to what now seemed like an absurd joke, I could be free. I could stop pretending, I could stop the grasping and the running, I could be happy.

I remembered trying to jump off a waterfall when I was a kid, standing on the edge too scared to take that one step over the side, even though I knew I would fall safely into the water and be better for doing it. I was feeling a similar sensation now, but something was holding me back. I couldn't take that last step.

My horse stopped, I opened my eyes and found I was next to the prayer flags — the top had come too soon. That night in my tent I wrote my diary and tried to explain what I'd felt on the mountain, but with every word I closed what my horse's steps had opened. I tried to rationalise, to understand something that perhaps didn't need to be understood, something that just needed to be. I was rebuilding the illusion of myself that had almost collapsed in the pass.

I thought about the Tibetan saying, *You must die once* and started to feel that perhaps I knew what it meant. *You* was *I*, the self-centred *I*, the greedy *I*, the craving, deluded, ignorant fool of an *I*, the *I* Khensur Thabkye Rinpoche had tried to teach me to see for what it was — a conman, a trickster, a fraud. It was this *I* that I constantly tried to satisfy, but its hunger was like a blazing fire, consuming all my energy and leaving me with a pile of ash. It was this *I* that must die, this was the *I* that I needed to leave behind in a mountain pass to freeze to death. This was the *I* that kept me in a constantly revolving sequence of false happiness and suffering. If this part of me died, I could escape the cycle.

I had told Jigme and Dhondup that my journey to Gang Rinpoche was like a pilgrimage, and a pilgrimage shouldn't just be a physical journey but also one of the mind; my mind should change so that when I reached the end I wouldn't be the same person, hopefully I'd be someone better. If I reached the end without *dying* then I would have wasted the opportunity to change. Whatever I might have achieved in terms of kilometres crossed or mountains climbed, whatever hardships I'd endured, would be for nothing.

I closed my diary and pulled the hood of my sleeping bag over my head. In the freezing darkness I decided that if I reached Kailas I would leave that part of myself to die at the top of the six thousand-metre Dolma-la Pass and walk down the other side another person. Now, with such a great distance between myself and all the worthless things I craved, I could see this part of me was nothing but trouble — it was bad company, like a wayward friend. But at the same time I knew it wouldn't be easy to let this old mate go, we'd been pretty close. He'd kept me going and we'd spent many nights together in bars.

It was a freezing morning; crunching around on fresh snow my fingers turned to painful ice as I packed my wet tent. I set off but it wasn't long before the cold drove me inside. I stopped at a house and was met by a young monk and his parents, who took me in to warm up by their stove.

'*Khyerang-la gompa kaba duk?*' I asked the monk, where is your monastery?

'*Seka Gompa,*' he said and pointed down the valley; his monastery was called Seka and it was in the direction I was heading.

'*Trapa katsay yawrey?*' How many monks are there?

'*Sum gya!*' Three hundred! It was a very big centre.

'*Seka Gompa lama su ray?*' Who is the lama at Seka Gompa?

'*Denma Locho Rinpoche.*' I was astonished — I'd heard the name before. Denma Locho was a high lama who had fled to India and I'd met him in New Zealand a couple of years earlier. I'd had no idea which part of Tibet he was from and until now I didn't even know Seka monastery existed. The monk told me there was a town about twenty kilometres away called Zadoi and the monastery was another ten kilometres past that. It was a long way, but I hoped to reach the *gompa* that night.

The valley continued to narrow and the mountains grew even more rugged as we slowly pushed on. Ridey was slow; he hated walking on the hard road but the valley was so slim there was no choice. Occasionally it would open out slightly into small river plains where people were living, but often they had fenced the land right up to the road and there was nowhere else to ride. There were small, scrubby bushes on the rocky hillsides, the first real vegetation I'd seen. The scrawny plants meant dry sticks to make a fire to cook my food and make tea.

In the early afternoon I started to see signs that we were close to a settlement — the land was covered in rubbish. It was heartbreaking to see pollution in what had been such a pristine place, but everywhere there were shredded plastic bags, soft drink bottles and empty noodle packets blowing in the wind; further on piles of human waste had been dumped by the river. Even if a town wasn't marked on my maps I could always guess when I was approaching one by the rubbish blowing across the landscape. The Chinese government had encouraged settlements but hadn't provided any infrastructure. There was no garbage collection, no sewerage, no thought given to the waste the increase in population would produce or how their unnatural by-products would be disposed off.

Soon I was leading the horses down the dusty main street of Zadoi, where mud-brick houses were built into the side of the mountain. Again I found a little Chinese noodle hut and before long I was enjoying another great feed with a group of Chinese men at the next table sharing their beer with me. There's not much entertainment in Zadoi and I quickly became the main attraction. The restaurant was jam-packed, but I was the only one eating — fifty people must have crowded in to see me and the windows were darkened by peering faces. When I went to check out the little shops I had a crowd of at least a hundred pressing around me. After spending days in solitude it was suffocating and after a few minutes I had to leave.

Beyond the town the weather closed in. Snow fell heavily and I kept hoping to find the monastery every time I rounded a bend. The horses were tired but I pushed them on; if I was going to reach the *gompa* that day I would have to keep moving. Late in the afternoon I met an old Tibetan man coming the other way on the trail.

'*Pala! Seka Gompa kaba duk?*' I asked him, Father, where's the monastery?

'*Seka Gompa,*' he replied and pointed up a side valley.

The old man disappeared into the swirls of snow. I crossed the river and rode into the narrow cleft in the mountains. As evening fell the snow became heavier; soon visibility was almost nil, I could only make out a few metres ahead. I felt like an adventurer searching for a fabled lost city, expecting it to manifest out of the mists at any moment. And despite the discomfort in the cold and snow I had to think that this was the perfect place for a monastery, hidden high in the mountains, and it was a perfect way to find it, struggling through a blizzard.

It was starting to get dark, my *chuba* was caked in frozen snow and I was shaking in the cold. Still there was no sign of the *gompa* and I knew I would soon have to find somewhere to spend the night. I peered through the gloom and falling snow, hoping to see something, but all I could make out was a snow-covered mountainside. I put my head down and kicked Ridey on.

A few minutes later I heard a deep sound ahead, a horn blowing from somewhere in the mist. I looked up but again, all I saw was white mountainside. The cloud parted for a moment and I saw the white of the mountain was actually the high whitewashed walls of Seka Gompa; temple buildings, monks' houses, *stupas* and hermits' huts appeared as if by magic. A short distance on I met two monks, probably as astonished to see me as I was to see them. They grinned wide, infectious smiles as I climbed out of the saddle.

'*Seka Gompa?*' I asked.

'*Rey, rey.*' They nodded. They took my horses and we walked towards the monastery, which covered the whole mountainside and valley floor. I followed the monks through narrow winding streets to their house, where we tied the horses in a little sheltered yard and went inside, up dark wooden steps and passageways to emerge in a lovely room with large windows made from a framework of small panes. There were comfortable benches covered in thick Tibetan rugs and a warm, crackling stove. A minute later I had a bowl of hot tea in my thawing hands and a pot of *tukpa* was bubbling on the stove. When I'd warmed up we unloaded the horses and stashed my gear inside. They would have to spend the night in the yard as it was too dark to try to find grazing, but the monks filled their nosebags and left them a great pile of straw.

The monks introduced themselves as Tsombo and Norbu. I showed them my maps and photos and tried to explain to them where I'd ridden from. We sat there for a while trying to communicate as snow continued to pat against the windows, but before long the strains of the day and the effect of warm food took their toll. I was exhausted and desperately in need of sleep. Tsombo insisted on giving me his sleeping space and I unrolled my sleeping bag and disappeared inside. It had been a great day and I looked forward to exploring the monastery in the morning. Outside the tiny streets rang to the sound of a hundred stray dogs. I shut my eyes and felt the unfamiliar luxury of being completely warm as I fell into a deep sleep.

I woke just after six to a rush of activity as Tsombo and Norbu hurried off to morning prayers. I went back to sleep for an hour, then I was woken by an elderly monk, who placed bowls of *tukpa*, tea and *tsampa* on the table beside my bed. The snow had stopped and the skies were a perfect blue. After breakfast I took Ridey and Packy up the valley above the village and left them on a hillside to graze.

When I got back the monks had returned and they took me to the main temple where a *puja*, or ceremony, was in progress. Outside the great doors two huge monks in special robes stood like guards; each held a heavy wooden staff. They were *geko*, monks whose job it is to keep order and discipline among the younger novices. Tsombo asked if we could go in; the *geko* lifted the greasy curtain over the door and looked inside. He made us wait for a few minutes until there was an appropriate pause so we could slip inside.

There were about two hundred monks seated on low benches inside the enormous room. Murals covered the walls, golden statues of Buddhas, saints and demons gazed down from every corner, vivid scroll paintings hung from the beams and on one side a thousand brass butter lamps flickered. The air inside was tense. I bowed my head and pressed my palms together in prayer, hoping to show I wasn't just a sightseer. Tsombo took me by the arm and led me closer to the walls into the shadows as if he was trying to hide me. We made our way slowly round the room as all the young monks watched me, the temple quiet except for the occasional whisper or cough. The leading lama seated on a throne at the front mumbled something and all the monks replied.

At the back of the temple behind a curtain was a large sand *mandala* laid out on the floor. Some three metres across, these complex and intricate designs are made completely of fine, coloured sand, and are painstakingly constructed by skilled monks. The sand is funnelled through long cones grain by grain. *Mandalas* mimic the creation of the universe in minute form; meditating monks can visualise themselves in the centre of a *mandala* as a Buddha or deity and so attain some of their qualities. This one must have taken four monks weeks to make, but it would only be kept for a few days; then they would run ritual instruments through the sands destroying it to show that everything is impermanent.

From the temple we went to another building where young monks were practising debating. As part of their spiritual training monks argue complicated points of Buddhist philosophy. One monk will attack a certain point of the Buddha's teachings while the other, with logic and reasoning, has to prove it was valid. Back and forth they argue until they exhaust all possibilities and arrive at the truth. By doing this the monks deepen their understanding of the *sutras* and at the same time impress on their own minds the value of the teachings.

We walked back through the monastery village with its cosy whitewashed houses piled on top of each other up the mountainside along little lanes. Tsombo pointed out a large house that had been the home of Denma Locho Rinpoche; he seemed to be saying he had left for India at the request of the Dalai Lama. Many important teachers have had to leave their homeland for India as they are restricted in their activities by the Chinese. They aren't allowed to teach or practise and many feel they can do more to preserve and spread the dharma outside Tibet. Also, more importantly, when these great masters die the Chinese often prevent their followers from searching for their reincarnations and the lineages are broken.

In the centre of the village was a large building that contained the monastery's offices. Tsombo took me inside and introduced me to the *khenpo*, or abbot. He asked me if I was planning to stay in Seka and become a monk. He also asked me if the police in Zadoi knew I was there and seemed amused when I told him I hadn't bothered to tell them. He was pleased to hear I had met his lama, Denma Locho, and that as far as I knew he was well and happy.

After lunch we went to a small shop in the village and I bought a couple of kilograms of rice. I had repeatedly offered to pay for the food Tsombo had given me and my horses, but he refused. He thought I was buying the rice for myself but I planned to give it to him the next day when I left. The weather was sunny and warm in the afternoon and the last of the previous day's snow melted away. Above the village there was a pilgrim circuit cut into the side of the mountain, a narrow trail at giddying heights where the faithful could circle the whole monastery in one go. Tsombo took me to the start of the trail and we walked slowly around. I took my *mala* from around my neck and let the beads slip through my fingers as I said the mantra: *Om mani padme hum*, Hail to the Jewel in the Lotus. The monk smiled when he heard me and gave me the thumbs-up.

Despite the absence of their precious teacher, Seka Gompa was very much an active centre. Tsombo and the other monks were serious students of the dharma and devoted to its practice. When I'd woken up I'd looked out the window to see another monk sitting on the snow-covered roof of the next house in the first light, diligently reciting *sutras*; another monk who visited the house whispered a mantra every time he breathed; each time he exhaled a prayer would be mounted on his breath, making each breath an act of virtue. There were others whose practice was simpler; the old monk who lived in the house was constantly cooking, cleaning and making tea, his spiritual practice was the act of giving food to others.

Just as it got dark I walked with Tsombo up the valley to bring the horses back to the yard. By the time we got back night had fallen and on the mountainside electric light generated from little solar panels shone in the windows of most houses. In the darkness only the squares of light could be seen; they looked so familiar they could have been anywhere in the world and reminded me of home. We filled the horses' nosebags and left them another pile of straw. Inside I was given another meal of meat and rice — I couldn't remember the last time I'd had three meals in a day.

That night I gave an impromptu English lesson. I sat with Tsombo and

Norbu and a couple of other young monks and taught them a few simple phrases in case another foreigner turned up at their monastery. The village was quiet and I'm sure the neighbours could hear us laughing as I got the monks to repeat the phrases over and over.

'Yes, yes, yes, YES!'

'No, no, no, NO!'

'Hello! Hello!'

We all laughed and I realised that for the first time in ages I was with friends. Tsombo had already told me to stay at Seka another day — it was tempting, but I would be on my way in the morning. It wasn't safe to stay in one place too long. The police in Zadoi might come and I feared myself becoming attached to the comfort of Tsombo's room and his company.

I had one more good sleep in the warmth of the house and another good breakfast. Tsombo helped me load up the horses, still insisting I stay another day before he walked me to the edge of the village. I shook his hand and took the bag of rice from the folds of my *chuba*.

'No, no,' he said, using some of the English I'd taught him.

'Yes, yes!' I replied and pushed the bag into his hands. He looked embarrassed but accepted it. *'Kali shu,'* I said, a Tibetan farewell. Stay slowly.

'Kali pay jolak,' he replied, go slowly brother.

I rode back the way I'd come until I met up with the main river and turned south towards a river known as the He Chu to the Tibetans, or the Tong Tian in Chinese — later it becomes the Yangtse. The spectacular rugged scenery continued — it was a beautiful place to ride. On the rocky slopes there were even a few scrubby green juniper bushes and in the afternoon the trail led me through areas of old broken stone walls. The height of the walls told me these were not just abandoned houses, these had once been small monasteries. In a couple of places I could see where reconstruction had begun on one or two small buildings, but basically what once must have been satellite temples of Seka Gompa were in ruins.

This was Tibet's broken heart. The temples had not been abandoned, they had been destroyed by the Chinese in the horror and madness of the Cultural Revolution. 'Religion is poison,' Chairman Mao had said and his Red Guards had taken this as their cue to destroy. Who knows what atrocities might have taken place here; the temples would have been looted, scriptures burned, statues smashed and broken, the monks forced to give up their robes and their vows, and those who refused dragged off to labour camps, prisons, or shot in the back of the head. I had read of this in accounts by refugees who had escaped to India. Now I could put a face to the stories. I shuddered as I imagined Tsombo being forced to shoot his lama.

By evening I reached the He Chu and camped next to the muddy river. It was too big to cross but I'd asked that day if there was a *sampa*, a bridge and was twice told there was one further upstream. In the morning I carried on and found a narrow suspension bridge of wooden boards a hundred metres long and thirty metres above the river. I tied Packy to a post and led Ridey slowly across — at first he shied at the hollow sound of wood beneath his feet but to my surprise he walked to the other side without any trouble. I left him and went back for Packy and we were soon on our way.

At the other end of the bridge was a small stone village. By now I'd been spotted and the whole town turned out to meet me. I was taken to the house of an old man I guessed was the village head and everyone who could fit inside crowded in to watch as I was given tea, *tsampa* and dried yak meat. I was told the village was called Lehe and high above the town was a small monastery called Latze, which I'd seen from the bridge. The old man said there was a trail up to Latze and then on over the hills to another *gompa* called Kaijin.

After half an hour I set off again towards the *gompa*, a young lad showing me the way. Past the village the trail turned steep and before long I was on foot, leading Ridey as the lad went ahead with Packy. Within minutes I was gasping for breath. The trail wasn't really a trail and we were virtually climbing straight up the mountainside. It must have been over four thousand metres and I could only walk for a minute before I had to stop and rest while the young lad skipped on ahead.

Finally we made it to the top. I was feeling unwell and concerned about altitude sickness. I'd just climbed several hundred metres in a short space of time, which could be extremely dangerous at this height; certainly I knew I would have to spend the night at a lower level. The monastery was small, just a couple of buildings and a few monks. Reconstruction was still going on — Latze must have also suffered in the Cultural Revolution.

One young monk gave me hot water to drink, which restored me. He opened the main temple, revealing beautiful statues and paintings; on the altar were two cups made from the tops of human skulls, probably past lamas. These ghoulish utensils weren't meant to frighten or repulse, but to remind us that even a great lama is mortal and impermanent and death is certain for all of us. No matter who we are, we all have to face it.

When I had recovered I set off along the 'trail' to Kaijin. I had to ride; I didn't have enough energy to walk for the rest of the day. Riding, though, turned out to be far from relaxing. The trail was a mere goat track with a sheer drop of hundreds of metres below. I gripped the reins and felt each of Ridey's steps as if it were my own, suddenly aware that death might be closer than I thought. If he'd slipped or the trail gave way someone might be making a cup from my skull, if there was anything left.

A few metres ahead I saw a section of the trail had already fallen away leaving just a couple of centimetres for the horses to walk on. I pulled the reins and stopped, wondering what I should do. I couldn't go back; the trail was too narrow to turn the horses. I couldn't get off; there was no room for me to dismount. There was no other way, up or down. I decided to nudge Ridey on; if he was game enough to attempt it I'd trust him and put my life in his hooves.

I also thought this might be a good time to pray. I recited the refuge prayer in which the practitioner entrusts himself to the Buddha, his teachings and those who teach them. If we fell I hoped someone would catch us, either in this life or the next. I closed my eyes as Ridey stepped forward; I could not bear to look. When I opened my eyes again we were safely across.

By that night we had made it back down to the river and I camped not far from Kaijin. In the morning I stopped at the small monastery and its village, where much of the land had been ploughed into stony fields and planted with barley, before heading on into the mountains and an afternoon storm with heavy snow. Soon I was on another goat track high above a frozen stream; this time the ground was wet and slippery. I led both horses and progress was slow and exhausting, but by evening we'd reached the top of the narrow valley and I camped in the lee of a high pass we would attempt the next day.

It was a freezing night and morning. I got up at nine but took two hours to load the horses — my fingers so cold I could hardly tie the packs and I had to stop every few seconds to try to warm them up. We finally set off, climbed onto a ridge and found a trail that would lead us into the pass. It was much too steep to ride and the ground was rough, loose rock. I clipped Packy's lead rope onto the back of Ridey's saddle so we could walk in a little train. This worked well as long as Packy moved when Ridey did; a couple of times he was too slow and the bridle was pulled off his head. The second time this happened it broke and I had to make emergency repairs.

The altitude quickly sapped what little energy I had — I could only walk fifty paces and then had to stop to rest for a full minute, it was definitely the toughest climb so far. Finally we made it to the top, where the views were staggering. I could see the valleys I'd ridden through in the last few days, almost all the way back to Seka Gompa. I could also see the climb to the valley floor on the other side was going to be just as tough. We made our way across the ridge in a wind almost strong enough to knock me down and then started to descend in an agonising climb over the same loose rock. It took hours and by the time we reached the first house I was absolutely spent.

Luckily I was met by five wonderfully kind women, three generations of one family. There seemed to be no men at home and they were reluctant for me to go inside, serving me tea and bread in the yard and feeding the horses. As I ate I told the women I was going to Gang Rinpoche and after that I would probably go to Lhasa. One of the young women said she wanted to come with me and we laughed and joked about it; she wanted me to take her photo and even went inside to change her shirt and put on make-up. However, when faced with the camera she giggled so much I could hardly get a decent shot. The happy encounter refreshed me and when I went to leave they gave me four loaves of flat bread and I gave them a Dalai Lama photo.

Later I crossed another river on a wooden bridge, passed through another small village and camped further downstream where there was a patch of reasonable grazing. Well, it was reasonable for Tibet — if I'd seen the same back home I would probably think the ground had been sprayed with herbicide. I found enough driftwood by the river to make a fire and had bread and tea for dinner. As I sat by the fire with a mug of hot fresh brew in my hand I realised I was worn out and decided to rest the next day.

Chapter Four

The next day I stayed put, sitting by the fire drinking tea and repairing the bridles. I had a constant stream of visitors; small groups would wander out as if I was a travelling circus. One old man sat on the other side of the river and watched me the entire afternoon; others wanted a closer look and waded through the freezing flow. While one group was there a sudden heavy snowstorm blew in; I retreated to my tent to shelter, thinking they'd go back to their warm homes, but they stuck it out in the blizzard waiting for me.

It was often frustrating being treated like a freak show but there was nothing I could do about it and I needed people's help; there was no way I could travel like this without them. I asked one old man if he could sell me some grain for the horses. In the afternoon he and a couple of other men came back with a few kilograms and I paid him ten yuan. He accepted the money and returned home, but a short time later he was back. He reached into his *chuba* and pulled out a packet of instant noodles as a gift, and gave me back the ten yuan note. It was very generous — I think he didn't want to show such generosity in front of his friends. Tibetans are taught to practise kindness and compassion in secret so their acts remain pure and are not tainted by thoughts of being praised or admired.

The grain he gave me was mixed with used tea leaves. The horses loved it; they scoffed down their nosebags that night and then in the morning they were clamouring for more. As I loaded them up they seemed unusually skittish and jumpy and I wondered if it was due to the small amount of caffeine left in the tea.

Over the next few days I continued through the mountains, spending nights in small *gompas* until the wild scenery fell behind and I came into an area of more open grassland. One morning I rode into the one-street town of Gyairong. After lunch, watched by a crowd of onlookers, I checked out the shops. I was trying to ask a shopkeeper if he had any chocolate, but he didn't seem to understand me.

'Excuse me, can I help?' I turned to find a young Tibetan woman standing in the doorway.

'Um, yeah, I'm trying to buy some chocolate.'

'Oh, I don't think you'll find any here!' She laughed. 'My name's Dolma,' and she held out her hand.

I was astonished to find someone speaking such excellent English in the middle of nowhere. Dolma had studied in Beijing and had foreign friends there. Now she worked in the government administration office in this tiny town on the plains.

We chatted as we wandered up and down the street. I had a hundred questions, things I'd seen in the past weeks I hadn't understood that she could explain, words I'd heard and wanted to know the meaning of, things I wanted to be able to say. Unfortunately, I suddenly couldn't think of a single one. It was such a valuable opportunity that I thought of staying the night until I remembered the police. If the town was big enough to have a government office it would probably have police as well.

'Are there any police here?' I asked, 'It's just that I don't have a permit.'

'Yes, that guy over there in the black suit, he's police.' I casually glanced around and saw the man watching me. 'But don't worry, I don't think he's interested in you, and if he tries to give you any trouble I'll take care of him.'

'Do you get tourists here?' I asked.

'Yes, in summer we sometimes get a few passing through, but I've never seen anyone like you. Dressed like that and riding a horse! Where are you going?'

'I'm trying to reach Gang Rinpoche.'

'What! It's on the other side of Tibet! It will take you months.'

'Yeah, I know. I've been riding nearly six weeks, I think it'll take another three months.'

'Are you crazy? Why don't you go by road?'

'Well, I'm trying to be a Buddhist, I'm hoping this will be a kind of pilgrimage.'

'Well, I'm sure the Buddhas are protecting you. I'll pray that you're successful.'

It was time to leave, it was too risky to hang around for long. Dolma walked me to the edge of town and we said goodbye.

'Take care, Ian. Good luck.' We shook hands. A sudden wave of nostalgia and loneliness washed over me; I wanted to hug her, I wanted to hold someone, I wanted someone to hold me, but of course I didn't. 'Yeah, it's been great meeting you, I wish we had more time, there're so many things I want to talk about, but . . . anyway . . . '

Dolma smiled and nodded, I climbed back into the saddle and rode out of town into the freezing wind.

A couple of days later I passed the tiny settlement of Ziqu. I'd been on the trail for six weeks and had ridden about twelve hundred kilometres. The weather had turned bad again, snowing heavily with a wind like iced needles. That night I camped in the foothills of a high mountain range. There was no grazing for my poor horses and I'd run out of grain. I could hardly find a flat place for my little tent and I had to scrape the snow off the ground before pitching it in the soggy dirt. I set the horses out on a hillside so they could forage for what little grass there was. Ridey started snuffling through the snow but Packy stood looking at me, waiting for a nosebag.

'Sorry, boy, there's no more I'm afraid.' I fed him some biscuits I'd bought in Ziqu and rubbed the underside of his neck. He loved this and stretched out his neck and quivered his lips. He was exhausted, and in the morning when I woke from a freezing night he was still standing in the same place. I knew he'd only last another day or so, and I knew I would miss him. He'd been so well behaved and had never given me any trouble, carrying me over some tough terrain.

I loaded up and we headed into the mountains. Every few hundred metres we would pass gangs of Chinese construction workers, chipping away with picks and shovels. There were no bulldozers, diggers or trucks — everything was done by hand and the workers lived in tents. I stopped at one camp and was given a bowl of tea and a steamed bun by a young Chinese lad. I think many of the workers were university students who joined the gangs for their summer vacation to help pay their fees. I smiled and tried to talk, but he looked miserable. I felt sorry for the poor kid, far from home in such wretched conditions.

At midday we reached the top of the pass and continued down into the valley. I passed a small village, just a few houses on a hillside, and started climbing yet another pass. Suddenly I felt the lead rope tighten as Packy stopped. I thought he must be going to take a leak, but when I looked back he was standing looking at me.

'Come on, Packy, *chu*!' I tugged on the rope, but he didn't move. I noticed his legs were shaking and I climbed off and walked back. I rubbed his ears and he turned his head and buried it in my chest. *I'm sorry boss, I can't go on, I just can't go any further, leave me here, please.*

He was totally exhausted and I would have to find another horse. I walked slowly back to the village. Packy would walk for a few minutes and then stop. I had to wait until he was ready to move again; I didn't have the heart to push him, I already felt guilty enough for what I'd put the poor animal through.

I stopped at the first house and when the family came out to see me I said, *'Nga ta chig nyo-deu yo,'* I need to buy a horse. The family didn't have any to sell, but a young monk with them told me his father might be able to help and we set off for his house on the other side of the hill. Again poor

Packy would only walk for a few minutes before stopping. The monk walked behind trying to urge him on, but there wasn't much point. When we got to the house we had to turn off the road and walk up a small hill to the monk's home. Packy just couldn't do it so we unloaded the saddlebags and left him tied to a fence.

Inside the monk's house I was given tea and *tsampa* as we waited for a boy to bring the horses in off the hillside. Soon three horses were run into the yard; two of them were too small to bother with but the other looked good enough. I couldn't afford to be choosey and negotiated a price of two thousand three hundred Chinese yuan. We swapped the saddle from Ridey onto the new horse and made him into the packhorse to give him a relative break, carrying the lighter load of the saddlebags.

By then one of the kids had managed to get Packy up the hill into the yard; he seemed to know his journey was over and was rolling on the dusty ground of the yard, rubbing his back in the dirt. The monk's mother gave him a large pan of grain and he buried his face in it, not hearing my thank yous and goodbyes. I snapped a few hairs from his tail — if I reached Gang Rinpoche I would leave them at the mountain as a blessing.

Before I set off the young monk took my hands in his and recited a short prayer wishing me good luck for the rest of the journey. He looked into my face and smiled and I had a strange and very clear feeling I'd met him before, although I knew it couldn't be possible.

I set off again; the new horse went well, although he was skittish and spooked easily but I guessed he probably hadn't been ridden for some time. Ridey was a dreadful packhorse; he wouldn't keep up and I dragged him for the rest of the day. We made it to the pass late in the afternoon in a heavy snowstorm; again I could hardly see a thing but by evening the storm had blown over and I camped alone in a hidden arm of the valley.

Over the next few days I headed into the mountains through massive gorges, the rocky slopes studded with small juniper bushes, houses or little villages on every other bend of the quick rivers, small *gompas* clinging to the mountainsides, where rocks and stones often bore the imprint of Buddha's teachings. As an act of religious practice Tibetans carve prayers and mantras into the stone, the most common being *Om mani padme hum*. I found this carved deeply into flat cliff faces, the characters in Tibetan script several feet high; elsewhere, flat slabs were covered in symbols and stacked into long walls. A couple of times I saw men camped alone in makeshift tents as they carved stones or built walls and in some areas it seemed that every stone I passed had been written on. They lay on the ground in a natural way as if they had always borne the inscriptions, as if the Buddhas had carved them themselves.

Soon I met up with the Zaqu river, which is in fact the upper reaches of the Mekong. The rough terrain had taken its toll on the horses, especially Ridey. I had given up using him as a packhorse; he was too slow and often pulled against me and I didn't have the physical strength to drag him. It was a constant struggle to keep him moving and he was so slow it was embarrassing; the frustrating pace was driving me insane. I'd been riding him for nearly six weeks and it was time to trade him in.

For three hard days, during which I walked much of the time, I tried to replace Ridey, stopping at every house I passed. Most of the villagers and farmers didn't have horses; these days they've been replaced with motorbikes. In this area it was often too steep to ride, and horses took up scarce grazing that could be used for more valuable stock.

I finally got lucky in another town called Zadoi, this one much more Chinese and much larger, where a family I stayed a night with sold me a small white mare for fifteen hundred yuan. She wouldn't have been my first choice, but Ridey was testing my sanity and my feet were killing me. The mare became the next Packy and Packy was promoted to Ridey.

As I set off out of town the next day it rained lightly, the first time it had rained during my trip. It was a sign that summer had arrived, but it was still bitterly cold. Again the mountains fell behind me and one evening I camped alone in an empty valley near a large *chorten* or *stupa*. It had rained heavily all afternoon and my gear was wet. During the night the rain turned to snow and it was still falling steadily in the morning so I let the horses off to graze and decided to have a day of rest.

It snowed most of the day, which kept me in the tent. There was no way I could light a fire and there was nothing to burn so I had to be satisfied with cold *tsampa*. I lay in my soggy home — hungry, cold, bored and cursing the miserable weather as I read the Dalai Lama's book.

In it he again told me I was to blame for everything negative that happens to me, it was my own fault it was snowing, it was because of me that I had nothing to eat and all my stuff was wet. How could I be to blame for the weather? I have no control over it, it's nothing to do with me! But as I read on he explained. Bad things happen to me because of bad things I have done in the past, and not only in this life but in countless others that preceded it. It's the Buddhist law of cause and effect . . . what goes around comes around.

Somewhere in the past I had done something to hurt others and now I was being paid back by being stuck in a tent in the middle of nowhere. Once I had done something wrong so now it was snowing, some time I had wasted food, or stolen food from others so now I had none, I had dumped a girl who had loved me so my girlfriend had dumped me. You only get what you give and somehow in the complex laws of karma it all catches up.

Why had all this happened? Why had I done so much wrong? Because I always thought about me first. My self-centred ego acted like the Devil, telling me it was all right to do something I knew in my heart was wrong. Again it came back to *I*, *I* want this, *I* don't want that, *I* want more money, *I'm* more important, *I* have to be happy even if you're not! *I'm* number one and *I* have to be able to do whatever *I* want!

If I could stop doing bad things and only do good things all this wouldn't happen, if I cared about those who cared for me, if I gave food to people who were hungry, if I kept the promises I made to girls it might be sunny and warm now, I might be sitting in a warm house with a bowl of *tukpa*, a nice old man might sell me a really good horse for a fair price, I'd reach Gang Rinpoche without too much struggle and when I finally returned home I'd meet a really nice girl, she'd stick with me and we'd have a really happy life together, no more snowstorms, soggy tents and cold *tsampa*.

But there I was, my nose running like a tap in the cold, my feet freezing in damp socks and snow still falling outside. And yet His Holiness told me I should be happy. He said I was lucky it was snowing, it could be much worse. I might meet this same snowstorm the next time I was at the top of a pass in the darkness instead of now, so I should be grateful. I could find myself with nothing to eat one day when I needed the strength to walk across that same pass instead of on a rest day spent lying in the tent; my partner might leave me when I'm old and all my hair has fallen out and no one wants to know me. Much better that it happened when it did, and now that these negative results have ripened they're over and done with. Better to have a cold now than pneumonia next week.

I recited mantras for a while and said my prayers and somewhere in the cosmos the karmic scales tipped a little, the snow stopped and the skies cleared and I was able to get out of the tent and dry my gear. In the evening I walked across to the *chorten* and did *kora*, walking round and round with my *mala* in my hand saying mantras. In the morning the skies were still clear and we set off up the long valley towards an easy pass. Near the top I saw a large fox trot across the trail. He was in no hurry to scamper away, stopping to scratch a flea. Later I saw a herd of about ten large hornless deer, which loped off a short distance before standing and watching me and my horses plod by.

Traditionally, Tibetans haven't been great hunters due to their Buddhist beliefs and many wild animals have little fear of man. This might be why it was easy for the Chinese to slaughter wild ass, wild yak and gazelles to feed their soldiers and road construction crews during the invasion.

I walked down the other side of the pass into an enormous valley that I would spend the next few days crossing. During the afternoon I met families moving their herds to summer pastures, although it was still bitterly cold and there wasn't a hint of green. I passed one old man pushing a herd of yaks along and saw one calf had separated from the rest and was snuffling its way along by the stream. The old man hadn't noticed and it was being left behind. A grey shadow moved on the hillside — a large wolf eyeing the calf. I called out to the nomad and waved towards the calf. He signalled his thanks and gathered the animal back into the herd. The wolf missed out.

A few days later I crossed some low hills and the Tanggula Shan mountains came into view on the opposite side of another vast sweeping valley; it was a great sawtooth range stretching as far as I could see to the east and west. I had been riding for eight weeks and was exhausted. I was beginning to think this land had no such thing as summer. Occasionally there would be a relatively mild day and I'd think this was a turn in the weather, but the next day it would plunge back into winter again.

The ground in the valley was a nightmare — rough, wet and a mixture of boggy holes and lumpy sod. We'd come to frozen streams the horses would refuse to cross; sometimes I had to lead them over one at a time, terrified we'd crash through into God knows what underneath. By afternoon I'd be hungry and cold. Sometimes I'd stop at houses and literally beg for tea and something to eat. I'd take my tea bowl from the folds of my *chuba* and give the people a double thumbs-up gesture saying *'Kuchi, kuchi'* which means 'please'. I'd seen beggars doing it in Lhasa. But often they shook their heads and waved me off. *'Cha mindu!'* they'd say. We haven't got any tea.

Snowstorms were a frequent unwelcome afternoon feature. By six or seven in the evening I'd look for somewhere to camp. If there was no one around it was another night on the frozen ground, struggling to put the tent up in the continuous gale. There was often almost no grass for the poor horses and they would grunt at me, waiting for a nosebag of grain I didn't have. I couldn't eat either; there was no vegetation so no sticks to make a fire and any dung on the ground was too wet to burn. Sometimes I tried, but it was impossible to get anything lit in the wind and I'd give up in frustration before crawling into the tent, still wet from the previous night.

I'd struggle to get my boots off over my thick socks and then fight to get the door closed. My whole body ached from the physical strain of trying to control two unwilling horses all day, my fingers cracked and raw from dragging the lead rope. Finally I'd crawl into my sleeping bag, completely drained. At last something that resembled warmth. I'd still be wearing all my clothes and I'd pull the hood over my head and draw the string closed, then the bloody zip would get stuck.

Late one afternoon I met three monks riding on the grassland, with ritual drums tied to their backs. They told me they were from a small *gompa* called Pe Mon, about ten kilometres away. Before long I could see a massive weather front closing in, a blizzard bearing down on us like a gigantic wave. The monks were in a hurry to avoid it and my tired horses were slowing them down. A couple of the younger lads went on ahead, but one of the others stayed with me. I'm glad he did; when the storm hit we could hardly see a thing. I struggled to keep up, knowing that if I lost sight of him I'd probably never see him again. In the blizzard I became very disoriented, sure we'd changed direction and were going the opposite way.

The monk ahead of me kept singing, I followed his voice and we eventually reached the monastery. I was taken inside and given tea and something to eat before the monks came outside to the yard to help me unload the horses. That night I slept in a broken-down shed, as rats scuttled in the corners. There was no door and the floor was made of mud. Still, it was fairly warm and better than another night in the tent.

The next day we spent another twenty kilometres crossing the bog. In the afternoon Packy stopped suddenly to have a leak, and my arm got tangled in the lead rope and almost wrenched out of the socket, straining the muscles in my shoulder and chest. Ridey stopped just in time; if he hadn't I think I would have broken my arm. By evening we were nearing some hills on the other side of the plain and I camped alone under a nearly full moon, so bright I could see for kilometres around my camp.

In the morning I woke up in pain. My chest hurt from the previous day's wrenching and I felt as if I'd broken a rib. Loading up took for ever — lifting anything was so painful — and climbing into the saddle I nearly cried out in agony.

Not long after we set off we found a road running vaguely southwest; it was just two wheel ruts in the ground but after the terrain we'd spent the last couple of days crossing it felt like red carpet. At last I had something to follow, a direction to go in, exactly where I had no idea, but it was a road and it must lead somewhere.

Late that afternoon I found a black tent before some low hills. When I stopped an old woman came out and stared at me. I took out my tea bowl and asked if I could have something to drink. She wouldn't let me inside but brought a kettle of tea out and I sat on the ground. The old lady crouched and watched as I drank. I thought showing her my photos might break the ice, but as I reached into my bag she shrank back. After that I kept still, finished my tea and rode on.

Soon the weather turned, clouds blew in suddenly and it snowed heavily for the rest of the day. I approached a couple of mud-brick houses and stopped, hoping to find shelter for the night but there was no one there and I set off on foot. It was too cold to ride a soggy horse. With my head down to keep the slush out of my face I felt as if I was crossing the Somme. I imagined my grandpa and great-uncle marching beside me. They'd served in the Second World War, and I pictured them in their uniforms, heavy packs on their backs and weighty rifles in their hands tramping across some God-forsaken European battlefield, in a hell a thousand times worse than I could ever imagine. They must have been terrified, but when the call went out they volunteered and when the battles began they stood up, took a step and moved forward. 'Come on cobber, chin up mate, we'll be home by Christmas.'

I kept hoping to find someone to stay the night with, but as darkness fell I started to look for a campsite. Eventually we stopped in the middle of nowhere. I unloaded the horses and tethered them out to forage for sparse grazing beneath the snow. I scraped the snow off a patch of muddy earth and set up my tent. By then everything was damp, especially my *chuba*, but at last in my sleeping bag I read for a while by candlelight.

Though the world and its beings be full of the fruits of misdeeds,
And unwanted sufferings pour upon me like rain,
Inspire me to see them as means to exhaust the results of negative actions,
And take these miserable conditions as a path.

This verse struck a deep chord with me: 'miserable conditions' was what was outside my tent — miserable, cold, wet snow. Enough to drive anyone to despair, enough to make me depressed and despondent, enough to make me give up this ridiculous idea and forget the whole thing, accept failure and admit it was too tough.

But of course His Holiness pointed out an alternative. Of course it was difficult, of course it was snowing — this was Tibet! What did I expect? I felt as if Tibet was testing me to find a weak point and when she did she would break me. But if she wasn't, what kind of trip would this be? What would I gain from this exercise if the weather was bright and sunny, warm with no wind? Hardly a test of endurance. What if the sacred mountain had only been a couple of weeks away? Hardly an epic journey.

What would it be like if I could stay in a cosy trekking lodge every night? Not much of an adventure. What if every time I approached a Tibetan house the people came running out, bowing and begging me to enter their simple homes? It would do nothing to reduce my pride and arrogance. What if my girlfriend had never left me? I would have learnt nothing, I would have continued hurting her and myself and we both would have become even more unhappy. If nothing bad happened to me, I'd keep making the same mistakes over and over and achieve nothing.

The Dalai Lama pointed out the obvious: I would never solve all my problems; there would always be something happening I didn't like; nothing would be perfect and the more I suffered and overcame the more I would gain and accomplish. Instead of bemoaning the troubles I encountered I should welcome them, the harder it was the better, no pain no gain, nothing ventured nothing won. I should invite Tibet to give me her worst, let it snow, let the wind blow and freeze me, put mountains in my way just to give me something to climb. This was supposed to be a pilgrimage and the harder it was the greater the rewards would be.

I blew out the candle and carefully lay down. My ribs ached and I could barely turn over, the pain kept me awake and I listened to lumps of snow slide down the tent walls. The thought of packing up in the freezing slush the next day was one miserable condition I could do without.

The skies were still grey in the morning but the snow had eased. We set off along the road again but made very slow progress. Ridey was worn out and Packy nearing exhaustion. I dragged her behind me, but she was so slow I pulled the bridle off her head twice. It infuriated me; each time I had to recapture her, fix the bridle and put it back on with numb fingers, my chest hurting so badly it was painful to lift my arm. I tried to think of what I'd read the night before. I tried to think that by having slow horses now, when speed wasn't really essential, I might have fast horses at another time in the future. Perhaps in another life I might be reborn in a lawless land and have to escape from bloodthirsty bandits on horseback. Hopefully by then my 'slow horse karma' would have been exhausted and I would be on swifter mounts.

In the early afternoon I arrived at a small group of houses where I rode into a courtyard and was met by a group of about twenty men. One of them took me inside to a small warm room where I met a young lama and his attendant monk.

'Where do you come from?' he asked. I was astonished he could speak English.

'I'm from New Zealand.'

'You are very far from home, where are you going?'

'Gang Rinpoche.'

'You are very far from that mountain too.'

'Yes, I know.' He said something to the monk, who poured me a bowl of hot tea.

'The weather is bad today.' It was snowing again. 'You should stay here and rest.'

'Thank you, I'm very tired, and my horses also.'

'Yes, I can see.'

I unloaded the horses and set them out to graze. Back inside, the lama introduced himself as Tenbi Nyimba. He was aloof and difficult to make sense of, despite his apparent ability to speak English. One minute he had a good grasp of the language and the next it was as if he couldn't understand even simple questions. During the afternoon he had a steady stream of visitors; the group of men I'd met when I arrived had come to see him and one at a time they came to receive his blessing and ask advice. Each man would offer money and then crouch on the floor in front of the lama. They addressed him as *rinpoche*, precious, and although he was only twenty-five he was already held in high esteem.

Later in the afternoon he sat on the sleeping platform reading a text and spinning a prayer wheel. Something struck me as strange and I realised he was spinning the wheel the wrong way. In Buddhist custom everything moves in a clockwise direction, but he was turning the wheel the opposite way. 'Are you *Bonpo*?' I asked.

'Rey, rey.' He nodded.

Bon is a shamanist religion that predates Buddhism; it was suppressed and almost wiped out by the powerful monasteries hundreds of years ago. There are great Tibetan legends in which the proponents of each religion challenged each other to contests of magic and cunning, flying about on magic drums, disassembling their bodies and putting them back together, bringing life to the dead. Eventually the Buddhists won and Bon was marginalised as a 'black' practice. The Tibetans once believed that reciting Bon mantras would turn your tongue black and even today some people poke out their tongues when they meet to show they haven't been saying the black mantras. Their faith was one of sorcery and secret ritual, magic spells and spirits, and the Bon were feared and respected. Today, Bon has mixed with Buddhism and at first glance there are few signs of difference — monks wear the same robes, temples look the same, but they do things the 'wrong' way.

In the evening most of the men left. The family were friendly, although the father seemed anxious. His mother was ancient and could hardly move — I guessed the lama had come to prepare her for the next life. The man would be paying the precious lama and was probably worried about getting his money's worth. I was exhausted and so were my horses. It was now eight days since we'd taken a break. I was in constant pain and even raising a tea bowl to my lips was distressful.

That night the family boiled up a great pot of yak bones. The meat was served into a large bowl, left to cool and placed in front of the lama. I was dearly hoping to be given something substantial, but I didn't want to look greedy. The father pulled out half a boiled yak's heart and handed it to me. I held the solid, dark organ in my hand, it wasn't very appetising but I knew it would be nutritious and I ate the whole thing.

That night I slept inside on a bench in the family's room. I was warm and comfortable but woke up with my stomach churning from eating too much yak heart. I felt nauseous and my chest hurt so badly I could barely move. I lay in my sleeping bag feeling as if I'd been hit by a truck. I couldn't sit up; I made several attempts but felt so weak and it was so painful I fell back onto the bench, gasping for breath.

Eventually one of the young sons noticed and helped me to my feet. I managed to get dressed and went into the room where the lama was staying.

'Good morning, Ian. How are you today?' He could speak English again.

'Not so good, I'm sick, do you think I could stay here today?'

'Yes, yes, no problem, stay, stay.'

I collapsed into a chair and his attendant brought me some tea. Not long after the father came and asked when I was leaving. I didn't like the situation — the lama could invite me to stay and the father would feel obliged to agree, but it was obvious I wasn't welcome. I was getting in the way of the lama's work, but I was desperately in need of a day off. It was snowing again and I felt awful. I thought of offering him money to allow me to stay, but I would still be unwelcome.

I made myself some strong black tea, which moved my stomach. I went outside and had a dump in the snow, after which I felt much better. I ate some dry bread sitting inside by the fire as the lama and his attendant made *torma* offerings, little sculptures made from *tsampa* shaped like tiny Christmas trees, which would be offered to whatever deity or spirit would be beneficial to help the old woman's passing. For the rest of the afternoon everyone disappeared inside a yak-hair tent pitched a short distance away. I went outside to move my horses and heard mumblings from inside. I wondered what ritual was being performed but didn't dare approach; the disruption of a stranger could scare off whatever spirits had been called and would be very inauspicious.

I waited back in the house. The father walked in and looked at me, said something I didn't understand and walked out again.

'What did he say?' I asked the lama.

'We have very much work to do,' he told me. It was time for me to leave.

I brought the horses in and loaded up and the *Bonpo* lama came out to see me off. 'Go carefully, Ian. My *gompa* is that way, maybe you reach in two days, you stay there and wait for me, maybe I come next week.'

'Thank you, I hope to see you there.'

A few days in the welcome comfort of a *gompa* sounded like a perfect solution. I thanked the father, he helped me into the saddle and I set off. Not long after the weather improved and I started feeling better. The horses hadn't recovered much, though. Packy was a dead weight and I couldn't drag her so I clipped the lead rope to a link on the saddle and let poor Ridey pull her along. The high plain slowly rose before us; we were heading for another pass. On either side of the plain snow-coated hills swept up towards the clearing skies.

By evening we were nearing the top of the valley and I camped at seven. I could see a group of houses nearby but decided I didn't feel like eating and was too exhausted to communicate with anyone. I could stop there in the morning and try to get something to eat. I put the horses out and set up my tent, crawled inside and fell into my sleeping bag, asleep in an instant.

The weather was clear in the morning but when I set off to find the houses they'd vanished, like an oasis. I followed the road and after a couple of hours stopped at a tent where an old woman served me two bowls of lifesaving *tukpa*. She was a kindly old *Bonpo* woman who sat by the fire watching me with a gentle smile as she spun her prayer wheel anticlockwise.

After I set off again I had to cross the wide expanse of a frozen river gully near the top of the plain. The horses nervously stepped across the frozen snow; I could hear water running underneath in a hollow cavern. Suddenly the ice gave way and Ridey crashed through to the riverbed; I found myself sitting on a horse up to his neck in a snow hole. Luckily there was only a metre of water in the stream and I managed to get my feet out of the stirrups and rolled off onto the snow. Ridey leapt out and we continued on foot to the other bank.

Eventually we came to a wide pass on the edge of the plain, prayer flags marking the spot where the high ground ended and the descent began. I headed down the trail, dragging the horses behind until we met the river in the valley below. With the drop in altitude the air thickened and became warmer, there was green grass and my mood lifted. We carried on following the river for the rest of the day. Before long it dropped lower and we found ourselves on a rocky road like a ledge, hundreds of metres above the river.

In the evening we got stuck behind a traffic jam of yaks being driven home for the night — the young man pushing them along told me the *Bonpo gompa* was only an hour away. I hoped to reach it that night, but before long we ran out of daylight and I camped alone in a little side valley. I put the horses out above my camp. Ridey started grazing but Packy stood staring at the ground, not even bothering to eat, the sign of an exhausted horse. We had been on the trail for ten days without a rest, the horses were finished and I had almost reached my limit. We needed to rest for three or four days and I hoped that when I reached the *gompa* I'd find the opportunity to do so.

We set off again in the morning and after thirty minutes rounded a bend to find a small village before us and the *gompa* high above on the hillside. I left the horses and crossed the river on an iron bridge to the village — just a few old concrete, semi-derelict buildings and a school. I walked into the yard and met the young yak herder I'd spoken to the day before.

'*Sa khang yawrey?*' I asked, is there a restaurant here?

'*Rey, rey,*' he replied, pointing to one of the shacks.

Inside several Tibetan men playing mahjong were surprised to see me swagger through the door. One of them pulled up a stool and I was soon drinking tea and scoffing a bowl of rice and meat. Before long a monk of about thirty poked his head through the door.

'Hello, how do you do?'

'I do very well thank you. You can speak English?' I asked him.

'Oh yes, but not so well. My name is Lobsang, nice to meet you.'

'Nice to meet you too!'

And it really was nice to meet him. Now I was more convinced than ever that this would be a good place to rest for a few days. With Lobsang to help me it was a great opportunity, the *gompa* above the village looked exciting and I looked forward to exploring it with him as my guide. There was an incredible feeling of calmness around Lobsang, and I felt an instant affinity, like meeting an old friend. Lobsang told me he'd spent five years in India with the refugee communities, hence his ability to speak English.

'Lobsang, I'm exhausted and my horses are nearly finished, do you think I could stay here for a few days and rest?'

'Oh yes, that will be OK, but we must get permission from the village head.'

Just then a Tibetan man in a shabby suit walked through the door; he was the assistant to the village head, who wasn't due back until four. He stared at me intently and exchanged words with Lobsang, the mahjong players went quiet for the first time since I'd walked in and looked back and forth between the man and the monk. Lobsang maintained his dreamy calmness, but I could feel tension, something wasn't quite right; instinct was telling me I should get back on my horses and leave.

'Is it all right for me to stay?' I asked Lobsang after the man had left.

'Oh yes, there's no problem, we just have to ask the head, but no problem.'

'If I have to I can go, I don't want to cause any trouble.'

'Oh no, everything is OK, we were just talking about where you can sleep.'

Lobsang's calmness rubbed off on me and I relaxed. I'd been travelling like this for two months without any trouble; I didn't see why it should be different in this tiny village. The place wasn't even on my map, and besides, my horses needed to rest. The official was overreacting and being overzealous and self-important and there was no reason for me to worry.

We led the horses across to the village and unloaded my gear in front of part of the school dorm. The children from the surrounding mountains would stay here over the long winter months when their herder families had less work; they'd go to school, then return home in spring to help with the newborn yaks and lambs. I asked Lobsang if he could take me up to the *gompa*, but he said he'd been told to wait until the village head came back. On the other side of the river a trader had set up shop in a tent and I stocked up on supplies before spending the rest of the afternoon lying in the sun.

The village head finally arrived in a jeep, an older man with a gun on his belt. I took off my hat and bowed, hoping to grease him up so he'd let me stay. He shook my hand warmly and invited me inside his home, ordering his wife to make tea. On the wall, instead of a portrait of the Dalai Lama there was a large picture of Chairman Mao, the Great Helmsman who had brought destruction and disaster to Tibet and caused the deaths of 1.2 million Tibetans. Again I felt apprehension, but Lobsang was called to translate and I calmed down.

'Can you ask him if I can stay for a few days?' He translated this to the headman, who grinned and gestured for me to stay put. 'Please tell him I can pay and I'll keep out of the way, I just want to rest my horses and I won't cause any trouble.'

'He says there is no problem for you to stay, everything is OK. Do you have a card like this?' Lobsang reached into the folds of his robes and took out the Chinese identity card all Tibetans carry. I should have shown him my passport but I was very reluctant to put that into anyone else's hands so

I handed him my New Zealand driver's licence. The headman seemed very impressed even though he couldn't read a single word and the formalities seemed complete.

The old man unlocked a room in the dorm and helped me lug my gear inside, before leaving Lobsang and me alone. 'Can we go up to the *gompa*?' I asked.

'Oh, perhaps we should go tomorrow, Ian. I will rest now.'

The monk gathered up his robes and started walking home. I watched him go — there was something strange in the way he moved, his actions very slow, almost as if he thought about every move before he made it, trying to decide how to take each step using the least amount of energy, and I realised he must be quite unwell.

I locked the room and walked across the river to where there was a large *mani* wall and joined a few villagers as they performed *kora* around the stones in *Bonpo* anticlockwise fashion. I felt strange walking the 'wrong' way but didn't think it would be polite to do otherwise.

As it got dark I went back to the village and found Lobsang's house. He invited me in and we chatted while his elderly mother cooked us a meal of yak meat and cabbage. I felt spoilt, two good meals in one day, and gobbled mine down.

Before it was too late I said good night and we agreed to meet the next day to visit the *gompa* if the village head gave me permission. I walked back to my room, looking forward to a quiet evening reading by candlelight. However, after a few minutes the headman knocked on the window and gestured for me to come outside. I opened the door and he signalled me to follow him. Thinking he was inviting me for a meal I tried to explain I'd already eaten.

'*Ma rey, ma rey!*' He shook his head. I locked the door and reluctantly followed. As we turned the corner a chill ran up my spine — parked in front of his house was a white jeep. We walked through the yard, I looked through the windows and my heart skipped several beats and sank to the pit of my stomach. Seated opposite the door were three uniformed policemen. *Oh shit, this is not good*, I told myself, *this is not good at all*.

Chapter Five

I smiled and greeted the three officers as I walked into the room, trying to play the innocent tourist. One of them, a Tibetan, jumped up and whisked my long knife out of my belt. I sat down and they started shouting at me in Chinese.

'I don't speak Chinese!' I told them. The youngest was Chinese and could speak a bit of English. He crossed the room, bending over so his face was in front of mine. 'This area, is closed, it is closed!' He shouted as if I was deaf.

'Oh, I'm so sorry, *gawn da, gawn da,*' I said to other two Tibetan officers. 'I didn't know, *hako-masong, hako-masong!*'

The Chinese cop was a spotty, fat-faced boy, but the Tibetans were more formidable. The elder, who seemed to be higher ranking, said something like '*Hako-masong*'. Bullshit!

I kept up my act of the simple and not too bright tourist, trying to make it look as if I had made an innocent mistake. The police were not amused. 'Passport!' the Tibetan next to me demanded. I took out my passport and he reached for it, but I pushed his hands away. One thing I'd learnt from previous experiences in Mongolia and Tibet was never put your passport in the hands of someone who might not give it back. Once the police have it you're stuffed. 'No, you can look but don't touch,' I told him. He growled at me like a dog but didn't try to take it again. I turned the pages and he examined my visa, writing down the number and my name.

I demanded he show me his identity card. I followed his example and wrote down his serial number, hoping this would make him nervous and give me an edge, but he scoffed and looked angrier. Then, like the village head, he wanted to see my Chinese ID card.

'I don't have one.'

He shouted something to the Chinese officer who said, 'You must show him this card.' I showed him my New Zealand driver's licence. 'No! Not this, show him your Chinese card! You must show him!' Things were becoming tense.

'I don't have one!' The Tibetan officer was obviously not clued up as to what documents foreigners are supposed to hold, as far as I knew the card he was demanding was only issued to Chinese citizens. He shouted something at me in Tibetan.

'I haven't got one! I'm not Chinese! How am I supposed to have a Chinese ID card if I'm not Chinese?'

The Tibetan officer shouted again and then turned his back on me like a sulky girlfriend. Meanwhile, the village head and his family had been watching in stunned silence. He spoke quietly to the other Tibetan and then to one of his boys, who ran outside. His wife served tea and we sat in silence for a few minutes. Things calmed down and soon the boy returned with Lobsang, who had been called to translate. The poor monk looked exhausted and nervous and didn't touch the tea placed in front of him.

'Lobsang, can you tell them I'm very sorry, I didn't know this place was closed, I don't want to make any more trouble.'

Lobsang sat with a dumb smile and didn't speak. I tried again. 'Can you tell them I'm really sorry, I didn't know this place was closed.' But again he didn't move. He was playing dumb, afraid of letting on to the police that he could speak good English. He was a monk who had been in India and may have already had serious trouble with the authorities; if a check was done on his background and they suspected he'd been helping an illegal foreign traveller he could find himself in strife, even be imprisoned. I didn't ask again.

The Chinese officer spoke. 'You must come to Naqu by jeep.'

I tried to explain I had two expensive horses, and I wasn't going to leave them. 'I'll ride my horses to Naqu, that's where I'm going anyway [a lie]. I'll report to the police in Naqu [another lie].'

'No! We will go by jeep tonight!'

'Tonight! But it's late, you must be very tired, let's go tomorrow.'

'We came from Lhasa, we've been driving since last night.'

'Then we should stay here tonight.' I was trying to buy a little time.

The police tried to argue but by now they were exhausted. They'd been in Lhasa when my appearance had been reported, by whom I'll never know, and had been sent to get me, a journey of at least two days. My guess is that one of the men I met at the house with the Bonpo lama reported me to the local authorities, who reported me to the police in Naqu, the region's capital. Without knowing it, some time in the last few days, I'd crossed from the Chinese province of Qinghai, which was mostly open to foreign travellers, to Xizang, what the Chinese refer to as Tibet, which is mostly closed. So there I was, under the guard of three Chinese police officers and my great journey to Gang Rinpoche in tatters.

Lobsang left and I was taken back to my room by the three cops. I tried to tell them I wanted to sleep alone but they insisted on staying with me, obviously not wanting to let me out of their sight. They unrolled mattresses and quilts lent to them by the village head, on the beds either side of mine, made themselves a meal of instant noodles and cracked cans of beer. I opened my notebook and started saying my prayers. They burst out laughing but I kept on reciting through to the end. Why should I care what they thought of me?

I tried to think of what my strategy should be in terms of dealing with the police. I certainly wouldn't make things easy for them and I decided to make a fuss if I was made to leave my horses. However, being nasty wasn't going to help much either. I could see no way I was going to be able to leave the village on my horses and decided to go along with whatever they said as much as I could — play the nice, stupid tourist, buy as much time as possible and look for a way out.

Certainly there was no use arguing with these three. They were just doing their job, they probably couldn't care less if I was out there but I'd been reported and they'd been sent to get me. There was no way I was going to risk trying to bribe them, it was too dangerous. The Chinese officer was probably there to make sure the Tibetans did their job properly.

'How far is it to Naqu?' I asked.

'All day by jeep, first we go to Liarong, then Naqu.'

'I see, is there a good hotel in Naqu?'

'Oh yes, very nice hotel.'

'How much does it cost?'

'Not sure.'

'Are there any other tourists in Naqu?'

'Oh yes, sometimes you can meet them.'

I kept asking questions about Naqu, hoping to give the impression I was happy about going there and not likely to cause trouble. After their beer the Tibetan officers calmed down and cheered up a bit. We talked about New Zealand and I showed them my photos, but not my maps. I didn't want to give them any more information than I had to about where I'd been and where I was hoping to go — the less they knew the better. After a while I joked them round a bit and lightened the mood. However, when I asked if I could have my knife back the Tibetan refused and instead asked me if I had a gun. They were all armed with handguns and carried an automatic rifle in their jeep.

The candles were blown out and the three cops were soon asleep, the Tibetans snoring blissfully while I lay awake cursing myself for being so complacent. I shouldn't have stayed here, I'd smelt trouble but I'd ignored it. But even if I'd kept riding they would have found me. I didn't sleep a wink trying to think of a plan to get myself out of this. I couldn't escape on my horses, how could I load them without anyone knowing? And besides, they were exhausted, I could hardly gallop off in a cloud of dust. I had mad ideas about locking the police in the room, but they'd break the windows and get out, or slashing their tyres, but it was pointless. I would be leaving tomorrow in a jeep.

We got up early, packed and loaded my stuff into the jeep. After breakfast with the headman I brought in Ridey and Packy. The police and the headman had arranged for an old man from the village to take my horses to Naqu. I told them they were too exhausted to be ridden and they promised the old man would lead them on foot. It was over two hundred kilometres to Naqu and all this seemed a very strange arrangement and a lot of fuss. The old man showed up before we left and I told him the horses were not to be ridden or loaded. I expected him to load them with goods to sell in town. He said he wouldn't but wanted me to give him three hundred yuan to get his teeth fixed. I refused. He complained but the police told him he had a job to do and he must do it. I felt sorry for the man, it would take a week to reach Naqu on foot.

I looked at poor old Packy and decided it was pointless taking her on the trek to Naqu. Without several days' rest she was finished and it was a waste of time taking her any further. I doubted she'd make the journey; she'd quite likely die from exhaustion along the way. I sent a boy off to find Lobsang. I took him aside and gave him Packy, although he wouldn't have much use for a horse himself; perhaps he could sell her and buy some medicine. I held his hands in mine and we talked in a whisper. 'I'm sorry, Ian. Last night, I couldn't say anything.'

'That's OK, I understand.'

'I'm sorry about all this. How will you go to Gang Rinpoche now?'

'Don't worry, I'll find a way. I'll go to Naqu and maybe get some more horses, I don't know but don't worry, I'll be fine.'

Before handing him over I took a few hairs from Packy's tail to leave at the mountain. I did the same with Ridey, now quite sure I wouldn't see him again and wondering if I'd ride again in Tibet, let alone reach Gang Rinpoche.

We squeezed into the little jeep and set off at eight, driving out of the mountains into open grassland valleys. The weather was bad and the road terrible, so rough and uncomfortable it would have been faster on my horses. The Tibetans took turns driving, not daring to entrust the difficult job to their Chinese junior; they smoked, drank beer — even behind the wheel — and played the same dreadful cassette of Chinese pop songs over and over; by the end of the day I would know every bloody song by heart.

In the middle of the day we stopped for lunch at some tents where some Tibetans were building mud-brick houses. While we ate and drank tea the police checked the workers' ID cards, and one man was severely chastised for not bringing his children's cards. It was very clear that administration in Xizang was much stricter than in Qinghai.

On we drove across good riding country, even ground and good grass; all I could think of was that I should be on a horse, not stuck in this damn jeep.

Often the driver would stop and talk to the Tibetans on the roadside; they would peer suspiciously through the window at me. I felt like a criminal, even though I didn't feel I'd done anything wrong. And every time we passed a nomad on horseback I felt jealous. We crossed a couple of passes and stopped on one to take a break. I walked around the prayer flags saying mantras and praying to the Buddhas to get me out of this as the police laughed. I tried to get them to line up in front of the jeep to take a photo; the Chinese was happy to but the Tibetans refused. In the end I got one of them to take a picture of myself with the Chinese man.

At about four we made it to Liarong. We stopped at the police compound where the wife of one of the Tibetan officers cooked lunch before we set off again, in a better jeep and on a better road. We joined the main Lhasa road and arrived in Naqu at about half past seven in the evening. I was nervous and tense; I knew I would meet more senior police officers who would decide my fate and could do whatever they wanted with me.

We drove to the centre of town and stopped in the main street in front of the Naqu Hotel. I was allowed out of the jeep but not allowed to move away from it until phone calls were made to another senior officer. He soon arrived, a short little Tibetan who, dressed in his dark blue uniform with shiny buttons, looked like a monkey. I was told I had to stay in the Naqu Hotel — it looked expensive so I asked someone to find out how much. The cheapest rooms were thirty yuan a night. I said it was too much — it wasn't really, but I was in a bad mood and felt like making things difficult and asked if there was another hotel.

'No! You must stay in this hotel!'

'What about that hotel?' There was another hotel next door, not more than twenty metres away.

'No! More expensive!'

'Really? It looks cheap, I'll go and ask.'

'No! You must stay here!'

'I just want to ask, you can come with me.'

'No! Stay here!'

'Can I stand over there?' I was playing now.

'No! Stay here!'

'I just want to stand over there.'

'No! Don't move!'

I stood next to the little Tibetan officer, even in his hat he didn't reach my shoulder. I made fun of his height. 'Ha! Look how short he is!' I stood right next to him, measuring up and showing how I dwarfed him. This wasn't going to help but I was enjoying myself.

'Yes, but he's very strong,' the Chinese officer said.

'I don't think so, he's too small!' A few people passing by stopped to watch me humiliate the pint-sized bobby; they giggled and the little cop grinned nervously.

Eventually I agreed to stay in the Naqu Hotel; it was pointless arguing. However, more calls had to be made before I was allowed to take my stuff out of the jeep, then more calls before I was allowed to move inside. Finally I checked into a dingy room on the ground floor facing the main street. I paid for two nights, guessing I would be here for that long at least, and the Tibetan officer gave me back my knife. 'Stay here, we will come back in the morning to see you.'

'What will happen to me?'

'Tomorrow we will decide.'

'OK, see you tomorrow, now fuck off and have a nice day!'

'Yes, thank you very much.'

The room was freezing, the toilet was a stinking concrete hole out the back and there was no running water. I stashed my saddles and riding gear in the corner; they looked ridiculous piled on the hotel floor. I suddenly felt very lonely. I was homesick for my little tent on a freezing windswept plain and missing my horses.

I crossed the road to a little Chinese restaurant for a meal; the only other diners were a couple of engineers from Lhasa, one Chinese and one Tibetan. We talked for a while and the Tibetan called his son in Lhasa on his cellphone. The young man spoke excellent English and it was nice to hear a friendly voice. When I tried to pay for my dinner the Chinese engineer insisted on paying for me and even bought me a can of beer. It was very kind and generous; it cheered me up and I felt much less friendless and alone.

Back in my freezing room I said my prayers and wrote my diary, recounting the day's mostly unpleasant events and not looking forward to the next. What a mess. I knew I might be fined, kicked out of Tibet and kicked out of China. In a few days I might be sitting in a bar in Hong Kong. Months ago I would have been pleased at that thought, but now it was the last place I wanted to be. I'd come to Tibet to deliver my lama's ashes to Gang Rinpoche and I had already ridden fifteen hundred kilometres in eight weeks. I couldn't give up. I refused to give up.

I still had my passport, all my riding gear and enough money. The idea of a pilgrimage was still worthwhile — we'd travelled two hundred and eighteen kilometres in the jeep and I could add an extra week's ride at the end to make up the difference I'd lost today. If I could just get out of town and buy some more horses . . . I might not get far but decided that if I got caught again, well, I'd have to take what I was dealt. I decided to see what happened the next day, play along with the cops and look for a chance to get away. I couldn't just lie down, I had to fight. Tibet was throwing another obstacle in front of me, the Buddhas were testing me, but only because they wanted me to succeed. I suddenly felt defiant and excited. I wrote in my journal: 'This is NOT over yet!'

I slept surprisingly well and managed to get a thermos of hot water in the morning to make tea and *tsampa* and wash in what was left. The police turned up at eleven — the midget Tibetan and two young Tibetan officers. One was a woman who could speak some English, and they seemed excited and pleased to meet me, as if I was a foreign guest rather than a criminal.

'Would you like some tea?' I offered.

'Oh, no thank you, please don't go to any trouble.'

They seemed very happy with my attempt at hospitality, even the little Tibetan was smiling and seemed to have forgiven my insults of the previous day. We chatted while I finished my second bowl of *tsampa*, then set off in a jeep for the police station.

We drove through an archway into a large yard past armed guards. I was taken inside and marched up the stairs to an office on the second floor. Every time we passed someone they'd stop and stare at the strange renegade cowboy — I felt like Billy the Kid. Inside the office I met one of the Tibetan cops from Liarong and soon another young Chinese officer who could speak reasonable English arrived with his own telephone, which he plugged into the wall. The phone was wrapped in a lacy cover with frills, which I guess his wife or mother had made for him.

'You have broken the laws of the People's Republic of China by travelling in a closed area without a permit, how do you plead to this charge?'

'Innocent.'

'But you were found in Liarong, you have no permission to be there, how can you say you are innocent?'

'How am I supposed to know that area is closed?'

'You could have checked with the correct authorities before you went there.'

'I did.' I was lying.

'Where?'

'In Zadoi.'

'Where?'

'Zadoi, it's a town in Qinghai, don't you know it?'

'Um, yes, of course we know it.'

'Yes, well, I went there, and as soon as I arrived I reported to the local police and asked permission to stay. It was given and I told them I was going to Liarong and they gave me permission to go there.'

This was all a complete lie — Zadoi was where I'd bought my last horse but I'd never dared report to the police. However, the police here would have no way of checking, so this was going to be my defence.

'What exactly did they tell you?'

'The police in Zadoi were very kind and friendly. After I reported to them we all had lunch and drank beer. When I told them I was going to Liarong they wished me good luck and said it was OK, so I was very surprised and angry to find that it's closed! How can tourists travel if we can't get reliable information on which areas are closed and which are not?'

The young cop translated all this to the others, who didn't seem impressed by my lies but weren't really able to argue.

'The police in Zadoi have no right to give you permission to travel in Xizang; you should have reported to the police in Naqu and asked for permission here.'

'That's what I was doing. When the police found me the day before yesterday I was on my way to Naqu to get permission.' That was another lie, of course.

The argument continued for some time, occasionally becoming tense and at other times quite jovial as we became locked in a debate that was something akin to 'which came first, the chicken or the egg?' Of course, there was no way I could find out if an area was closed until I actually entered it and then it would be too late to get permission, I would have already broken the law. Besides, none of this mattered much; I'd expected to be travelling in closed areas and I'd never had any intention of getting permission. I certainly didn't feel I'd done anything wrong. I hadn't hurt anyone and I'm sure that if I'd asked the Dalai Lama for permission to ride across his country he would have given it. Naturally I kept this opinion to myself.

Finally I was told I'd have to pay a fine of five hundred yuan.

'I'm not paying that, I've done nothing wrong and I've already lost one good horse, that horse was worth fifteen hundred yuan, so you owe me money!'

The Chinese boy-officer looked stunned by my audacious statement; he translated it to the others who laughed and went into further discussion.

'All right, so you must pay two hundred yuan, the road from Liarong is very bad and our jeep was damaged, so you must pay to get it fixed.'

'That's your problem, not mine.'

'What?' He looked astonished.

'It's not my fault your jeep is broken. I didn't ask to come here by jeep, I was quite happy to come by horse.'

'But . . . you were in a closed area, you have broken the laws of the People's Republic of China! You have to pay!'

'But how was I to know that area was closed?' Comfortably back to square one!

Eventually I agreed to pay two hundred yuan for the jeep; it wasn't too expensive and a concession on my part would help move things along. I handed the money over and was given a receipt.

'Here you go,' I said, 'now you can all go out and have a big lunch on me!' I was insinuating they were going to put the money in their pockets and not into the official coffers of the PRC. The young officer turned red with rage and stood in front of me, visibly shaking with anger.

'I am an officer of the People's Republic of China police force, we do NOT do things like that!'

'Oh, come on! I was only joking, I know you're a very good man and a very good policeman. Sit down, I was just joking.' The poor lad recovered his composure.

'Oh, by the way,' I continued, 'is it OK for Chinese police officers to drink beer while they drive a jeep on official police business?'

'Oh, um, yes, sometimes they do that because it is very cold.'

'But yesterday wasn't cold, was it?' At this he became very serious again.

'If that is the case then I must take action!'

'Oh never mind, it was just a question.'

Next there was the problem of what to do with my horse, which was set to arrive in seven days' time.

'You can stay in Naqu until your horse arrives but then you must leave Tibet and in the meantime you must surrender your passport.'

'I'm not staying in Naqu for seven days and I'm not giving you my passport.'

'Then what about your horse?'

'Is there a *gompa* in Naqu?'

'Yes.'

'I want my horse to be given to the head lama of the *gompa*; he can sell it or do whatever he wishes with it.'

The police were quite impressed with this plan and an official contract was drawn up, signed and stamped. When the old man arrived with Ridey he was to be given to the local monastery. At last I was the only problem left to solve.

'You must leave Tibet.'

'Can I go to Lhasa?'

'It's not possible, we have already discussed your case with the Lhasa central police and they say you cannot go there. You must go to Golmud, from there you can go wherever you like in China but not Tibet.'

Golmud is an enormous truck stop in the middle of a desert in Qinghai, thousands of kilometres to the north. I'd passed through on my way to Lhasa last time and had no desire to go back. I also knew that if I went there my journey to Kailas would be over.

'Fine! When can I go to Golmud?'

'Oh, um, tomorrow if you like?' The Chinese officer was expecting another argument and was surprised and pleased not to receive one.

'Tomorrow is fine, where can I get a ticket?'

'We'll help you get one in the morning.'

'Thanks, that would be great! How much are they?'

'Oh, about thirty yuan I think.'

'OK, good. How long does it take?'

'It's very far, but the road is good, about twelve hours I think.'

'Wow! It's a long way, can you recommend a good hotel in Golmud?'

And so the argument was over. I'd paid to fix the jeep and my horse was going to the local monastery and the next day I'd be on a bus to sunny Golmud, problem solved. The young Tibetan policewoman served us tea and it turned out the Chinese lad knew a lot about New Zealand. 'You have many sheep,' he proudly told me. When he was studying English at university he'd had to study one English-speaking country and luckily for me he'd chosen New Zealand.

'Oh great! Why don't you visit New Zealand some day?'

'I'd love to! But it's very difficult for me.'

'Come on, I welcome you to my country. When you come I'll be your guide!'

'Oh! Mr Robinson! Thank you so much!' And I gave him my address.

We all shook hands. 'Thank you all so much for your help, you've been very kind and I'm sorry I caused such trouble.'

'Oh no, never mind, it was just a mistake. Good luck and I hope you'll enjoy the rest of your time in China.'

I was driven back to the hotel and the young Tibetan woman told me they'd be back in the morning at nine to take me to the bus station.

'Great! Thanks a lot, see you then!'

I went back to my room in the hotel, 'Like hell you'll see me then,' I said to myself. I'd fooled them. The police trusted me, they hadn't bothered to take my passport and they weren't keeping an eye on me. It was time to put the escape plan into action.

Most of the main street of Naqu was a market of little shops and stalls, where I spent the rest of the afternoon stocking up on supplies. I bought candles, some new gloves, a full-face balaclava, some bread, a small jar of instant coffee, and some large sacks to put all my gear in. I had the heels on my boots fixed and had a huge lunch before packing up my gear. Earlier in the market I'd met a young Tibetan who could speak some English. I'd asked him if he could help me get a jeep to take me into the countryside, to buy horses. He couldn't, but wrote the name of a small village called Tarin on a piece of paper in Chinese characters. The village was about eighty kilometres north and if I could get there I might be able to find some more horses.

I walked back onto the street, just away from the hotel, and started trying to wave down jeeps and cars. Whenever someone stopped I'd show them the name on the paper and ask how much they'd charge to take me there. Most shook their heads; it was already after six and starting to get dark. Some said they'd take me tomorrow but I knew that would be too risky; I had to get out now. Eventually a sort of taxi stopped with two men inside, one Tibetan and one Chinese. I told them I wanted to go to the *gompa* at Tarin and we negotiated a price of a hundred and eighty yuan.

I got them to back the car up to my window at the hotel; I had to get my stuff out without the staff on reception seeing me. They'd probably been told to call the police if they saw me trying to leave. I went inside and passed my sacks of saddles and my saddlebags through the window and the men stashed them in the car boot. I closed the window and sat on the bed for a moment. This was it. I was escaping, from now I was knowingly breaking the law and I would have no defence. I was disobeying the Chinese police and if I was caught I would find myself in serious shit.

Do you know what you're doing, Ian?

Yip.

Are you sure about this?

Yip.

There's no turning back.

I know.

OK, let's do it!

With my heart thumping and my hands shaking I walked calmly out of the hotel, smiling to the guy on the door. The drivers were waiting, I got in the back seat where the windows were tinted, pulled the balaclava over my face and we set off out of town.

An hour later we turned off the main road and stopped in front of a small temple ten kilometres south of Tarin. One of the men went through the gates and came back a few minutes later to say all the monks had returned home for the summer and the place was empty. This didn't bother me; all I wanted was to find someone to sell me horses. They told me there was another much larger monastery further on and offered to take me there, for a renegotiated price. I agreed, thinking the further we were from Naqu and the police the better.

We carried on and stopped at Tarin to ask directions to the *gompa*. I liked this; if I was in an out-of-the-way place there would be less chance of anyone finding me. The driver asked an old man, who got into the car with us to act as a guide. We drove on another thirty kilometres then turned off the main road and started into the hills. Snow had recently fallen and several times we had to get out and push the car as the wheels spun on the icy ground. I was really lucky to have got a ride with these guys; most would refuse to take their car off the main road. As it was we were driving on a grass track that I could barely see in the headlights. All this reassured me even more; I was going to spend the night in a remote and hidden place.

Just as it got dark we topped the last hill and Drugu Gompa lay below, built on a rocky outcrop in the middle of the valley, like a fortress. It was perfect. We stopped the car in front of the main temple and several monks came out to greet us, welcoming me in and helping me carry my stuff up the hill to the monastery. As soon as I heaved my saddlebags over my shoulder and started trudging through the mud I felt better. *This is where I should be.*

Soon the monks were serving me tea and bowls of *tukpa*. I told them I wanted to buy two horses and although they didn't have any themselves I hoped word would go out and some might turn up the next day. I was exhausted, it had been a dramatic day and I felt drained. I was terrified but thrilled at the same time. I knew I was doing the right thing — if I got caught I would have to accept it, but at least I was doing all I could to get going again.

It snowed all night and the valley was white in the morning — again this made me feel more secure, as if my tracks were being covered. After breakfast I walked down the hill to the small village. Word of my interest in horses had spread and a couple of men told me they'd sent their sons off to bring me mounts they wanted to sell. This sounded very good and I started to think I could be away faster than I'd thought. The horses wouldn't arrive until the afternoon, so I spent the time wandering round the monastery. I was taken to see the abbot in a little sunroom next to the main temple. He didn't seem surprised by my arrival and told me I was welcome to stay as long as I needed.

Out in the valley I could see another monk sitting by a stream under a sun umbrella. He'd been there all day and I wandered over. He was making water bowl offerings — seven little brass bowls were laid out on a bench before him, each representing a different offering to Buddha. Although he was only offering simple water taken from the stream, in his mind he visualised other substances, beautiful flowers, incense, lamps and food. This was the most religious practice I had seen any monk undertake at the temple. At Drugu Gompa, like many of the smaller monasteries I visited, there seemed to be little formal religious practice. Without the strength of realised lamas to guide them, many of the monks seemed to pass their days lazing about drinking tea and eating. The monastery was of the Gelukpa order, the order the Dalai Lama heads, yet nowhere could I see a photo of His Holiness. I realised this was another example of how strict the authorities were in this part of the country — his image was banned and having one would probably get you arrested.

Later in the afternoon a couple of horses turned up and were offered for sale. I refused both — for the prices the men were asking for the walking bags of dog food I could buy a share in a race horse back home. Obviously this wasn't going to be easy. Later another old man said he'd show me two horses the next day, so I resigned myself to another night with the monks. However, I could feel my novelty was beginning to wear off and I wouldn't be welcome for much longer. By now the police would know I'd escaped and I wondered if they'd be looking for me. Hopefully they would think I'd gone to Lhasa or was trying to get back to my horses.

In the morning I walked down to the old man's house. His son led the horses in from the valley but again they were unfit to ride; one was so small it was still a foal and the other looked like its great-grandfather. Unbelievably, the old man wanted fifteen thousand yuan and refused to bargain. It would be pointless buying them — they'd be exhausted in a couple of days and if they were all I could get I might as well give up and go back to Naqu. Whether the men of the village had colluded to try to rip me off or whether they thought I was stupid I didn't know. However, it must have been obvious I was stuck there and relying on someone to do me a favour and sell me two reasonable horses for a fair price.

No one else offered to sell a horse and I walked back to the *gompa* feeling dejected. I was stuck here and knew that if I stayed too long the police would catch up with me. I went back to the monk's room and packed my gear. I decided to hitch back to Tarin and buy horses there. It was a long shot but I knew it was pointless staying at Drugu. I rolled up my *chuba* and made a swag with a saddle blanket, a bridle and a rope — enough basic gear to ride one horse. I asked the monks if I could leave the rest of my gear in the room, but by now their compassion seemed to have run out, they shook their heads and waved me out. I had to drag the sacks down to the village to the old man's house. I gave him a ridiculous story about how I was going back to Naqu to get some money from the bank and I'd be back the next day to buy his horses. Equally ridiculously, he believed it.

I set off on foot with my swag on my back — I must have been a pathetic sight as I slowly made my way over the hills towards the main road. It must have been about five kilometres to the road and the walk at this altitude exhausted me. There was little traffic, and as I waited I worried that a police jeep would come by, until I realised worrying was pointless. I couldn't run away and if they came, they came. I sat on my bundle on the edge of the road and eventually an old truck stopped. I climbed into the cab with the Chinese driver and we set off towards Tarin. When we arrived at the tiny village I offered to pay for my lift but he kindly refused.

I walked across the road to the village and was met by the old man who had shown us the way to the *gompa* a couple of days before. He invited me into his home and served me tea and *tsampa*. I told him I wanted to buy two horses and he went off to ask his neighbours, returning a short time later to tell me he'd found one. The horse was small but stocky and in good condition. Its owner wanted four thousand five hundred yuan but I managed to bargain him down to four thousand. It was still too much but better than the rip-offs at the *gompa*. I had one horse, I was halfway there!

The old man's son had a little truck and in the evening I paid him to take me back to Drugu to get the rest of my stuff. We didn't get back to Tarin until well after dark, and when we arrived a neighbour was offering another horse for sale which he said he'd show me in the morning. Before going to bed I wrote a letter home, telling my family what had happened but that I had escaped, which the old man said he'd post the next time he went into Naqu. I was given a bed in a room next to the main house. It was pointless getting my hopes up but I felt more positive than I had done in the last few days. If I could get another horse I'd be away again.

I slept well and woke late, lazing in my sleeping bag for a while before forcing myself to get up. (I should have got up earlier.) The old man's wife served me *tsampa* for breakfast and I asked them for some hot water and made myself a couple of cups of coffee. (I should have skipped the coffee.) The old man took me across to another house to see about the horse. It was very small, not fully grown, but again it was in good condition and I was eager to buy it and get going. The Tibetan who owned it asked for four thousand two hundred yuan, which it wasn't worth, and I spent ages trying to bargain him down to an even four thousand, but he wouldn't take a yuan less. Now I only had four thousand five hundred yuan left, enough for one more horse, so when these two were finished I'd have to walk with my gear on a packhorse.

Anyway, I'd done it! I'd bought two more horses and in a few minutes my escape would be complete. I took the horse back to the old man's house and loaded them both up ready to go.

'*Cha tung, tukpa sa.*' The old man invited me inside for tea and something to eat before I set off. I sat down inside next to the fire feeling very pleased and the old man's wife handed me a bowl of tea.

'*Kan an dro?*' The old man asked, where are you going?

'Lhasa,' I told him, it wasn't true of course, but if anyone came to find me I hoped they would look in the wrong direction. Suddenly he stood up and looked out the window behind me. I looked around to see what he was looking at and felt the blood drain from my face. Just outside the yard walls was a white jeep and three police officers were walking up to the front door.

'Oh my God! This can't be happening!' I muttered to myself as they walked through the door and sat down. I was literally minutes away from leaving, five more and I'd be gone; how could they turn up now? I could feel myself shaking, but once again I greeted the police and smiled calmly, playing the happy, innocent tourist.

The three officers, two Tibetans and one Chinese, sat and talked to the old man as his wife served them tea. My mind was racing, how could I get out of this? What the hell was I going to do? How had they found me? Was it a chance encounter or were they looking for me? Had they found out I'd been at Drugu, gone there, and then followed me here? I'd never find out, and at the moment I didn't really care.

'Passport?' one of the officers said, finally addressing me.

'*Rey, rey.*' I smiled and nodded.

'Passport!' he demanded and held out his hand.

'Oh, you want to see my passport? Oh, yes of course, it's in my saddlebags on my horse, wait here and I'll go and get it.' I indicated this to the officers and stood up to go outside. Thankfully they sat and waited. Someone was protecting me.

I walked through the yard and round the corner to where the horses were tethered ready to go. I untied them, picked up the lead rope for the packhorse, jumped into the saddle and took off.

Seconds later we were cantering across grassland heading west, the thump of my heart louder than the hoof-beats. I heard shouts behind but didn't look back. *Oh my God, what am I doing? Buddha, please protect me!*

When I reached the low hills on the other side of the grassland I looked back. The jeep was coming after me on a track around the side of the plain. I turned the horses and doubled back; the ground was rough and boggy and I knew the jeep wouldn't be able to cross it. I passed within a few hundred yards of the village and saw the old man in front of his house waving out to me. I felt awful, he'd been so kind and could get in trouble for helping me — I was an escaped fugitive and he'd aided me in getting away. Of course, he had no idea who I was, but the Chinese might not be so forgiving. *'Gawn da pala!'* I yelled, I'm sorry father, though he was too far away to hear.

The jeep turned back and I found myself on a track heading into some hills as a front of light snow blew in. The horses were running well, though this was certainly not the way I liked to become acquainted with new horses, but both were well trained and gave me no trouble. I was terrified the saddlebags would come loose but they held firm. My 'good fast horse karma' had ripened sooner than I'd thought — I didn't need to wait for the next life to be chased, it was happening now! The jeep was gaining, though, and I had to get off the track.

I headed into the hills just as the jeep came close enough for the police to shout to me. I kept riding but looked over my shoulder to see them jumping out of the vehicle and waving at me to come back. I put my head down and kept riding to the top of the ridge. To my dismay the track the jeep was on led around the hill and continued below. I rode along the ridge parallel with the track; the jeep turned off and headed towards me. The cops had picked up a couple of boys from the village and within a couple of hundred metres the ground became too steep for the jeep. It stopped and the nimble-footed boys started chasing me.

I took off, pushing the horses up the slope. The hill turned and one of the boys cut across and came within a few metres of me. He ran across the hillside shadowing me but not getting any closer. I could see fear in his face — he must have thought I was some kind of dangerous criminal. He stopped and picked up a rock to defend himself with.

'Ma rey! Ma rey!' I yelled, and turned the horses higher out of his reach.

I crossed the track ahead of the jeep and carried on further into the hills; still the police shadowed me, stopping every so often to let the boys out, but they still couldn't get close enough. I started up another gentler slope. The police saw their chance, turned off the track and headed after me. The hills before me were lower, the jeep could have covered them and there were enough hands in the jeep to surround me on a hill top.

I could hear the gears change down just behind me. I didn't think I'd get much further, and I was losing my nerve. I wanted to give up. I didn't want to be in any more trouble, I just wanted out of this awful situation. Although I still didn't feel I'd done anything wrong, I was now firmly on the wrong side of the law.

The jeep's wheels spun, the driver chopped it down and tried again, and

I looked back to see it sliding sideways across the hillside — there was just enough snow on the ground to stop them! *Thank you, Buddha! Thank you! Thank you!* I felt like crying. I carried on to the top of another ridge and turned the horses to face the jeep, the police and the boys now standing in front of it in resignation.

They yelled out and waved at me to come down. I yelled back and waved at them to come up. Something changed inside me. I still wasn't safe, I knew they could still catch me — all they needed were a few more hands, and I fully expected to be back in Naqu that night in police custody. The situation seemed hopeless. *Oh what the hell, I might as well have some fun with this!*

I rode on at a slower pace, and the jeep shadowed me at a distance, the officers knowing they couldn't chase me into the snow-covered hills. They stopped every so often and called out for me to come back and show them my passport. 'No, you come up here!' I'd yell back, and we'd ride on and repeat the little game a short time later.

Finally the hills steepened and became rockier. The jeep couldn't pass through and stopped at a group of houses below the hills and everyone got out. I thought that would be the end of it; they would come after me on horseback and I knew there was no way I could outride a Tibetan. I carried on slowly, beginning to accept my inevitable fate and trying to enjoy my last ride, constantly looking back over my shoulder expecting to see the Tibetan cavalry bearing down on me.

Chapter Six

It didn't happen. They'd given up. I rode on for the rest of the day expecting see a squad of police jeeps waiting for me round every hill, but I hardly saw anyone the whole afternoon. I had no idea what happened. Did they go back to Naqu and report the incident? Were they too embarrassed to tell their superiors I'd got away? Was it just a chance encounter after all, they didn't know who I was and chose to ignore it? I'd never find out. One thing I do know is that the letter I'd given the old man to post never arrived.

It snowed heavily in the afternoon, which I was glad of, as it would slow down any jeeps, but cleared again into warm sunshine. I only stopped once, to jettison the stack of Dalai Lama photos. If I was caught again I'd be treated more severely and be searched. If the police found the photos I could be accused of spreading anti-government propaganda, or some other bullshit. I placed them on a large rock and made a pile of stones on top; hopefully they'd be found by a curious local and end up in respectful hands.

I crossed the Naqu river in the evening, then covered a wide flat grassland and camped at the base of some hills at about eight. I set the horses out to graze but waited until it got dark before putting up the tent. My new horses had done me proud; I was sure I wouldn't have made it on less willing mounts. New Ridey was small but strong and walked well and Packy was a good packhorse, often trying to walk in front of Ridey. I made tea and *tsampa* and ate some bread and a tin of greasy, unidentified meat — not very appetising but I had to keep my strength up.

I fell into an exhausted sleep, the police turning up in every one of my restless dreams. My worst fear was the police catching me in my sleeping bag, so I'd set the alarm on my watch for five hoping to be away at daybreak, but I slept right through it and didn't wake up until after half past six, a sign of my exhaustion. It had snowed heavily overnight and visibility was near zero when I stuck my head out of the tent — a cold blanket for me to hide under. I took my time packing up and the snow clouds quickly cleared into warm sunshine.

Before I set off I scorched a cork in the flame of my lighter, waited for it to cool and then smeared black soot on my face to darken my skin. The plan was to avoid people as much as I could; the more people who saw me, the more of a trail I left. I hoped that with a dark face under the balaclava and my *chuba* I wouldn't look like a foreigner from a distance; if people saw me ride by on the other side of the valley they'd think I was Tibetan, then if the police came asking the locals if they'd seen a foreigner they'd say no. That was the plan.

I loaded the horses and crossed the hills above my camp; they were high and the snow at the top knee-deep — another barrier between me and Naqu. In the open valley on the other side fog caused by the warm sun on the snow hung low; long, thick ribbons stretched above a tangle of streams and slowly washed over me as the wind rose and stirred the air.

I rode all morning and into the afternoon without stopping and made good time. However, as the day got older I became hungry and felt like some human company. I stopped behind some rocks in the floor of a valley and watched a couple of houses on the other side through my binoculars. I was nervous. These would be the first people I'd met since I'd escaped and I still felt like a criminal on the run.

I rode up and was greeted, invited in and served butter tea and yoghurt. Now that summer was supposedly beginning the Tibetans had a surplus of butter, which they use to make Tibet's most famous drink. First tea is boiled in a great kettle and poured into a long wooden tube, salt and butter are added and it's vigorously churned and returned to the kettle. This is *cha suma*, or butter tea. It's an acquired taste. Most Westerners can't stand the stuff, but its very warming and nutritious and I was rather fond of it, especially if the butter wasn't too rancid.

As I took off my balaclava the family exchanged mutters at the sight of my blackened face. I tried to explain it was some kind of sun block. They seemed to accept this, but I decided not to bother again; I must have looked a fright and it would probably make the locals even more suspicious. And besides, even on horseback with the balaclava and *chuba* and a Tibetan knife in my belt the locals weren't fooled for an instant. Even from kilometres away I could see them stand and stare as I went by, instinctively knowing there was something very different about the passing rider.

I decided my best defence was to behave normally, avoid towns and main roads and not stop at any houses with vehicles parked outside. From now on I wouldn't tell anyone I was going to Gang Rinpoche, instead I'd say I was on my way to Lhasa or some imagined far-off monastery.

The family wished me well as I set off and I appreciated the kindness they'd shown me much more than I had done in the past; now that I was in need of a friend those I met seemed all the more precious. In the afternoon it turned grey and rained heavily. I continued through the hills and grasslands on foot, saying mantras, my *mala* in my hand. Instead of following, Packy and Ridey walked beside me, one on either side, as if they were trying to protect me.

Over the next few days I kept heading west towards the vast salt lake Siling

Tso; the region was desolate and remote, with no settlements and very few people. This suited me fine, I doubted I would run into the law out there and I calmed down and got back into the rhythm of the journey. The people I came across were mostly living in black yak-hair tents at their summer camps. Sometimes they would serve me tea on the ground outside; I'd sit in the dirt drinking bowls of tea with the horses behind me. Often Ridey would nudge my shoulder and reach his nose over towards my tea bowl as if he was trying to drink. Once I stood up and went inside the nomad's tent and he tried to follow me and another time a Tibetan woman gave him a lump of stale bread, which he wolfed down while Packy turned his nose up. All this made me wonder if he had been a human in his previous life and still wanted to be part of things in the human world.

I carried on heading west across vast barren grasslands intersected with low hills. The weather alternated from brilliant sunshine to sudden bitter snowstorms. I'd often have to camp in places where there was no water and it became rarer to find people living in the area. At one camp I was given butter tea and *tsampa* and I bought a large tin can off the head of the family. After I'd set up my camp that night on another empty plain I made the large can into a stove. I hadn't seen any vegetation in days and although dry yak dung burns well it needs to be enclosed in a stove where it's hot enough to combust. In this region it was also difficult to find stones to make a fireplace. I cut an opening in the front with my knife and punched ventilation holes in the top and bottom by hammering one of the iron horse stakes through with a rock. It was usually easy enough to collect a small pile of dry dung. I filled the little stove and after a few attempts managed to light it with dry grass. It worked a treat and soon I was sipping hot coffee and slurping instant noodles.

The horses were beginning to tire and I took the next day off to rest them. I camped alone on the edge of a vast plain and spent most of the day sitting in the sun next to the stove. I read my book and through the pages the Dalai Lama talked about developing patience and compassion to the point where we can see those who harm us as a teacher and a spiritual friend, someone to be thanked and loved solely for the harm they have caused us.

I immediately thought of the police who had arrested me, taken my horses and almost ruined my whole trip. They were only doing their job and furthermore they were just tools of an oppressive government. I didn't hate them, but it was hard to feel anything positive towards them or their masters. My quarrel was with the Beijing government, which continued to abuse the Tibetans, slowly eating away at their culture and religious freedom. If I was to hate anyone and feel anger towards anyone, it should be them. This is where His Holiness made his point of seeing such people as helping me to practise patience and loving kindness.

What! How could I feel love for such tyrants, responsible for the atrocities that still go on in Tibet, who keep the poor old Dalai Lama in exile, who imprison innocent monks like Jigme and Lobsang, who took my Ridey and Packy, who tried to stop me reaching Gang Rinpoche and sprinkling the ashes of Khensur Thabkye Rinpoche? How could I see such bastards as spiritual guides helping me? Get real! If I met any of them I'd like to grab them by the throat and shake them, rub their noses in the filth on the streets and show them the poverty they claimed to have eradicated!

But as I read on the Dalai Lama explained that those who mean to harm me give me the greatest opportunity to develop spiritually; when I encounter such people and circumstances I naturally feel hatred and anger, and through them I am given the chance of refraining from these feelings. If everyone was nice to me all the time I'd never have the opportunity to practise patience; it's easy to feel compassion for those who are kind and whom I like, but the real test comes when I meet someone who tries to hurt me, someone who tries to stop me doing what I want, someone who takes something from me, someone who insults me. If I can feel love for someone like this then I am making progress. This person has given me the chance to grow, and so I should thank him. Even someone like Khensur Thabkye Rinpoche, in all his wise teachings, cannot give me this opportunity so my enemy should be seen and respected as my greatest teacher.

I'd heard incredible stories of lamas who had taken this way of viewing their enemies as teachers to the extreme — lamas imprisoned by the Chinese during the Cultural Revolution who had been horribly tortured by their guards. Every time the Chinese took them away to be beaten they prayed the punishment would be severe, knowing that the harder they were beaten, the stronger their patience and compassion would become. Later, some even said their time in the Chinese gulags had been the best in their lives for spiritual development.

Such sentiments seemed unimaginable; it sounded good on paper but when it comes to putting it into practice I felt it was completely beyond me. I couldn't bring myself to thank those who had put me through the last week's stress and fear. Even sitting quietly next to my stove with a hot mug of coffee in my hand I gritted my teeth when I thought of the Tibetan collaborator who must have dobbed me in to the Chinese. I'd love to get my hands on that bastard, I'd give him a golden opportunity to practise patience.

A couple of days later I camped next to a small lake marked on my map as Nei

Mu Ko Tso. It was cold and very windy. I was hungry and although I could see a couple of houses on a hillside in the distance I was still too nervous to ask to stay the night. In the morning I set off around the side of the lake, intending to stop and get some tea and something to eat. Once again during the night the houses had vanished. Had they just been hallucinations, caused by my overly hopeful and hungry mind?

A couple of hours later I spotted a real house in the distance. A few hundred metres away I met a little girl of about four. I walked with her towards her home, leading the horses behind as she prattled away non-stop in rapid Tibetan I had no way of understanding. She was sweetly unaware of the fact I couldn't speak her language. From what I could pick up she was telling me her family had gone away somewhere, leaving her at home with her old grandmother. I nodded and made noises whenever she stopped for a second to take a breath. A few minutes later I stood in the doorway. Her old grandmother wasn't as sweet — she wouldn't let me inside and refused to give me any tea.

I starved for the rest of the day, not finding any occupied houses until late in the evening when I arrived at Pan Ko Tso lake on the edge of an expansive saltpan. That night I pitched my tent near a family who were about to milk a flock of sheep. The animals were tied together by their horns in a herringbone and the women went along the row on either side, placing a pot between the animals' back legs before milking a small amount from each one. Some of the sheep must have been rather nervous, as they defecated into the pot. This didn't bother the women; they picked out the droppings with their fingers and went on to the next animal.

I was given a meal of yak meat and in the morning I set off above the lake in light rain, onto a high plain flat to the horizon. It reminded me of the vast and empty steppes of Mongolia. I headed westwards towards the lake, Siling Tso, which I hoped to reach that day. Before long a freezing storm of torrential rain and sleet blew in. I walked much of the morning to try to keep warm, but before long I was soaked and bitterly cold. I stopped and put on my *chuba*, but my fingers were so numb it took ages to do it up.

Early in the afternoon the weather thankfully cleared as we topped a low rise and a staggering sweep of deep cobalt blue spread out before me. Siling Tso — seventy kilometres long. I couldn't see the other end and the great body of water looked more like an inland sea. The area surrounding the lake was barren and empty; from the rise I stood on as my horses rested I couldn't see any sign of life. I carried on heading southwest around the bottom of the lake and rode onto the vast plain. In the afternoon we camped in a lovely spot next to a small stream in a sheltered ravine. It was only four o'clock but

I'd achieved the day's goal of reaching the lake and the sun was warm so I spread my damp gear out to dry.

The next day was long and tedious. I set out across the plain under clear skies, but a fierce wind blew all day. I was hungry but there was no one living there and no chance of anything to eat. We travelled on a track on top of a long sandbar that stretched into the distance and vanished. The landscape was a monotony of emptiness, a void except for the changing moods of the lake. Every time I looked at her she seemed to have changed to another shade of blue as the wind ruffled the surface and clouds crossed the sky. Several times I was teased by the sight of what looked like dwellings in the distance, but we'd plod on only to find deserted cattle pens.

Finally in the evening we reached the edge of the plain and started to leave the lake behind. The ground dipped before it slowly rose into some low hills and the landscape held enough moisture to make the final part of the day's ride an exhausting slog through mud. The horses would sink up to their bellies, panic at the sensation and I'd have to fight to keep them under control. Meanwhile, I'd be up to my knees in the stinking, salty muck, making only a few metres before I was drained of the little energy I had.

Thankfully as it got dark we entered a small greenish valley where there were a few whitewashed houses and I set up my tent. I collected some dry dung but before I got a chance to get the stove going the wind began to howl, making it impossible to light. After a few minutes' trying I gave up in despair and went to bed.

It was pouring with rain when I woke late the next morning so I decided to take a day off. Luckily for me the skies cleared. I let the horses off to graze and set about getting the stove going. Unfortunately, the dung I'd collected the night before was damp and to make things worse my lighter was running out. As I was swearing and cursing trying to get the damn fire going a couple of young women wandered by with their sheep. They stared at the strange angry stranger for several minutes. I smiled and tried to wave them over, but they shook their heads and went back to their flocks. When I eventually hit on the right combination of profanities I got the fire going and made coffee and *tsampa*.

A short time later the two women returned; this time they were less shy and offered me a small sack of dry dung and a box of matches. They joined me by the fire and one of them kindly offered me a small *khata*. I was overwhelmed; we had hardly spoken during our first encounter but they had seen I needed a hand. I showed them how to make coffee — black with sugar. I tried to hand the steaming mug to them so they could have a taste, but they turned shy again, giggled and shook their heads.

Later, they came back as I was enjoying my last mug. This time they offered me a lump of butter, indicating I should put it in the coffee like they do with tea. This could be something new, a butter latte? I regretted I had no Dalai Lama photos and offered them my empty coffee jar. They giggled, thanked me and returned to their homes.

I spent the rest of the day checking my maps and watching the lake, an enormous turquoise jewel in the distance. From here I would head further southwest through a more mountainous region to the next large lake, Gyaring Tso. The horses grazed and enjoyed their day off, but it was clear they were tiring. Packy spent half the day lying flat on his side in the sun.

The area I rode through the next day was more populated; I made a couple of tea stops and in the evening came to a river valley about a kilometre wide. It was nearly seven and I picked out a spot on the other side of the valley above the river, which I decided would be my campsite. We started across the valley floor but before we got near the river the ground turned boggy. Suddenly, Ridey was up to his belly in mud and panicking.

I kicked my feet out of the stirrups and tried to jump off, but it was too late, he kept stumbling about and went over flat on his side in the mud with me trapped beneath. My leg was firmly stuck and I couldn't pull myself out. I tried to sit up and look about to see if there were any houses near enough to call out to, but there weren't. I was stuck there alone, in the mud under my horse.

'Come on, Ridey! Get up!' I yelled at the poor animal and kicked him in the rump with my free leg. He made a couple of feeble attempts but fell back onto his side, panting. I'd lost the lead rope for Packy, who had wandered off and was grazing on the side of the valley. I kept booting Ridey in the arse but it was no use, he couldn't, or wouldn't, get up.

I had only one option — I drew my long knife and jabbed my poor horse in the rump. He tried again but fell back. I jabbed him harder, this time breaking the skin with a sickening pop. But it was the motivation he needed; he heaved himself up and leapt to his feet. I rolled out of the way of his hooves and crawled through the mud to the edge of the valley.

Ridey wandered off to join Packy as I lay on the ground with my face in the dirt, crying. This was just too much. With all the other stresses and struggles I had to endure every day something like this made me feel it was all too difficult. After a few minutes I pulled myself together, got to my feet and gathered up the horses. Ridey seemed fine, his wound hadn't bled much, but everything was caked in sticky mud. We set off, again heading for the campsite; this time I walked, leading the boys. When we got to the main branch of the river I waded through without bothering to get into the saddle; the water came over the tops of my boots and soaked my socks but I didn't care. I set up camp and spent the rest of the light scraping mud off in a tiny stream. Everything was damp and smelly. I felt beaten. Tibet had won the day. I crawled into my sleeping bag, thankful it was over.

I was camped below a mountain I later found out the locals call Chepo Ri, a spectacular peak of eroded rock capped with snow. All night the mountain rang with the howls of what sounded like dozens of wolves. I woke to heavy rain, it was pointless trying to pack up in these conditions; everything would be soaked in seconds so I lay in my sleeping bag and waited until it stopped. The horses played up as I loaded them — Packy got loose and headed off across the mountainside. I had to saddle Ridey and go and recapture him. When I finally climbed into the saddle Ridey played up so much I had to drop the lead rope to avoid being pulled out of the saddle. Again, Packy took this as his cue to head off on his own. It was midday before we started making progress.

We headed on up the valley, which quickly narrowed into a rocky chasm. I rode along the base of formidable cliffs where streams of perfect spring water rose straight from the bottom of the rocky walls. In the afternoon I stopped with a large family who treated me with wonderful hospitality, feeding me all the milk, tea, rice and *tsampa* I could eat and even giving the boys an armful of straw.

Later in the evening I camped a few kilometres short of a small village. I didn't want to get any closer. To make me even more nervous a white jeep went past just as it got dark, but thankfully it didn't stop. The next day was the seventeenth of June and my visa would expire in less then twenty-four hours — I would be illegally in the People's Republic of China, and if I was caught again there would be no way I could argue my way out of it.

The next day I carried on through the hills and on my first day as an illegal alien I crossed a low pass in the mountains. A long stretch of blue water lay before me — Gyaring Tso. I had hoped to be further north, as just south of the lake was the town of Xianza, which I dearly wanted to avoid. As I made my way on foot down towards the lake I still couldn't see the town, but I knew it must be a reasonably large place by the amount of rubbish. The ground was covered in green plastic bags and discarded noodle packets.

I rode down to the river, north of the town but still several kilometres from the bottom of the lake and pushed the horses into the water. It was deep and we had to make several attempts at crossing before we found a suitable place — even then the water came halfway up the saddle and my boots filled with water. In the middle of the valley I found a small monastery, just one building and one lama, a kindly old man who let me into the temple. I made an offering of a few yuan on the altar and made prostrations to the images of the Buddha to give thanks for my successful escape.

The lama served me tea and bread and I headed to the other side of the valley. Before we'd gone far I found myself in some of the worst terrain I've ever ridden, the whole area a maze of lumpy sod with deep holes of mud in between. Soon I was lost in the jumbled confusion, the horses refusing to cross the patches of mud. I must have spent a couple of hours staggering round in a circle getting nowhere until I was spotted by a helpful local who led me out of the mess further south towards the town. I now had a clear view of Xianza spread out along the side of the hills I had already crossed. It was large and would certainly be policed. I crossed the rest of the valley and hurried north away from the town.

That night I camped alone a couple of hundred yards below the lake and in the morning I climbed into some hills on the western side, crossed a low pass and stopped for tea with a family. I was given tea and *tsampa* and stocked up on supplies, buying bread, dried yak meat and noodles from the old man for a few yuan. The elderly Tibetan was a kindly and dignified fellow. *'Ngai bu,'* my son, he said to me after we'd had tea and gestured for me to follow.

We went to a small hut where he unlocked the door and ushered me inside. He had set the room up as a shrine; there was an altar with pictures of various Buddhas and deities and even a large portrait of the Dalai Lama. He had pasted paper over the windows and seemed very keen to keep what he had inside a secret, forced to practise his faith underground. Again I realised how lucky I was to have been born in a land where I can openly follow whatever faith I choose. I felt guilty and spoilt; this old man would probably do anything to receive teachings from someone like Khensur Thabkye Rinpoche. Given the chance he would meet him every day, whereas I attended his lessons only when I found myself with nothing else to do.

I carried on and was soon riding alongside the lake above its stony shores, surrounded by high barren hills. The lake gleamed a perfect blue, the weather was warm and sunny, much too hot for the *chuba* and with Xianza dropping further behind me with every step I started to relax. Gang Rinpoche still felt impossibly distant and the thought of reaching it seemed an obscure fantasy. Still, that afternoon, as a light wind blew off the lake, I felt free and incredibly fortunate.

Early in the afternoon I rode behind some hills on a wide peninsula in the lake and found the perfect campsite. I could pitch my tent hidden by a rise just a few metres from the water and far from the road; there was reasonable grass for the horses and an old pile of dry dung. I hobbled the horses, left them to graze and set up camp. The horses were tired and I decided to stay for three nights so we could all take a decent break.

The next day I lazed in the sun by the stove, eating and making tea as the horses grazed; it was so hot in the afternoon I even took my sweater off. The land along the lakeside had begun to turn green with new grass; finally, summer had arrived. In the afternoon I was visited by a couple of young guys camped further up the lake as they herded their grazing yaks. I shared my tea and bread before they went off with their shaggy beasts, leaving me in blissful solitude to stare across at the mountains on the other side of the lake.

The following day was just as idyllic. Ridey and Packy grazed and rested while I skipped stones on the surface of the lake. In the afternoon I was sitting by my stove mixing *tsampa* and drinking tea when I heard a gentle hum in the distance. Suddenly it grew louder and I looked up to see a police jeep come flying over the rise. There are hundreds of thousands of words in the English language but at that moment only one came to mind: *Fuck!*

The jeep skidded to a halt in front of my camp and four police officers jumped out; with them they had one of the young guys I'd met the day before, who must have been conscripted to show them where I was. I felt myself begin to fall apart, the awful feeling of being in trouble, just like a kid being sent to the headmaster's office, but one more time I smiled and pretended nothing was wrong, although I knew the act was wearing thin.

'Tashidelik! Cha tung?' I greeted the officers and offered them tea.

'*Ma rey!* Passport!' the Tibetan who seemed to be in charge shouted.

I showed them my passport. They inspected my visa, which was now expired by four days, though luckily everything was written in English, although I knew it wouldn't be long before they figured it out.

'Xianza!' the cop in charge growled. He shook my tent, indicating I had to pack up and go with them back to town in the jeep.

'Machine ma-dro, ta nyi yo,' I said, I can't go in the jeep, I've got two horses, and pointed to the boys.

'Ma rey! Ma rey!' he shouted, gesturing I'd have to leave my horses.

'Ma rey, ngai ta gong chenpo!' No way, my horses were expensive! None of the men could resist laughing and the mood lightened.

I told them I'd stay put for the night, as it was already nearly six, and ride into Xianza the next day. Remarkably, and quite stupidly I thought, they agreed. I told them my horses were tired and slow and it would take a day and a half to reach the town and they seemed to appreciate this. They all climbed back into the jeep and drove off. I sat there rather stunned and feeling very fortunate to still be in possession of my passport and horses.

I sat by the fire and made another cup of tea while I decided what to do.

It was obvious they didn't know who I was, so I guessed the police in Naqu hadn't put out a bulletin on me, but I knew they soon would.

'I'm sorry, boys,' I said to the horses as I led them in to be loaded up, 'we're on the run again.' Our little holiday was suddenly cut short. I wearily loaded up and we set off at half past six. I rode off the peninsula and then walked along a dirt road around the side of the lake heading west, away from Xianza, before turning away and into the hills. It was still and quiet and I walked slowly, feeling strangely at peace and somewhat detached. I knew the police would come back. I knew at best I would only get a couple of days' head start. But at least I was giving it my best shot. This was the third time I'd disobeyed orders and escaped and things were out of my control now. I couldn't avoid being caught. I wasn't afraid any more, I was beyond caring, let them come and catch me, I won't be intimidated, what the hell!

We walked until after nine, crossed a river and I put the horses out for the night and pitched my tent in the darkness behind the sod walls of an old cattle pen. I hoped I would be hidden from the road, but of course there was no way I could hide the horses. I woke up very early, even before first light. It was a freezing morning and sleet fell as I packed. I hoped to be away and over the hills, but it seemed the police had got up even earlier. They arrived before I even had the chance to catch the horses. Again four of them piled out of the jeep, the Tibetan officer in charge looked positively livid as he stamped up and down beside the jeep; this time they'd brought a Chinese officer who could speak a bit of archaic English.

'How do you do?' he asked me, his formality and politeness absurdly comical given the tense situation.

'Oh, I'm very well thank you, kind sir, and how are you?'

'I'm fine, thank you.'

'Oh, good! Jolly good! And what can I do for you today?'

'Where are you going?'

'Xianza, of course.' It was clear to anyone I wasn't going to Xianza, I was heading in the opposite direction.

The senior officer barked something. 'You must give him your passport.'

'He can look but he can't touch it,' I replied, desperate to hold on to my papers. I took it out ready to show the grumpy cop; obviously he wasn't pleased about having to be out of bed early and wasn't in a mood to be disobeyed. Before I got a chance to open it the Tibetan grabbed one end of the document. 'No! You can see it but don't touch!' But he started shouting at me furiously in Tibetan.

'No! Just fuckin' wait and I'll show it to you!' We stood there for several moments in a tiny but angry tug-of-war.

'Give it to him!' the Chinese officer yelled and joined in to wrestle the passport out of my hands. Together they ripped it from my grip.

'Oh, fuck it then, you arseholes! Take the fuckin' thing!' I turned and walked towards my horses. I was furious and took my time messing about with the horses as the triumphant police waited in the falling snow. When I returned to start loading up the Chinaman started at me again.

'You must go to Xianza! You must go only to Xianza!'

'I heard you the first time! Now fuck off!'

'You had better not go that way!' he said and pointed towards the hills.

'Yeah, yeah, I understand. Now fuck off, I've got work to do!'

'Do you understand, if you don't come to Xianza you will have a serious problem.'

I turned around and stood face to face with the cop, my face centimetres from his.

'I understand perfectly, I already have a serious problem, now FUCK OFF!'

The police drove away leaving me to fume as a freezing wind started to blow. I loaded up the boys with frozen fingers and sat on a lump of sod wondering what to do next. I looked towards the hills in the west — high mountains rose behind them. I still had a choice, so what if they had my passport? They could keep it, I could carry on without it and turn myself in later. No doubt it would be sent to Lhasa, where I planned to end up anyway. My first instinct was to jump into the saddle and ride, just say to hell with it and keep going, next time they'd have to put me in bloody handcuffs!

Then reality set in. Yes, I could keep riding, but how far would I get? The police had already come out to find me twice, and next time they would probably handcuff me and confiscate Packy and Ridey. My horses weren't up to another dramatic escape — even on a good day we could only travel thirty-five kilometres and a police jeep could cover that distance in an hour. There was nowhere to hide; the country was so open. I thought of trying to find an isolated nook in the hills and holing up until the fuss died down, but I knew the area was well populated. Before long a local herding his yaks would find me and by the end of the day the whole valley would know there was a foreigner camped in the hills.

I sat in the middle of nowhere and agonised. I couldn't bring myself to say it wasn't still worth trying to reach Kailas. I'd had almost no chance of making it when I started out from Garilang and even the slimmest possibility of success I had now would still make it worth a shot. But did I even have that slimmest of chances, was there any hope at all? If I went back to Xianza and played along with whatever the cops said, would another chance to escape present itself? Perhaps I could still make it to the mountain, though I knew that if I rode my horses into that damn town it would be certain I wouldn't leave on them, or that I'd ride again in Tibet.

It had been three months since I'd set out and I'd ridden two thousand kilometres. I thought of the hardships I'd endured, how I'd struggled through every single day. I stood up and made the toughest decision of my life. I'd never failed like this before. I climbed onto Ridey's back, turned him round and headed back towards Xianza. With every step I felt my heart break a little more as he carried me away from Gang Rinpoche.

I reached the lake again and was so cold, hungry and depressed I stopped at an old campsite and fired up the stove for tea and *tsampa*. It took up a fair amount of time but I felt as if I was in no hurry. I carried on and as we rode I counted all the things I was going to miss and all the things I wasn't going to do. Crossing a small plain by the lake I passed a pretty young shepherd girl with her charges, who stared at me from under her shawl. I waved to her and her face lit up into a beautiful smile as she waved back. I realised how much I was going to miss the people. As we headed into the hills at the end of the lake I got off and Ridey walked up beside me with his head by my shoulder as if he wanted to comfort me. 'I'm sorry, boys.' Tears on my face again; I was going to miss them too.

I stopped for tea at a tent with the two young men I'd met at my campsite. The one who had been with the police when they'd found me said they'd stopped at his camp and asked if he'd seen me, then ordered him into the jeep and made him lead them to me. He could hardly lie and say he hadn't seen me or didn't know where I was, he'd had no idea anything was wrong and he'd only have got himself in trouble. Later I stopped at the house where I'd met the old man with his secret shrine. He also said the police had asked if he'd seen me; it seemed that someone near Xianza had reported me to the authorities, who had gone door to door until they tracked me down. The old man was sympathetic and I got the feeling he wasn't a big fan of his local police force.

That night I camped on the river plain below the lake. I knew it would probably be my last night in my tent and I made *tukpa* and tea under the ripening moon. As I stared into the dying embers I tried to think more positively. I knew I should still feel proud of what I had achieved; two thousand kilometres across Tibet alone was a success in itself but I couldn't shake the sense of failure and an awful feeling in my gut that there would be things left unfinished.

I made tea in the morning before loading the horses for the last time and heading up the valley. After a couple of hours I stopped with a nomad family

Ian wearing a *chuba*, with his first horses, about to set off from near Garilang.

Yak riders near the Yellow River.

'I say, anyone for billiards?'

Ian with Ridey and Packy.

Ian with a group of monks in front of their temple.

From vice to virtue: the mantra *Om mani padme hum* is painted on the top of an old pool table as part of a *mani* wall.

Village ladies in traditional amber headwear near Seka Gompa monastery.

Crowds of onlookers in the town of Zadoi near Seka Gompa.

Sharing tea with a local lad by the campfire.

Crossing a pass near Ziqu.

Pious Tibetan carving mantras onto stones.

A different 'Ridey' and 'Packy' in a snowstorm.

Ian with a Chinese police officer after arrest and on their way to Naqu.

Drugu Gompa, to where Ian escaped from Naqu.

Ian in disguise with his new horses.

Nomads milking sheep.

in their tent for a last bowl of butter tea and one of the men showed me where to cross the river. I arrived in Xianza in the middle of the afternoon.

The town was a dusty jumble of small streets, concrete Chinese buildings and huts surrounded by garbage. I rode my horses up the main street, feeling like a high plains drifter as everyone stopped to watch.

I tied the horses to a power pole outside a Chinese noodle hut and went inside for something to eat. Afterwards I asked the young woman who worked there to show me where the police station was, but when we arrived it was empty. Instead she showed me to a little hair salon. The pretty Chinese girls inside giggled shyly as they saw their first exotic head walk through the door. However, a moment later they were offering me tea and some ghastly Chinese wine as they argued over who was going to cut my hair.

I hadn't washed it in months — it was dry and a complete mess. The young lady held my head over a basin as she soaped my hair with warm water and shampoo. Her experienced fingers gliding over my scalp felt delightful; apart from the odd handshake this was pretty much the first physical contact I'd had with another human in over three months. She sat me in front of a mirror and started snipping away.

'Oh, to hell with it, darling,' I said and pointed to an electric shaver, 'just take it all off!'

A few minutes later I had a haircut to rival any monk in Tibet. I ran my fingers over my skinhead — I felt so smooth and clean, it was fantastic.

I went back to my horses and the Chinese woman showed me to a hotel across the road from the restaurant. I checked into a dusty little room for twenty yuan a night. There were a couple of beds, a chair and a table, but the best feature was a tin stove and a box of yak dung. I walked the horses up to the door and unloaded them, surrounded by a crowd of locals. I stashed my gear inside and took them down onto the river plain below the town. We walked out to where the garbage was thinner and I tethered them for the night before going back to the police station. This time there was one officer there who didn't seem to know who I was, but one of the kids who had been following me told him I was staying in the hotel. I told him that when his colleagues returned they could come and find me.

After another meal in the restaurant I went back to the hotel to wait for the police. Four of them, including the Chinese officer who could speak English, arrived in the early evening.

'Your visa is expired.'

'Yes, I know, I was going to Lhasa to extend it when you found me.'

'We will call our headquarters to decide what you must do; tonight we will come back and tell you. You must wait here, don't go away from the hotel.'

'All right.'

They left and I stoked up the stove to make tea. I wasn't feeling very hopeful about what was going to happen. The headquarters the cop was talking about was in Naqu — and I really didn't want to go back there. Going to Lhasa wouldn't be a complete disaster, and there would be a chance I could escape and still make it to Gang Rinpoche by road.

The police didn't return until ten thirty. 'We have called our headquarters in Naqu. They are very angry you disobeyed their orders.'

'Yes, so where will I go now?'

'You must go to Lhasa, there you will be dealt with by the Lhasa police.'

I could hardly believe it. Although I knew the situation could change in a moment I felt as if the day hadn't been a complete disaster.

'You must sell your horses before we leave Friday.'

Today was Sunday. I wasn't looking forward to being stuck in Xianza for five days, but I had no choice, and at least it would give me time to do something with the horses.

'You must stay in Xianza, you must not go anywhere else. Do you understand, Mr Robinson?'

'Yes, thank you.' And they left.

I slept quite well and was having *tsampa* for breakfast when there was a knock on the door. I opened it to find one of the policemen, a short Tibetan. I thought they'd changed their minds and were about to take me off to Naqu, but he smiled and unfolded a large sheet of white paper with Tibetan characters written on it in blue ink. It was a sign saying: 'I want to sell two horses.' I felt touched he'd gone to the trouble to do something to help me.

I spent the morning wandering round the dusty streets of Xianza showing the sign to men who looked as if they were from the countryside. While there was considerable interest, none of it was in the horses, just me. I was the first foreigner to visit the town and the fact that I'd arrived on horseback dressed like a Tibetan made me even more of an oddity. Although any of the villagers would have gladly taken the horses, none of them had any money. They were worth five thousand yuan and I expected to sell them for much less, but for a Tibetan herdsman even this is an enormous amount of money. And while the traders and shopkeepers may have had cash, they had no use for horses. I tried again over the following days, but it soon became obvious I wasn't going to be able to sell the boys. I gave up for the time being and went back to the restaurant.

The Chinese woman and two men who ran the little noodle shop were very kind, sharing their lunch with me. I was given a plate of fried rice and cabbage, more green vegetables than I'd seen in months. During the days I spent in Xianza I visited them every day and often one of them would wander over to the hotel when they weren't too busy.

In the corner of the single room of their restaurant there was a small bed behind a curtain. I guessed one of the men slept there at night in case the place was broken into; however, one rainy morning I arrived at the restaurant to find everyone still in bed. The woman was still dozing behind the curtain with one of the men, while the other was under a quilt on the floor. All three of them lived on the premises, which doubled as their home. I guessed the woman must be married to the man she was lying next to; however, later in the week I found her in the same position with the other man. We didn't have enough language in common for me to make polite enquiries into what the exact situation was, other than to say they all seemed fairly happy.

Like the other Chinese I met in the small towns on the plateau, they had come to the frontier to start a new life. They had probably been given incentives from the government, tax breaks and relocation allowances, larger rations and the option of having more than one child. They seemed to get on well with the locals, often being visited by Tibetan friends. On the whole from what I saw, the Chinese immigrants and their Tibetan hosts lived happily in a symbiotic relationship, trading and dealing with each other, exchanging goods and labour. I never detected any hostility or resentment. Life for the Chinese must have been difficult in such a harsh environment and far from their homes and families, but they had come to make the best they could of it.

I spent the afternoons lazing in my room making cups of tea. Every so often a Tibetan would open my door and stand on the threshold staring at me until I waved them away and closed the door. Most of the time when I went out I'd be followed by groups of kids who waited outside my room with their faces pressed against the glass. After three months of solitude this became tiring and I felt myself becoming lazy and lethargic; sometimes I'd spend half the day sitting in my room staring into space, unable to motivate myself to do anything. The rhythm of my journey had been broken and the thought of the tension and effort of trying to escape again made me despondent. Sometimes I would wander along the street to a little 'hole in the wall' shop in a mud-brick building where a pretty Tibetan girl worked. Someone had set up an old pool table on the street and in the evening some of the village men would gather there to play. I'd join them, struggling to understand the rules of Tibetan pool, but usually beating any challengers.

The next evening as I sat alone in my room there was a knock at the door. This time I opened it to find a young Chinese police officer.

'Good evening, I am Wang Huang. I am an officer of the Public Security Bureau of the People's Republic of China.' What he meant was: 'I'm a cop.'

'No kidding, I guess you better come in.'

The young officer marched into the room and sat down. I guessed there had been developments in the plan to take me to Lhasa. However, for several minutes he sat staring at the wall above my head taking deep breaths as if he was desperately trying to compose himself. I realised he was extremely nervous. 'Is everything OK?' I asked quietly.

'Yes,' he gasped, without looking at me.

'Do I need to go with you?'

'No.'

'Is there a problem?'

'No.'

'Do I need to go to the police station?'

'No.'

This continued for some time. Every so often he would open his mouth to speak but before he could get a word out he would lose his nerve.

'Would you like some tea?'

'No, thank you.'

Finally he managed to get himself together enough to speak. 'When I was a university student in China I studied English. My teacher was a woman from America. I would like to invite you to my home for tea and something to eat, if you don't mind please come with me.' At last he looked at me, his eyes almost pleading. He wanted to practise his English and it had probably taken him all day to get up the nerve to come and ask me.

'Thank you, I'd love to.'

The young man sank back with relief and his face broke into a smile.

On the way he told me he'd graduated from police training college two years earlier and Xianza was his first posting from his home in the south of China. I felt sorry for the poor boy, sent to this miserable hole; it must seem like the worst place on earth and I could imagine he'd be terrified of the Tibetans, wild, rough people who live in tents and never wash. He was bored, lonely and homesick.

In his little concrete room he served me tea and dried plums while he showed me photos of his home and family.

'This is my mother and father, and this is my girlfriend. I haven't seen her in two years but this December I will have a vacation, two weeks! I can go back to China to see them.'

'You must be very excited.'

'Yes, it has been a long time, my life here is difficult.' He lowered his voice as if someone might be listening. 'I don't like it here, I want to go home.'

Friday was drawing closer and I knew I was going to have to get rid of my horses. On Thursday morning I led them up to the hotel yard, where I tied them to a pole. I saddled them for the last time, walked them out to the street and climbed on Ridey's back. I suddenly felt so high off the ground, even though Ridey was tiny, and so proud to be in the saddle. One thought instantly came to mind: 'This is where I should be!' And then I was brought back down knowing that when I returned to town it would be without my boys. This would be my last day with horses in Tibet and I wanted to enjoy their company.

We rode out onto the plain and soon reached the river; again it was wide and swift and I rode downstream for a while until I found a place to cross. The water was deep in the middle, right up to the saddle and Packy was almost swimming behind us. We made it to the other bank but then had to wade through soft mud, both horses sinking up to their bellies. I jumped out of the saddle and waded through the muck, leading them behind me. Ridey followed on but a few metres from solid ground Packy stopped and just stood there. I left him, leading Ridey onto the grass and then returned to get Packy.

We made it over the last few metres and were almost on the bank when Packy started to panic. In his fear he struggled against me and ended up stumbling into a wet hole of soft, sticky mud. He started sinking and began thrashing about, which only made it worse. I grabbed his halter and tried to pull him onto the bank but he was becoming a dead-weight. I was desperate to keep him on his feet, but within seconds his legs went from beneath him and he was lying on his side in the mud, panting and shivering and unable to move, exhausted and going into shock.

I climbed down beside him and tried to get him on his feet, but it was impossible, he couldn't move, no amount or method of encouragement had any effect. He closed his eyes and lay there.

'Come on, Packy, get up! Come on, boy, you've got to get up, if you stay here you'll die!'

But it was useless. I sat on the bank and cried — this was the last straw. I was supposed to be enjoying my last ride and trying to find someone to give my horses to, but here I was with poor Packy dying in a mud hole. Any thoughts I had of escaping and sneaking off to Gang Rinpoche were wiped away. Tibet had beaten me; she'd won the battle. I couldn't take any more. I felt dejected and broken and finally defeated.

But I had to do something to help Packy. I caught Ridey and set off towards a group of houses a kilometre away. I'd been noticed and a Tibetan man was on his way out to meet me. We hurried back to where Packy lay and the man looked shocked. He climbed back onto the bank and started yelling towards the houses, waving his hat above his head and calling for more help. Before long three more men were on their way.

Without hesitation the men stripped off their *chubas* and boots and climbed into the mud. First they turned Packy round so his head faced the bank, then three of them got behind his back while the other shoved his legs underneath him to give him a chance to get on his feet. I took hold of his halter and on a count of three we all heaved. Packy struggled and got halfway to his feet before sinking back; we heaved again, his front legs scrambled and hit the solid ground of the bank, the men pushed from behind and my little packhorse pulled himself onto the grass.

I shook the men's hands, *'Tujachay! Tujachay!'* They just smiled and nodded and one of them led Packy to a large puddle of rainwater in the grass, where all the men scooped up water in their hats and washed Packy down. He soon stopped shivering and within minutes seemed none the worse for his experience, happily nibbling on the grass. We set off towards the houses and before long I was enjoying a bowl of butter tea by the fire.

I showed the men my sign: 'I want to sell two horses', but they shrugged and said, *'Gong mindu.'* We haven't got any money. I was beyond caring; tomorrow the police would take me to Lhasa and I had to do something with the horses. Selling them was impossible so I decided to give them to the man who had first come out to help me. After tea we went outside, I untied Ridey and jumped into the saddle and cantered round the village for a last ride. He'd been rested for the last few days and had some fire in him again. After a few minutes I pulled him up in front of the house and climbed out of the saddle for the last time.

'Sangnyi nga Lhasa-la dro,' I told the man, tomorrow I'm going to Lhasa. I pushed the lead ropes into his hands. Their new owner looked confused and somewhat embarrassed that a total stranger had just given him two good horses and a complete set of riding gear.

'Cha tung,' he said, have some more tea.

'Ma rey.' I shook my head and pointed back towards Xianza.

I rubbed Packy's chin and scratched the hair on Ridey's forehead: 'Thanks, boys. Good luck.'

And then I turned and walked away. This was the end of this part of the journey, it was the end of this part of my life, and as I walked across the grassland I forced myself to accept that this was the end of my dream. I wouldn't reach Gang Rinpoche.

I thought about the last three months, all the kilometres I'd ridden, all the kind people who had helped me, every frozen day I'd made it through, the passes I had crossed, the cold sunsets and the bright moons, the humble joy of making tea on a fire, the promises I'd made to others and myself. Had it all been for nothing? Had anything changed inside me or was I still the same deluded fool I was when I set out from Garilang? I thought of what I was losing by not reaching the mountain, of the achievement that wouldn't be mine. I tried desperately to be proud of myself and think positively on what I had done, but the thought chewed at my heart that reaching Kailas would have been the greatest event of my life. Now that chance was gone.

I walked up the river until it met a road and hitched a ride back to town on a truck. In the afternoon I packed up my gear before going back to the restaurant for the last time.

The Chinese woman had made a huge bowl of dumplings for me and we shared a couple of bottles of beer with the two men. Before I left we took photos together and exchanged addresses. When I tried to pay they refused and insisted the meal was on the house. I was deeply touched; these three were some of the kindest people I met on the whole trip. I guess in view of the Tibetan situation one could see them as the 'enemy', or at least as part of the problem, but as much as I'd love to see Tibet emptied of her Chinese visitors, I could never bring myself to think so, they were just openly good, honest people. They were friends.

At eight thirty the next morning a police jeep pulled up in front of my room. To my relief I saw the officers who would be taking me to Lhasa included the little Tibetan who had made me the sign and a couple of the friendlier members of the local constabulary.

We set off in two jeeps along with a couple of women, wives of the police I guessed, and their kids. As we drove out of town I looked across the valley to where Ridey and Packy must have been; of course, they were too far away to see, but I knew they were two of those black dots. 'Goodbye, boys.'

We drove out of the Xianza valley and climbed slowly into the mountains across grasslands finally beginning to flush with spring green. In the afternoon we started up a high pass and when we reached the top one of the men in the front seat of the jeep turned to me and pointing back the way we had come, said, *'Drokpa'*, nomads, then pointing down the other side of the pass said, *'Po-pa'*, which means the crop farmers of the lower climes of Tibet. I was about to enter a very different part of the country.

The road fell quickly; we must have dropped several hundred metres in a couple of hours and when we stopped at a little wayside lodge for lunch I saw the first real trees I'd seen in three months, great lanky poplars with lush green leaves. I felt as if I was seeing trees for the first time. I walked over and rubbed their rough trunks, rubbing the smooth green leaves between my fingers and listening to the wind rush through the branches.

Further on the landscape became even more surprising. By evening we were travelling through warm valleys — bare rock mountains rose on all sides, but the valley floors were layered with lush green barley fields tipped with bright yellow flowers. Leafy birch and poplars lined the roadside and streams. Everywhere farmers headed home after their day's work. There were no yaks, just skinny cows, and no horses, only the occasional donkey cart. Villages of high-walled, grey-painted mud houses clustered on the river bends and *gompa*s like citadels perched on the hilltops. I felt totally lost, I couldn't believe I was still in Tibet. I felt as if we had crossed the border into Nepal or India, everything was so different.

We stopped for the night in a small town called Namling and checked into a lodge in an open yard lined with trees. It was so warm I had to shed half my clothes; children ran about in the streets in T-shirts, cicadas chirped in the trees and mosquitoes swarmed above the open drains. Dominating the town was an impressive monastery — I asked the officers if I could visit it and they nodded happily. They had been friendly all day, even stopping the jeep so I could take photos.

I walked along the main street and headed up through the old Tibetan village, past little stone houses in cow yards, narrow passageways and stone steps leading high above the town to the *gompa*. Towering above the monastery were the remains of a *dzong* or ancient fortress. Namling Gompa is a large centre with about eighty monks. I met one young novice outside, who ran off to find his senior with the key to open the great doors of the main temple. I made prostrations in front of the main altar and was taken through some smaller shrine rooms. I was told one small room was where the Dalai Lama stayed on a visit, which must have been more than fifty years ago when he was a teenager. The room had been kept exactly as he'd left it, even the bed was still made up as if waiting for his return. It was good to stand in a real temple again, but as I walked back out the main doors I had a pang of regret that my horses weren't waiting.

Back in the village I found a noodle shop and got something for dinner. Before going back to the lodge I bought a couple of bottles of beer to give the police to thank them for their efforts behind the wheel. They were embarrassed and at first refused, but I pressed the green bottles on them and insisted. Inside their room they were all enjoying dinner and I could tell they wanted to ask me to join them. Despite being cops they were still Tibetans and wanted to offer me hospitality, but I was still a criminal and that prevented us from becoming too cosy. During the day I tried to break the ice with the women and kids, but they shied away, perhaps under instructions not to talk to me.

We set off at eight the next morning and before long we'd reached the Yarlung Tsangpo river, Tibet's greatest waterway, known as the Brahmaputra further down the subcontinent. We crossed the river on a vehicle ferry and were then on the main Lhasa/Shigatze road. Cut into the sides of the great cliffs with the muddy flow of the river far below, the road is mostly sealed and busy with traffic.

All day we followed the river through bare rocky hills and past villages, any flat space ploughed and planted with barley. By late afternoon we were approaching Lhasa and I began to feel steadily more apprehensive.

Chapter Seven

But ready or not we were soon on a four-lane highway heading into the city, the road thick with traffic, like some manic Grand Prix with trucks, tractors, jeeps and cars all jostling for position in a mad dash to get to the city. Finally the Potala came into view, the colossal whitewashed palace/fortress that was the winter home of the Dalai Lamas, a building which still dominates Lhasa and symbolises the city. The last time I'd seen it was twelve years earlier and I'd burst with joy at arriving in the Holy City, but now any emotion had been dulled by my sense of failure and smothered by kilometres of Chinese shops and housing blocks. The billboards and neon lights and the surreal sight of Chinese women in skirts and short sleeves had me asking myself, 'Is this really Tibet?' Twelve years earlier Lhasa had been a Tibetan city, now it had been reduced to a Tibetan village surrounded by kilometres of Chinese sprawl.

We drove straight to the Lhasa Central Police Station and waited outside while one of the cops went off to try to find someone to deal with me. Raised gardens filled with blooming roses graced the entrance to the building, but the yard was full of jeeps. After an hour's wait an officer arrived but he didn't seem to know who I was and couldn't speak English. Phone calls were made and soon a young Tibetan girl from one of the hotels arrived to translate. There wasn't much to say, other than that since tomorrow was Sunday there would be no one on duty and I was told to come back on Monday.

'When will I get my passport back?' I asked.

'I don't know, you'll have to ask on Monday,' she told me. 'The officer here doesn't know anything, just come back on Monday.'

My saddlebags were taken out of the jeep and loaded into a black Chinese saloon car; the driver opened the door but before I got inside one of the officers from Xianza tapped me on the shoulder. I turned around to find them lined up to farewell me like old friends. This was the last time I'd see them, their duty was done and from now on I'd be the concern of the Lhasa police. We all shook hands. There was no animosity, they had just been doing their jobs and throughout the whole ordeal I'd been treated kindly and fairly for the most part.

'*Tujachay*, goodbye.'

'Good-a-bye!'

The car drove me and the Tibetan girl to the Yak Hotel, one of the more popular backpacker hangouts, or so it had been twelve years earlier. Now I couldn't believe it was the same place. I was greeted by a marble foyer, garden furniture among the trees under an awning and rooms ranging up to four stars in value. There were no dorm beds left so the girl directed me down the street to the Hotel Kirey. I told the girl to tell the police where I was if they came looking, heaved my saddlebags and *chuba* over my shoulder and set off into the darkening street.

The footpaths were crowded with stalls selling everything from butter and yak meat to nylon socks and everything in between, buyers, sellers and streams of people heading home in the falling night. As I swaggered through the throng everyone stopped to stare, not because I was foreign this time but because of the way I was dressed — in my high boots and black hat I wasn't your average tourist.

I made it to the Kirey and filled in the registration form; where it asked me to state where I was coming from I wrote Garilang; of course, the woman had never heard of it and shrugged. She gave me the key to the three-bed dorm and I lugged my saddlebags across the yard to my room. There were a few other foreign travellers sitting about on benches chatting in the twilight, but as I walked by they fell silent and watched me pass. I was sharing the room with two young Japanese backpackers. When I opened the door they looked so startled it was as if a *Khampa* bandit had walked in. We introduced ourselves and shook hands. I told them I'd spent three months crossing the plateau on horseback but they just nodded as if they didn't understand what I was saying. I dropped my gear off and headed back out into the streets towards the Jokhang Temple and Barkhor market.

Twelve years ago I could have found the place blindfolded, I visited it so many times during the three weeks I'd spent in Lhasa. I was sure I could find it again, but I was soon so disorientated I had to stop and ask directions. The Jokhang stands in the centre of Lhasa and is one of Tibet's oldest and most hallowed religious sites. Some say it's built on an underground lake and it is used by the faithful of all the different sects of Buddhism in Tibet. The pilgrim circuit-cum-market known as the Barkhor runs around the outside between the temple and the surrounding buildings, and streams with pilgrims and shoppers all day and half the night.

I stood in front of the main doors where the flagstones have been polished as smooth as mirrors by thousands of worshippers making prostrations for hundreds of years. I found a space among them and made three full-length prostrations, laying my whole body on the greasy stones, much to the bemusement of the locals. I was beyond bothering by then and after finishing I joined the current of Tibetans as they made their evening circuits of the Barkhor.

The crowd consisted of monks and lamas, Lhasan Tibetans in Western dress or light summer *chubas*, nomads and country folk from every corner of Tibet clad in sheepskin, hair still matted by the winds of the wilds, perhaps travelling for weeks or even months on a once-in-a-lifetime pilgrimage to the Holy City, all with *malas* in their hands and mantras on their lips. Here and there groups of wide-eyed tourists from Hong Kong trailed like sheep behind their flag-waving guides, terrified they'd get lost and never be seen again. There was the occasional odd Westerner, large Americans on package tours, backpackers who had come overland from Kathmandu, and in amongst all this a bewildered freak who longed to be back on the plateau with a couple of scrawny horses.

The market was about to pack up for the night, stalls stacked with carpets and bolts of cloth, souvenirs and antique odds and ends, *thangkas* or Buddhist scroll paintings, fake coral and turquoise jewellery, monks' robes and fur hats, knives and brass butter lamps. On the corners sat groups of young monks cheerfully chanting prayers in exchange for alms from the passers-by while real beggars, elderly pilgrims without enough money to get back to their distant homes, cripples and lepers held out their crooked hands, hoping to catch whatever was left.

I suddenly realised there were no longer any dogs roaming about; there used to be hundreds but the Chinese have cleaned up the market's image. The lane has been widened (some say to allow them to get tanks around should there be another uprising), stalls have been licensed and their size standardised, and the dogs have been destroyed. Instead there are Chinese security personnel with radio-telephones, the eyes and ears of the police, perched on stools at regular intervals. Every time I caught sight of a uniform my heart automatically skipped a beat.

Back in front of the Jokhang the air was filled with smoke from juniper burnt by the pilgrims; the sweet, pungent smell reminded me of nights when I'd burnt sticks of it in the mountains on an open campfire. I suddenly felt utterly exhausted, as if my whole body was about to fall apart. I looked at the darkened doors of the great temple. Inside was the Jowo Shakyamuni statue, Tibet's most sacred treasure, said to have been made during the lifetime of the Buddha himself.

To many Western travellers in Asia, Lhasa is the ultimate destination. Any who make it this far must feel like I did the first time, elated and thrilled to walk the streets of this almost mystical city. But this time I felt like an intruder, like an infidel at Mecca, a fraud who didn't deserve to be there, not having earned the right, let alone the right to go home. I felt I had let myself down and I was letting down all those who had tried to help me reach

Gang Rinpoche, all those who had wished me good luck and prayed for me. Now I would have to go back and tell them I'd failed. And worst of all I had disappointed my lama. I still had Khensur Thabkye Rinpoche's ashes with me. I'd said I'd sprinkle them at the holy sites at Gang Rinpoche, but now there was no way I could keep my promise. And although perhaps there had been a change inside me, only time would tell, but I knew *I* hadn't died, I could feel that *I* was still alive.

I wandered back to the hotel just as my two Japanese roommates were heading out for dinner, so they invited me along and over noodles we talked about my trip. They were surprised and impressed with what I'd done and after a few glasses of beer I cheered up a bit. I didn't sleep well, the room was too hot and the street outside noisy with traffic. I got up early and had breakfast before heading off to the Barkhor again; after a circuit I wandered round the back streets and found a couple of little temples I remembered from last time. I had lunch in a Tibetan restaurant, solid simple food my stomach could handle, and then went back to the hotel for a snooze.

Again the few other Western travellers stopped talking and stared as I went past. They were dressed in bright T-shirts and shorts with trekking sandals while I was still stalking about in my boots and oilskin coat. At the back of the yard was a shower block; the Japanese had told me there was plenty of hot water during the day. I hadn't had a shower or done any more than wash my face and hands in over three months. I always thought it would be the first thing I'd do when I got back to 'civilisation', but strangely I had no desire to wash; I almost felt it would be a betrayal, I'd be turning my back on what I'd been through and if I washed I would break the spell of the horseback journey. I knew that as soon as I washed it would really be over.

On Monday morning I walked to the police station. I hung around in the lobby waiting for someone to come and deal with me. Leaning on the counter I glanced over the other side and saw a stack of blank Alien Travel Permit cards. There was no one about so I grabbed one and stuffed it in my bag, just in case I might need it someday. Finally I was told the officer who would deal with my case wasn't there and I'd have to come back at four o'clock.

After a late lunch I went back. This time I was taken to an office upstairs where I met the young Tibetan officer who had been assigned to me. Dressed fashionably in jeans and a T-shirt, he spoke very good English and didn't waste time. He told me I had committed three crimes: illegal travel, failing to register my accommodation, and allowing my visa to expire.

'Mr Robinson, I have the report from Naqu headquarters. It states that you were found travelling illegally in Liarong without a permit, you were taken to

Naqu and told to leave Tibet; however, you disobeyed and bought two more horses. What do you have to say to that?'

'Nothing much.'

He looked annoyed, expecting me to argue more vigorously. 'Do you admit you disobeyed the orders of the Naqu police? They told you to leave Tibet but you didn't.'

'They just told me to leave Naqu, they never said I had to leave Tibet.'

'But that's not what I have in my report, it's very clear, they ordered you to leave Tibet!'

'Then that report is wrong, they told me to leave Naqu. I don't remember anything about being told to leave Tibet.'

This argument went on for some time. I wasn't going to admit I'd been told to leave Tibet and told him the officers in Naqu couldn't speak English very well and it must have been a misunderstanding, their explicit orders somehow lost in translation.

'Yes, well, perhaps it was just a misunderstanding.' The young officer conceded — round one to me. I slouched in my chair, casually crossed my legs and looked bored.

'However, you were found travelling in Liarong, which is a closed area, without a permit. What do you say to that, Mr Robinson?'

'How was I to know this place is closed?'

'You should have checked with the government authorities before you went there.' And I told him my lie about having been given permission to go there by the police in Zadoi. 'The police in Zadoi have no right to give you permission to travel anywhere in Xizang!'

'How am I supposed to know that?'

'You should have checked with the Central Government.'

'How?'

'Um, you could have used the Internet before you came to China. I'm sure you know how to use a computer, you're not an idiot, are you?'

'No, I'm not!'

It was ridiculous to suggest you could find this kind of information on the Internet. You couldn't get it from the Chinese government, or even from an embassy, you'd be lucky to get a straight answer from anyone in a face-to-face meeting. I told him how in 1990 I'd been in Lhasa and had been given permission by the police to go to Tsedang, a small town several hours by bus from the city, but on arrival I'd been arrested for being in a closed area. 'How can I trust the Chinese authorities to give me accurate information? It's impossible!'

'Nevertheless, you were also found in Xianza; this place is also closed. You could have asked the police in Naqu if you could go there, but you didn't. The fine for travelling illegally in a closed area is five hundred yuan!' Round two to him. 'Next, you failed to register your accommodation. It is required by the law of the People's Republic of China that all foreigners must register their accommodation. What do you have to say to this?'

'I was living in a tent, how can I register my tent?'

'You should have reported to the local authorities.'

'There were no local authorities! There was no one, sometimes I didn't see anyone for days!'

'Really? What did you eat?' The young man looked shocked, almost concerned.

'I took *tsampa* with me.'

'Weren't you afraid?'

'Not really.'

'You're very brave, Mr Robinson. Well, yes, perhaps it wasn't possible for you to register with anyone. You have still broken the law but I won't impose a fine for that.'

'Thank you.' We'll call that even, shall we?

The final point was my expired visa. 'I was on my way to Lhasa to extend it when the police in Xianza found me,' I told him. 'Tibetan horses are slow and my visa expired before I could arrive.'

'That is your problem, you should have left your horses and gone by road. Your visa is now expired by fourteen days; the fine for an expired visa is five hundred yuan per day.'

That was more money than I had left. I'd have to argue this one down. 'But I should only pay for four days, my visa was only expired by four days when I met the police in Xianza.'

'But your visa is expired by fourteen, you have to pay for fourteen days!'

'But I had to wait five days in Xianza, that wasn't my fault, was it?'

'Yes, all right.' He started adding this up on a piece of paper.

'Then it was two days by jeep to Lhasa.'

'All right.'

'Then I had to wait another day in Lhasa because you were on holiday.'

'Oh, all right then, that leaves six days. Where are the other two days, Mr Robinson?'

'The other two days were spent riding my horses to Xianza.'

'But why didn't you go by jeep with the police?'

'They refused to take me. I had to ride my poor horses.' Of course this was bullshit.

'So that's four days, very well, that's two thousand yuan, plus five hundred for the illegal travel. You must pay a fine of two thousand five hundred yuan. If you cannot pay you will be taken to prison, do you understand?'

I handed over the money and was given a stamped receipt. The officer had taken a detailed statement recording his questions and my answers, which I had to sign. Of course, it was all in Chinese and I couldn't read it but I didn't care. I was also given a form detailing my crimes, which, if I chose to, I could take to the People's Court to appeal my case.

'Thank you, I think that will look nice hanging on my wall at home!' I said and the Tibetan laughed.

Now that the arguments and formalities were over the young officer relaxed and he told me that when he'd studied English at university in China he'd had a teacher from New Zealand. 'Do you have any questions, Ian?'

'Yes, can you tell me why these areas of Tibet are closed? There is nothing there, why can't tourists visit?' I knew I wouldn't get a satisfying answer but I was interested to hear what he'd say.

'Well, you know what happened in New York on September 11, we worry that we could have trouble here. The Tibetan people in the countryside are not used to meeting foreigners like you, they don't understand another people's culture and we worry this could cause misunderstandings and problems.' As I expected, a load of rubbish.

'When I was in the countryside,' I told him, 'I met many Tibetan people, I believe there was friendship between us. I don't feel I've done anything wrong, I didn't hurt anyone, I didn't take anything from anyone, I feel my time in Tibet has had a positive effect.'

'Yes, I understand, and I believe you didn't do any harm, but just as in your country, we have rules and laws and they must be obeyed. I'm sorry, Ian, but you did break them.'

'Yes, but I have cooperated fully with the police and done everything asked of me.' This wasn't true, especially my dramatic escape from Tarin, which this young man seemed to have no knowledge of — obviously it wasn't in the report.

'That's true, I think it must have been very difficult for you. I think the police in Xianza must have been very rough.'

'No, not at all, they treated me very well the whole time.'

I was given a visa for five further days and told I must leave the People's Republic within that time.

Back at the hotel I bit the bullet and had a shower for the first time in more than three months, and it did feel good. Over the next couple of days

I managed to book a seat to Hong Kong and each day I visited the Jokhang, joining the crush of pilgrims lining up with butter lamps and making offerings to the Buddha statues in the cavernous temple. One by one we filed past the Jowo Shakyamuni, where I touched my head to the base of the statue and recited a short prayer for the happiness of all sentient beings. I also laid the *khata* Dhondup and Jigme had given me across the base of the statue; inside I had wrapped the tail hairs I'd taken from my horses and as I left them behind I prayed for their safety.

On my last evening in Lhasa I sat outside the Jokhang on the flagstones with a family of pilgrims from Kham in eastern Tibet, who shared a thermos of tea with me. Within a week I would be sitting with my own family in New Zealand; my mind was mixed with thoughts of anticipation and apprehension at the feelings I would have to confront. Breaking down in tears at my mother's dinner table when I tried to describe the cold, harsh conditions, and the heartbreak when I'd been forced to give up. Not knowing what to say when friends asked, 'How was your trip? Did you have a good time?' I'd be at a loss as to how to answer, knowing I hadn't finished what I'd set out to do — the nagging fact that there was something left undone.

Before dawn the next morning I took a taxi to the airline office, then a bus to the airport a couple of hours outside Lhasa. Eventually the check-in counters opened and I followed a huge group of Hong Kong tourists into the customs hall. I was the only non-Chinese on the flight and the only person to be searched. As the flight took off I looked out the window at my last view of the mountains and valleys of Tibet.

Soon the flight attendants served tea and biscuits; as one, a young Chinese girl, leant across to pass a cup to my neighbour I smelt her perfume. As she served me she smiled, she was really very pretty — just a few months ago I would have tried to catch her eye and speak to her, but now I just smiled back and was happy to let it be. After she'd gone I smiled again, to myself this time; perhaps something had changed inside me. I knew it wouldn't be easy being faced with the distractions of home, bars, restaurants and pleasant company. Would I soon go back to my old ways? Would the temptations I'd tried to leave behind seduce me again? All that would remain to be seen. I was sure of one thing — I would never see Tibet again. I was finished with this place.

Part Two

*Just to leave one's homeland
is to accomplish half the dharma.*

(Milarepa, Tibetan saint)

Chapter Eight

Several months later I woke up one Sunday morning, hung-over and next to someone I didn't really know that well and realised of course I was going back, I'd always been going back, there was never truly any doubt I would return. I needed to finish what I'd started.

On 24 June 2004 I found myself back in Lhasa. I'd come via Hong Kong where I'd been given a three-month tourist visa for the People's Republic, taken a train across the border to Guangzhou, flown to Xining in central China, boarded an overnight train to Golmud and finally spent twenty-one hours on a bus full of smoking, hoicking Chinese. I had been worried my name might have been on a computer and I'd be refused a visa or the permit to Lhasa, but everything had gone smoothly. To get the permit in Golmud I'd had to sign up for a two-day tour of Lhasa. I was met by a driver with a minivan and taken to the Hotel Kirey. After I checked in to the three-bed dorm my guide turned up.

'Mr Robinson, welcome to Lhasa! Your tour starts tomorrow at ten.'

'I'm feeling really sick, the bus ride was terrible — I think it's the altitude. Perhaps I should just rest tomorrow.'

'Oh yes, maybe that's a good idea. My office is on the second floor, just tell me when you feel better and we'll start then.'

In fact I felt fine, but I had no intention of joining the tour. I had no desire to pay again to see places I'd already been to several times on my own. The next day I bumped into the guide; he asked me how I was feeling and I told him I still wasn't up to starting the tour. I never saw him again. The 'tour' had been expensive and was now money lost, but all that mattered to me was that I was back in Tibet and free to do whatever I wanted.

In the months that followed my return to New Zealand I'd tried to put Tibet behind me, I'd tried to accept it was over and I'd tried to put the feeling of failure to rest, to leave the trip as it was, unfinished. But I hadn't been able to. I'd hardly spoken to anyone about the journey, I hadn't even shown my family my photos. Part of me felt that if I talked too much about it I would be bragging about something I hadn't done. I wouldn't allow myself to be proud of what I had achieved, even though others told me I should.

All the while I could feel Kailas waiting for me, quietly drawing me back. Before long plans started forming in my mind, I started making lists of equipment I'd need to buy or make, things I needed to do before leaving.

I knew this would be my last chance to reach the mountain and I staked everything on it, spending everything I'd saved and borrowing the rest.

I decided to travel with only one horse. I could move faster and having only one mount would make it easier to escape if I ran into trouble. And the chances of running into trouble would be high; from the moment I left Lhasa I'd be in restricted areas. With one horse I'd also be severely limited to what I could carry and would have to strip my equipment down to a bare minimum — a lightweight sleeping bag and a 'bivvy bag', the kind of shelter mountaineers use when they sleep out on a tiny ledge on the side of a peak. It had no frame or poles and wasn't much bigger than a sleeping bag. It was light, less than a kilogram, and folded up small enough to almost fit in my pocket. Although my horse would have to carry both me and my saddlebags I reasoned that my weighing in at less than sixty kilograms would still make the load lighter than most adult male Tibetans.

I would carry one thing with me that I hoped might get me out of serious trouble — the Alien Travel Permit I'd stolen from the police station two years earlier. In New Zealand a Chinese friend filled it in for me and wrote a covering letter which basically said I'd been given permission to go wherever I wanted and do whatever I liked in Tibet. We'd even forged a rubber stamp — it all looked very official and impressive. While I knew the police in Lhasa would know it was fake I hoped they'd never have to see it and I was guessing it would fool a country cop for long enough to give me time to get away. I was reluctant to use it though, as being caught using forged documents in the PRC would get me into serious shit.

And again I would carry Khensur Thabkye Rinpoche's ashes with me. For the last two years they had been sitting on the altar in my living room. They'd sat on the small table surrounded by lamps and images of various Buddhas and deities, all meant to remind me of their sublime qualities and inspire me to practise. For all the notice I'd taken of them they had become little more than beautiful souvenirs as once again I'd allowed myself to be distracted. I still had hopes of improving myself on this journey, but what I desperately wanted to do was to keep the vows I'd made to my lama and see his ashes laid to rest at the sacred mountain.

In New Zealand a new lama had been sent to teach at the centre Khensur Thabkye Rinpoche had founded and through him and another young Tibetan student I'd managed to get a couple of contacts in Lhasa, people I hoped might be able to help me get a horse. I called Nyima from a payphone on the street.

'Wei?'

'Hello, is that Nyima? My name's Ian, I'm from New Zealand.'

'Aa! Hello, hello, I've been waiting for you! Where are you now?'

'I'm at the Hotel Kirey, do you know it?'

'Oh yes, it's near my house. I'll come in ten minutes!'

A short time later we were sitting in a cafe with his brother and a beer each. We talked about my plans and how I needed to get out of Lhasa to the grasslands, where I could buy a good horse.

'No problem,' Nyima told me. 'We can go my village, west of Lhasa. There are many *drokpa* there and we can find a horse.'

'Great, thank you so much for helping me.'

'It's no problem, we can hire a jeep and go the day after tomorrow.'

Things were happening quickly, which suited me. I was still worried about the tour I was supposed to be on; the guide would become suspicious when he saw I had no intention of taking the tour and perhaps report me. I also realised I was paranoid. After what had happened last time I wasn't taking any chances.

'Nyima, please don't tell anyone what I'm doing. I'm worried the police will hear and try to stop me, please don't say anything to the people at the hotel.'

'Yes, of course I won't say anything. Do you have a permit?'

'No.'

I saw no reason to tell Nyima about my fake permit. He didn't need to know and if I got into trouble I would have to be extremely careful it didn't lead back to him as he could be arrested for helping me travel illegally. At least if he didn't know about the permit he would be innocent on that count.

Later I called my other contact and we met at the hotel and went out for dinner. Tseyang was a young and very attractive Tibetan woman who spoke excellent English. She worked for a tour company that dealt with foreign climbers and trekkers and often spent weeks at a time in the summer months at the base camps of Everest and other peaks. Luckily for me she was between tours. She was the other side of Tibet, young, modern and sophisticated. She almost didn't look Tibetan; when we were out together even other Tibetans mistook her for a Japanese tourist.

'Do you really think you can ride a horse to Gang Rinpoche?' she asked. 'I've never even heard of a Tibetan doing that! Do you need my help to get a permit?'

'No, it's OK, I'm not even going to bother asking.'

'What will happen if they catch you?'

'Then they'll catch me, whatever happens will happen.'

'You're very brave, Ian.'

'No I'm not, I'm terrified.'

The next day we had lunch before spending the afternoon in the market buying gear I would need. With her help bargaining with the tenacious Tibetan stallholders I bought a saddle, bridle, ropes and saddle blankets, a *chuba* lined with lambskin and a long knife. We stuffed everything into a large sack and lugged it back to the hotel.

In the afternoon Tseyang returned to her office leaving me to visit the Jokhang. At that time of the day the place was much less crowded and I made prostrations in front of the statue of Jowo Shakyamuni and prayed for a safe and successful journey. I was more apprehensive about setting off into the wilds of Tibet this time than I had been two years ago. Now I knew what I was letting myself in for; I knew how hard it was going to be and how the conditions would try to crush me. But at the same time I felt an edge of confidence. Now I had a much better idea of what I was doing; I was better prepared, I felt aggressive, almost angry and defiant. I pictured myself riding hard and fast, light and mobile on one good horse. For the moment the idea of reaching Gang Rinpoche seemed distant and unreal, but I was determined to give it my best shot, and most of all I wanted to do it without being caught by the Chinese.

That night Tseyang took me out to dinner. The evening was very warm and after dinner she took me to a park behind the Potala Palace where there was a small murky lake called the Dragon Pool. As we walked around the lake I instinctively wanted to reach out and take her hand in mine.

'I hear that in Western countries divorce is very common, is that right?' Tseyang asked.

'Yes, it's very easy to get a divorce. I think in New Zealand about forty per cent of married couples end up getting divorced.'

'Why?'

'I don't know, it's not such a big deal these days.'

'Yes, in Western countries people are easily attracted but easily separated, people don't take relationships seriously.'

'I agree, but I also think young people should enjoy themselves.'

'Relationships are not just for fun. People shouldn't be together if they can't commit for a long time.'

'Yeah, I guess so.' My hand stayed in my pocket.

The evening was still light but the moon shone romantically on the dark waters of the lake. We were alone and it would have been the perfect place for a moonlit kiss. I was grasping again, trying to find something familiar to hold on to; in twenty-four hours I knew I could be alone on the plateau or at best in the company of strangers. I wanted to hear someone say they loved me, that they'd miss me, I wanted someone to ask me not to go, to beg me to come back soon. Kailas may have been quietly drawing me back but I still clung desperately to what I knew best, to what only made me unhappy, to what I needed to leave behind.

As darkness fell we took a rickshaw back to the hotel. 'Good luck, Ian. I hope everything goes well for you, please take care and be careful.' She draped a *khata* around my neck.

'Thank you, and thanks so much for all your help, I . . . um . . . it's been really good to meet you, I hope to see you again when I get back.'

'I'm sure I'll be here.' We shook hands.

The next morning I was up before the sun. I waited outside the hotel and Nyima arrived just before seven with his brother and a driver in a little van. We threw my gear in the back and set off heading west out of the city. A couple of hours later we stopped at Nyima's home near the town of Yangbajian; his elderly parents greeted us and took us inside for tea and *tsampa* before his father went off around the village to ask his neighbours if they had a horse to sell. I sat and waited in the gloomy, dusty little room mixing my *tsampa*. The smell of burning yak dung filled the room and I already felt I was back on the trail.

The old man returned to say no one had any horses and we set off again. We spent the rest of the day driving up and down valleys, stopping at villages along the way to ask about horses. While there were plenty of horses around, no one seemed interested in selling. 'I think they worry about what you will do with the horse, Ian,' Nyima told me. 'Some people think that maybe you sell the horse to the Chinese, they will eat it!'

It was a very hot day. I couldn't believe Tibet could be so hot and it was frustrating trying to find a horse. Either the villagers had good horses but refused to sell or they only showed me horses that would be finished in a week. Eventually we met an old man who told us his son had a good horse to sell at another village further up the valley. It was six o'clock when we arrived and at last we had some success. The horse was a white gelding, well behaved and in good condition. Nyima negotiated a price of six thousand yuan; it was expensive but I was so excited to have found a good mount I counted out the sixty notes. I would have to carry all my money with me in Chinese renminbi cash as there was no way I'd be able to change money and my stack of bills was enormous.

We went outside and unloaded my stuff from the van. Nyima presented me with *khata* and we shook hands. He touched his forehead to mine and whispered something in Tibetan, a prayer or blessing for my safety, then climbed into the van with his brother and headed back to Lhasa. I was on my own.

I spent the night in the home of the man who'd sold me the horse. We tried to sort out my riding gear but the separate bits of tack I'd bought didn't go together so he swapped his old saddle for my new one. This was actually better as it was worn in and would fit the horse more snugly. I was given a meal and several bowls of tea before I unrolled my new sleeping bag on a bench on the side of the room. Finally the lamps were put out and the family slept while I lay wide awake in the darkness, thinking about what I was about to face.

I was terrified of failing. I dreaded not reaching the mountain and returning home unsuccessful. I couldn't keep coming back to Tibet — I had to get it over and done with now and I could feel a sense of urgency, almost a recklessness. It was at least fifteen hundred kilometres to the mountain, a ride of two months or more on which I would face all the obstacles and hardships I'd met with two years earlier all over again, of which I feared the Chinese police the most. Before I closed my eyes I recited a short prayer to the Buddhas asking for their protection. It did little to reassure me. I felt no one was listening.

It was a beautiful morning as I loaded up my horse, whom I'd named Whitey. It was almost two years to the day since I'd stopped riding in Xianza and as Yangbajian was over two hundred kilometres east of the town I figured it would make up for the time I'd spent in the jeep from Liarong to Naqu. The Tibetan walked me to the edge of the village. We shook hands, I climbed into the saddle, pointed Whitey west, kicked him in the ribs and restarted my pilgrimage to Gang Rinpoche.

We headed out across the grasslands towards a row of high, snow-covered peaks. Whitey walked well, keeping up a steady pace all day. I'd been directed towards a narrow valley in the range that would lead me to a pass called Gurum-la. I'd been told it was high and that the snow would be deep at the top, but I was sceptical of this given the warm weather. And anyway, I was keen to get stuck into it — lofty peaks and the challenge of a pass sounded perfect.

We entered the range following a fast river of snow melt into the tight and rocky valley. By mid-morning the sun was already high and hot and before long the ground was so stony I couldn't ride. I led Whitey, shedding layers of clothes every time we stopped for a break. I was soon down to a shirt that on the previous trip would have been several layers below my *chuba*, and for the moment the thought of wearing the heavy garment made me feel faint. I never imagined I'd ever be too hot and decided I preferred the cold. The heat was exhausting, and combined with the altitude and physical exertion on a body that had done little exercise in the last two years, left me worn out by the middle of the afternoon.

We stopped at three thirty — although we still had about six hours of daylight I'd done enough for the first day. I set up my camp in the lee of a large boulder, let Whitey off to graze and gathered sticks for a fire. I spent the rest of the day making adjustments to my riding gear and gazed around the valley as I waited for the water to boil. The river roared below us and the land swept up to the base of the mountains — bare grey rock studded with squat, scrubby bushes. Unlike two years earlier, the grass was green and fairly thick, and my horse was soon standing in the sun with a full belly.

It wasn't until after nine o'clock that the sun slipped behind the mountains and the darkness of the Tibetan night began to descend. I stoked up the fire and made one last cup of tea. Looking up at the brightening stars, I felt satisfied. I'd only made it through one day, but every day was an achievement; I had come back to give it another shot.

When the fire died I crawled into the bivvy bag to sleep. It was cramped and uncomfortable and I dozed on and off all night. Whitey was nervous about something whining in the mountains above our camp, perhaps a stray dog. He paced up and down all night and I kept waking up, worrying he was going to escape. He was tethered on a long rope staked deep in the ground with an iron peg. I didn't have any hobbles; the herdsmen in this part of Tibet didn't seem to use them and I hadn't been able to buy any.

I lay in my sleeping bag, now wet with condensation, and waited for it to get light, which didn't occur until after seven. I started the fire and made tea before loading up and setting off.

As we headed up the widening valley, the ground became easier — there was a faint trail and I was able to ride most of the day. In the afternoon I found a few families camped high in the mountains. They were probably from the villages on the grasslands I had started from, but in summer they drive their herds to the top of the valleys to take advantage of the grazing. The mountainsides were dotted with yaks; sheep and goats grazed along the riverbanks as their young herders sang at the tops of their lungs and flicked stones at their animals from slings to keep them moving.

At one tent I stopped for tea — I was welcomed in and a fresh pot of butter tea churned. I took out my little world map and photos and showed the puzzled family. My tea bowl was constantly topped up and I was offered *tsampa* and bread. It all felt very familiar, as if I'd never been away. However,

I also had a strange sense of it all being old hat. Now I was back I had a job to do and I wanted to get it done so I could go home.

I rode on into the afternoon and reached the base of Gurum-la pass; from here the going became much heavier. The entrance to the pass was a jumbled mass of loose rock that looked as if it had tumbled out of the mountains the day before. It was like crossing a maze and would have been almost impossible if a passing nomad hadn't stopped to help. He walked ahead, scouting a way through the mess before guiding me across. Finally we reached better ground and I turned around to thank him, but he walked away before I had the chance.

I was alone in a high valley, a great crescent of bare rock and snow. I tried to walk on, leading Whitey, but we were several hundred metres higher than when we'd set out in the morning, probably close to five thousand metres, and the altitude was crushing me. I had to ride, but I wasn't sure which way I should go. I scanned the ridges ahead, trying to sight the pass out of the valley, but I could see nothing but walls of rock. Soon I was riding poor Whitey across bare, loose stone as we made our way towards the still unseen pass.

Finally we stopped; there was nowhere else to go. I gazed around in confusion, unable to see any way out. Then I made out three sets of tracks rising above me in a massive bank of frozen snow a hundred metres high. It looked like two Tibetans and a yak had crossed the mountains in the last couple of days — the pass must be somewhere above the snow bank.

I climbed off Whitey and stood gasping in the thin air as I looked up at the daunting barrier ahead; cloud drifted over the peaks and the skies darkened. We started up the bank, following the footprints. It was an exhausting climb. The top layer of snow was frozen but it would only hold my weight for a moment before I'd crash through and sink up to my knees. I'd pull myself out only to sink again on the next step as I half-crawled up the steep slope. Whitey struggled behind me, up to his belly in the snow. His saddle slipped off twice and each time I had to completely unload him and start again.

After what seemed like an age we made it to the top of the bank. There the ridge levelled out, but on the flatter ground the snow became deeper, reaching up to my waist. Still I followed the prints leading ahead of me, hoping the low ridge above would mark the top of the pass, only two hundred metres away. But that short distance might as well have been kilometres as I could only make two or three paces before having to rest for several minutes to catch my breath. I was losing energy and if we didn't reach the other side soon I knew I wouldn't make it.

The day was getting older, and colder. Most of my clothes were wet, my hands and feet were freezing and I was starting to shiver as an icy wind blew off the peaks. Three more laboured steps, rest and breathe, then three more, rest and breathe, then three more, collapse into the snow and gasp for breath. Finally the top of the ridge lay before me. I hadn't reached it yet — to my horror I saw the pass was still another snow-filled high valley away. The ground dipped for another kilometre at least before it rose again to where the pass lay. The snow ahead would be even deeper; it was starting to get dark and to make things worse avalanches of snow and ice were crashing down the mountains on the other side of the valley. How the Tibetans and their yak made it across I'd never know.

I stood up to my arse in snow, leaning on Whitey and trying to think what I should do. My next step was crucial — up or down? And then it hit me. I didn't have any choice. If I kept going there was no way I was going to get over the pass; in an hour it would be dark, the temperature would plummet and I'd perish in the snow. I had to turn back, and turn back now. It was impossible to go on and while I was disappointed, dying of altitude sickness and hypothermia on the second day of my trip didn't strike me as being very cool.

I turned poor Whitey round, sorry I had put him through such a difficult climb for nothing and we started back down. However, before I'd even completed my first set of three steps I dropped back into the snow. I was totally drained, I didn't have the strength to go on and it was frightening to feel so weak, too weak even to save my own life.

I crawled into the saddle and pushed Whitey on over our own tracks, relying on him completely to get me out. I have no doubt Whitey saved my life that day. By the time the last of the day's light was fading I was setting up camp on a grassy patch not far below the snow bank. I crawled into my sleeping bag, too exhausted to think of bothering to eat or even write my diary, my prayers left unsaid as I collapsed into a dead sleep.

Coming this way had been a mistake. I had seriously overestimated my ability and underestimated the conditions. Did I think I would be able just to pick up where I'd left off two years earlier? Trying to cross such a high pass before I was fully acclimatised was foolish and disregarding the warnings of the locals plain stupid. I'd wasted two riding days, but decided I had to put it down to experience and start again when we got back onto the grassland.

Over the next two days I rode back down the long valley, ending up not far from the village where I'd started. I went further south before turning west again on a road that would lead me to a high pass called Hugu-la. For the next couple of days I followed the road over high grasslands that eventually turned into a rocky valley between enormous peaks. The road was busy with all manner of traffic. Several times I was passed by police jeeps; if I saw them early enough I'd get off Whitey and use him to hide behind by bending down and pretending to make adjustments to the saddle. Often I had little warning; the valley was too narrow to be able to get far from the road and I would have to put my head down and hide under my hat.

Early one afternoon I was riding next to the river on the opposite side to the road. On the other side a group of Chinese tourists had stopped for lunch. I rode slowly past. Before long they'd seen me and, realising I was a Westerner, they started taking photos. I stared back at them beneath the brim of my wide black hat feeling very cool, my hand resting on the long knife stuck in my belt like a sword. Not for me the guided bus tour — that was for softies — I had my own horse, I was a real nomad. I was a cowboy!

Someone called out to one of the Tibetan guides, who watched me through a pair of binoculars. I quickly turned away and kicked Whitey on, suddenly realising how stupid it was to draw attention to myself. The guides would know I wasn't supposed to be in these areas alone on my own horse and any one of them could report me. If the police came looking I wouldn't be hard to find. Further on I stopped at a tent for tea. Climbing out of the saddle the stirrup leather broke, I lost my balance, got tangled in the reins and fell flat on my arse as my nomad hosts roared with laughter. In this case pride literally came before a fall!

Late in the afternoon I started into the pass. A rough switchback road had been hacked into the side of the mountain; jeeps roared down, somehow avoiding collisions with ancient trucks and buses that moved like giant tortoises up the other side. I travelled on a horse trail below, mostly hidden from the road. Before long I had to start walking as it was too steep to ride. Again the altitude made it feel as if my boots were made of lead, but for the moment the weather was good, overcast and cool, and I paced myself, walking for a few minutes before stopping for a few more to rest.

This would be the first pass I'd cross on this leg of the trip; it was a tough challenge but one I knew I could complete and I felt confident and strong. Just before seven we found ourselves below the top of the pass as the weather closed in with driving rain and wet snow. At the top, thousands of prayer flags flapped in the gale. I was cold and wet but elated at making our first successful summit. Right on top of the ridge two brothers were camped in a flimsy plastic tent from which they were selling prayer flags and wind horses to passing motorists who had forgotten to bring their own. They let me inside and gave me a bowl of hot water before I carried on; I was hoping to get down into the next valley before nightfall.

The rain and snow continued and by the time we reached the river in the valley below I was soaked and freezing cold. I desperately wanted to spend the night inside, but there were no houses or camps in sight so I had to unroll the bivvy bag on the wet ground. I tethered Whitey by the river where the grass was better and squeezed inside as the snow began falling heavily. It took me an hour of breathless wriggling to get out of my boots and oilskin riding coat and into the sleeping bag. Everything was wet — the sleeping bag, my clothes, the *chuba*, the saddle blankets I used as a mattress, all my gear, everything. I was as miserable as I was damp.

It snowed heavily all night and I hardly slept. I pulled the hood of the bivvy bag over my head to protect me from the snow and zipped it shut — there was supposed to be enough ventilation to allow me to breathe, but during the night the hood of the bag became soaked and stuck to the outer cover like a wet shower curtain. Every few minutes I woke suffocating and scrambled to open the bag to catch my breath — it was like sleeping inside a wet plastic bag. By the time the cold, grey dawn finally arrived I was buried under several centimetres of snow.

I lay in the bag as cold water dripped onto my face, not wanting to move. I was cold and felt groggy and weak, not having eaten much in the last couple of days. I had to get down the valley and get something warm inside me. Eventually I sat up and shook the snow off the bag. I turned around to check if Whitey was all right only to see that he wasn't where I'd left him. I jumped up in panic, thinking he'd escaped or been stolen. I pulled my boots and oilskin on and scanned the valley with my binoculars, finally sighting him further up with a small herd of nomad horses. I packed up my sodden camp and then set off through the snow to catch him.

He saw me coming and turned round, but I caught him with no trouble; he'd pulled the stake out during the night, possibly when the other horses had wandered past, and had gone with them. He was hunched over in the cold with his head down; even he was miserable in these conditions, shivering and wet and wanting the comfort of his own kind. I led him back down, loaded up and set off on foot.

Walking warmed me up a bit and after a couple of hours the snow began to thin on the ground and the skies slowly started to clear. I was starving and we stopped at the first house we saw, where the people welcomed me in and served me tea. They were kind and sympathetic to the dreadful weather the night before, even feeding Whitey a bundle of straw, which seemed to cheer him up. The old woman offered me *tsampa*, but I needed something more. My body was crying out for protein, I needed to eat meat.

'*Tukpa yawrey?*' I asked her, do you have any *tukpa*?

'*Tukpa mindu.*' No *tukpa*.

'*Lug sha yawrey?*' Do you have any mutton?

'Rey, yawrey.' She nodded. I asked her if she could cook me a meal and indicated that I'd pay. Before long I had wolfed down two bowls of meaty, fatty noodles and felt much better.

By afternoon the sun was shining and I started to dry out. We reached the bottom of the valley and came to a small village next to the road and below the ruins of an ancient fortress. One family had set up a small restaurant on the roadside to serve passing buses and truck drivers and I bought another meal of rice, potatoes and yak meat. In one day I'd eaten more than I had in the previous week.

The road drifted away somewhere to the south, but after leaving the village I headed further north and by evening I was camped alone, hidden in the corner of a valley next to a little stream. It had been six days since we'd set out from Yangbajian; we were both worn out and so the next day was a day off. It poured with rain again all night and much of our rest day. Apart from the bivvy bag I had no shelter and spent most of the day hunched in the rain, cursing the fire that wouldn't go and making repairs to my tack. Occasionally the sun would make an appearance. I'd get things dry or nearly dry and then the clouds would sweep over and drench everything again. Whitey spent half the day rolling in the damp dirt and by evening wasn't looking very white at all.

The next morning we loaded up in the drizzle and set off northwest over the hills, up another long rocky valley and across another pass. That night I stayed with a family of nomads in their tent, grateful to be able to sleep out of the weather, then carried on down the river for all of the next day. The whole area was a maze of rugged mountains, slender valleys, passes and wild rivers. I soon lost track of where I was on the map and felt completely confused and disorientated. Asking directions was hopeless; no one could understand me or else didn't seem to know which way to go. I'd been asking for directions to Xianza — I knew it couldn't be far from where I was and while I had no intention of getting too near the town, I wanted to be in the same region. The Tibetans I asked had heard of the place, but no one was able to give me any clues as to how I could get there.

One evening I set up camp under the lean of a large rock by the river. I'd hardly seen anyone all day and hadn't eaten much. It was too wet even to bother trying to light the fire and I went to bed. On one side of the rock some faithful local had carved Om mani padme hum into the surface of the boulder. At least I felt I would be protected sleeping there.

In the morning I packed up and set off down the valley on a rough road; the weather was good for most of the day but as we slowly walked on I felt something was wrong. I could feel that I was heading in the wrong direction, everything felt too low, too warm, too south. The valley contracted into a massive gorge; in places by the river jets of thermal steam and hot water shot out of the banks, spooking Whitey.

Around the middle of the day I stopped by the road to take a break and let Whitey graze for a while. Behind me another branch of the road led into the mountains and a passing herdsman told me it led to a monastery called Sebu Gompa, about an hour's walk away. It wasn't in the direction I was hoping to head, but I decided it might be worthwhile visiting. I guessed there would be a village there with people who might be able to help me with directions and besides, after days of uncertainty I wanted to be in a place that was 'somewhere'.

Sebu Gompa was small but impressive; a huge, round, whitewashed *stupa* stood above the main buildings, and retreat huts and hermitages had been stuck to the cliffs and mountainsides. I tied Whitey outside and walked into the courtyard in front of the main temple, where a group of Tibetans were trading sacks of *tsampa*, grain and wool. I bought a basin of wheat from one of them for a few yuan and offered it to Whitey before asking if I could see inside the *gompa*. Someone went off and came back a few minutes later with a young monk who had the key.

He unlocked the huge doors — they reluctantly groaned open as if they'd been asleep for years and didn't want to wake up. The monastery was of the Nyingma sect and seemed to be devoted to the memory of the Tibetan saint Padmasambhava, who is still revered and worshipped for his role in promoting and spreading Buddhism across Tibet in the seventh century. The temple had been built around a small cave, where it is said the great saint had meditated. In the wall of the cave a simple image of Buddha was carved into the solid rock. The monk indicated that Padmasambhava had made it himself with his bare hands.

There were apparently two lamas in residence at Sebu and I guessed only a few monks; it looked as if the place had seen better days. The inside of the chapels were filthy and thick with dust. The altars hadn't been cleaned or tidied in a long time, butter lamps that had long ago burnt out lay about in disorder, piles of old and probably valuable *thangka* were scattered in the corners.

Back outside I asked my young and very friendly guide if there was a restaurant or shop in the village. There wasn't, but he took me to his room below the *gompa* and served me tea, *tsampa* and dried meat. The monk sat next to me on the sleeping platform, closer to me than I felt comfortable with in fact, and we talked about where I'd been in Tibet and where I was going. Then he asked me another question I couldn't understand. He repeated it over and over. I could pick up that he was asking how many, but I had no idea how many what.

'*Gawn da, hako masong.*' Sorry, I really don't understand.

What he was asking me was how many women I'd slept with and he made the question clearer by crudely using his fingers to model a couple having sex. I told him I didn't think it was an appropriate question for a monk to be asking and stood up to leave.

When I collected Whitey and asked the villagers for directions to Xianza I was told I would have to go back the way I'd come and start asking for a pass called Gubu-la. I walked all the way back down to the road and then started heading upriver again. It was late afternoon by the time I'd made it back to the rock where I'd spent the previous night. We carried on, crossing the river on a swing-bridge made of thin steel cables and logs, and rode on into another valley.

It was getting late; the skies were darkening with thick clouds ripe with rain. There were several families camped in the valley. I asked for directions to Gubu-la and was pointed northwest to a corner of the valley. By then the wind had picked up, usually a sign a storm was about to break; I could feel it in the air, a sense that time was running out and something calamitous was about to happen.

The storm hit just as I reached another camp. As I rode up and dismounted a young boy came outside. '*Tashidelik!*' I greeted him. He didn't reply. '*Pala yawrey?*' I asked him, is your father here? He stuck his head inside the tent and yelled something. A moment later an older Tibetan man came out, either his father or grandfather.

'*Tashidelik pala, cha tung?*' I asked him if I could have some tea. He disappeared inside and came back with a kettle of tepid tea. The rain was getting heavier and I was freezing. I pointed towards the tent: 'Do you think it would be too much trouble for me to come inside, it's bloody raining!'

He shook his head, gave the kettle to the boy and went inside. I took out my tea bowl and the lad poured for me. I was desperate to get out of the weather, hoping to find somewhere to stay, as it was obvious the storm would last most of the night. I stepped past the boy, opened the flap and invited myself inside. The old man was sitting in the corner, spinning a prayer wheel. I crouched by the almost-dead fire and the boy gave me another bowl of tea.

'*Nga nang-pa yin.*' I'm a Buddhist, I told him, trying to break the ice. '*Khyerang-la Gelukpa?*' I asked him if he was from the Gelukpa sect of which the Dalai Lama is the head.

'*Hako masong!*' he growled, not even trying to understand me.

'*Nga Gang Rinpoche-la dro,* I'm doing *ne-kor*.' I told him I was doing a pilgrimage to the sacred mountain.

'*Hako masong!*' he repeated and with his free hand waved me towards the door, telling me to get out.

'*Tering charpa yawrey.*' It's raining today, I said, gesturing that I wanted to stay in his tent.

'*Ma rey!*' he shouted and waved me off again.

'*Kuchi, kuchi!*' Please!

'*Ma rey! Ma rey!*' He sat there, waving me out of his home into the storm with one hand while the other spun the prayer wheel, inside of which would be a roll of paper printed with prayers for the benefit of all beings. I don't know how he reconciled the two, but he refused to give me shelter.

I finished my tea and went outside. Whitey stood with his rump into the wind, looking as cold and dejected as I felt. I looked up the valley towards where the pass must be. The mountains above me were colossal; there was no way I was going to get across, probably not even on a good day, and today certainly wasn't turning out to be anything close to good.

I took Whitey's lead rope and started walking back down the valley as the rain fell in steady streams whipped along by the wind. I was cold, hungry, tired and close to despair, with no idea where I was and no clue as to where I should go. I was wet, depressed and I'd never felt so lonely in my whole life. I couldn't believe the old man had sent me out into the storm. I thought of asking at one of the other tents, but the possibility of being turned away again was too much to contemplate.

We crossed the bridge and headed back towards the rock. And just to make sure it was a completely disastrous day the rained turned to thick, wet lumps of snow and the heel came off one of my boots. By the time we reached my sorry little campsite I was close to tears. Tibet could be a cruel land and her people as hard as the mountains they lived under. I set Whitey out to graze and as the snow reverted to rain I unrolled the bivvy bag and set up my camp. I took off my boots and unzipped my sleeping bag to get inside. Everything was wet again and I endured another dismal night with nothing resembling real sleep.

The valley was still draped in low cloud in the morning, but at least the rain had stopped. I packed up, stuffing my wet sleeping bag into its cover and shaking the worst of the water off the bivvy. I was still feeling totally dejected from the day before and stopped at the first camp I came to, where I found an old woman on her own. '*Cha tung?*' I asked her, '*kuchi, kuchi amala, kuchi, kuchi!*' Please, mother, please! I was nothing short of desperate.

She didn't say anything but motioned me inside the tent by the fire. I sat on the ground and held my hands out in front of the embers as the old lady placed a kettle back on the fire and waited for it to heat. I was too exhausted to try to make conversation and she looked nervous. A few minutes later I held out my tea bowl, she filled it and passed it back. I sipped while the old woman watched me across the fire. I looked up at her, she managed a half-smile and there was kindness and compassion in her eyes. *'Tujachay amala, tujachay,'* I put my head in my hand and sobbed with relief and gratitude. Her simple act of generosity at that moment felt as if she had just saved my life.

I cheered up a bit after that and was soon on my way back down the river. I was sure there was no way I could go north from where I was, so I resigned myself to riding south until I found a passage through towards Xianza. In the afternoon the clouds cleared and for a while the sun shone. I stopped and spread my damp gear out to dry, but no sooner had I unrolled my soggy sleeping bag than it started to rain. No breaks in this land.

By evening the skies were dark and I dreaded another night in the open. Ahead on a rocky pinnacle above the river I could make out the ruins of a *dzong*, an old fortress, where I hoped I might find shelter. When I reached the base of the outcrop I saw there was little left of the *dzong* and realised I was unlikely to find a dry corner. On top of that the trail leading up to the ruins was cut into a cliff face and looked unstable; however, on the other side of the river, connected by a log bridge, was a large village of double-storied houses.

I watched the village through my binoculars. I was nervous — the last time I'd stayed in a village I'd been arrested. I had my home-made permit but I was terrified to use it. I could make out what looked like a school, but there didn't seem to be any other official-looking buildings. Still, I knew I would be taking a risk; even if there were no police someone might report me, or word might spread that there was a strange foreigner riding around on a horse.

I walked down to the river to the foot of the bridge. Behind me on a flat cliff face several images of Buddha had been carved, as if to protect travellers crossing the river. I crouched in front of them for a moment and prayed. 'Buddhas, please help me find somewhere to stay tonight, and please don't let me get caught by the cops!'

I led Whitey across and we climbed the steep riverbank to the village.

A few minutes later I was sitting on a rock in the middle of the settlement surrounded by kids, and soon a group of women arrived on their way back from the fields. One of them sent a little girl home, who returned with a kettle of tea. There seemed to be no men in town. I guessed they must have gone off for the summer to work, perhaps to Lhasa or on road construction crews.

'Dru khang yawrey?' I asked if there was somewhere I could sleep, thinking there might be some kind of lodge or guesthouse in the village, or that

someone would offer to take me home for the night.

'*Mindu,*' they told me, but then another kid was sent off to find the local schoolteacher. He duly arrived and managed a few simple phrases of English: 'Let's go!' We led Whitey into the schoolyard, where he was given an armload of straw and left to graze on the playing field. All my wet stuff was lugged inside the teacher's small room, where he stoked up the fire. I spread my sleeping bag and wet clothes out to dry, as the young Tibetan prepared *tukpa*.

'*Ganla kaba?*' I asked, where's the village head?

'Lhasa!' he replied waving his hand towards the east. This relaxed me and I guessed I would be safe as long as I didn't stay longer than a night.

That night, for the first time since leaving Lhasa, I slept right through. When I woke to find the sun had already risen I could hardly believe my luck and remembered the prayers I'd made to the Buddhas carved into the rock face the previous afternoon.

After breakfast of reheated noodles and tea I was away again down the river. The valley widened and dropped and by the next day I was at a much lower altitude. Although still over three thousand metres, most of the land had been sown with barley. Stone villages stood at regular intervals above the river and though I was still drenched by frequent showers, when the sun shone it was very hot.

Whenever I asked for Xianza, or the Xianza Tsangpo river, although people seemed to have heard of them I still had trouble getting reliable directions. I felt uneasy; there were too many people, it wasn't horse country, there was little open grazing land and it didn't feel like 'my' Tibet. I wanted to be in *drokpa* lands, in high valleys and grasslands.

One morning I crossed the river on a concrete bridge and carried on downstream until the afternoon, when I met a lively group of women who told me they were on their way to the local monastery, Beddo Gompa. I tagged along and the women sang all the way — several were carrying bottles of *chang*, home-made beer made from fermented barley. We arrived at the *gompa* mid-afternoon, where there seemed to be some kind of event, as there were other groups waiting. Later they all went up to a flat space on the hillside to drink *chang*.

I met a couple of monks who took me in for tea and asked me where I was going. When I told them I was trying to get to Xianza they told me I was on the wrong side of the river. They seemed to be saying the trail on this side had been washed out. I was told I'd have to go kilometres back up the river and cross to the other side. It was a stinking hot day and once again I found myself heading the wrong way. I couldn't be bothered going any further and when one of the monks invited me to stay the night I accepted. We unloaded

Whitey and put him out to graze for the rest of the day and I spread my stuff out in the courtyard to dry.

I wandered down to a stream to have a wash and a shave but was soon called back by the monks. Two old women had arrived at the *gompa* with a couple of emaciated horses loaded to the hilt with sacks of grain. They were on their way to a village in the direction of Xianza and said they would show me the way. I packed my stuff and loaded poor Whitey again ready to leave. Before we got going an old man and another younger woman joined the group. We set off, but after only a few minutes the Tibetans stopped for a picnic by the river. They gave me some tea from a thermos while the old ladies giggled and coaxed each other into drinking several cups of *chang;* by the time we got going again they were both tipsy.

Our little group headed on down the river through fields of barley and past little villages. I soon felt worn out in the heat and altitude, but I was desperate to keep up with the Tibetans, fearing they'd become impatient if I lagged behind and go on without me. I had a chance to finally get myself on track and I didn't want to lose it.

The trail was good except for one place where it had washed out and we had to climb a ridge high above the river. By late afternoon the old ladies were tiring and the old man and the younger woman helped them climb onto the backs of their poor little horses, where they perched precariously on the sacks of grain. Every so often we would have to cross rushing streams strewn with slippery boulders. I would ride Whitey across to keep my boots dry and then dismount on the other side. I could barely watch as the ponies staggered under the weight of grain and elderly women. A fall could have been fatal, but every time the horses stumbled and threatened to throw their loads into the flow the women would cackle as if they were riding on a merry-go-round!

Further on we had to cross a series of muddy holes where the rain had collected in ditches. I watched in horror as one of the horses slipped and stumbled into one of these holes. It started to sink into the mud and the old man tried to pull it onto solid ground as the woman clung on for dear life. Before it could take another step the poor animal collapsed onto its side, trapping the woman underneath in a pool of muddy water.

I dropped Whitey's rope and rushed to help her out, but I was beaten to the spot by the old man and the younger woman. The scene was alarming, the horse thrashing about in the water trying to get up and the woman half-submerged with her leg wedged under the animal; she could have broken her leg or hip or even been killed, but she lay there laughing as if it was a huge joke. Even the others were cracking jokes and giggling as they worked to extract her from the mud.

Tibetans must be the hardest people in the world to upset. I often saw things that would have made me furious — yaks losing their loads and running off, horses misbehaving, broken-down jeeps or trucks stuck in the middle of nowhere for days, sudden storms which soaked belongings, accidents and mishaps of all kinds. But the Tibetans never lost their temper — these things happen, there's nothing you can do about it, it's just bad luck or karma and getting upset won't change a thing, what's the point of panicking or getting angry? It will only make things worse and won't solve anything. Their calm and patience in the extreme must be the most admirable quality of the Tibetan character.

Before long the little horse was back on its feet and the old lady out of danger. She was caked in stinking wet mud, something that would have pushed me into a rage, but she shrugged and laughed and we set off again. Heat clouds continued to build throughout the afternoon and the temperature suddenly dropped. I stopped to put on my oilskin to keep warm, but my inner layers were wet with sweat, and as the sweat cooled I started to shiver. The clouds darkened and I knew a downpour was imminent. I worried again that my guides would pick up the pace and I'd be left behind; however, they were totally unconcerned and stopped by the river for a few more shots of *chang*.

A few minutes later thunder roared in the valley, announcing the arrival of the latest downpour. Soon I was trudging through mud, soaked to the skin, exhausted and freezing. But at last I had met a river that would lead me to a high pass and into the valley of the Xianza Tsangpo river. It was nearly dark by the time we arrived in the Tibetans' village. The old man invited me to his home for the night, for which I was extremely grateful. Whitey would have to spend the night in a muck-filled yard though, as the land all around was planted in fields. He was given a pile of straw to see him through the night, but I knew he'd still be hungry. There was nothing I could do about it and I was almost beyond caring; the day's march had completely worn me out.

It turned out the old woman who had nearly come to grief was the old man's wife and despite her misadventures she was still expected to cook dinner. She boiled up small pieces of fatty mutton mixed with flour, which by the end of the evening had become a thick, dark, oily soup. She scooped out a bowlful and handed it to me. It tasted fine and was very nutritious, but I'd eaten only a few spoonfuls when I started feeling nauseous, breaking out in a sweat and gasping for breath so much I had to go outside. I'm sure there was nothing wrong with the old lady's cooking; I'd pushed my body to its limits, I was probably dehydrated and the greasy brew was more than it could handle.

I lay on a pile of sacks for several minutes; the old man came out to check on me a couple of times as I fought my churning stomach to try to hold on to my dinner. After a while the nausea passed and I staggered back, unrolled my sleeping bag and crept inside.

I woke in the morning feeling as if I'd eaten a sack of rocks. I had no energy and struggled to sit up, in a state that reminded me of the time I'd stayed with the Bonpo lama. I managed to get up and made myself some black tea. I felt slightly better but didn't feel like riding and the weather outside was abysmal, with steady cold rain. *'Nga nagyi du,'* I told the old man, I'm sick, and I asked if I could stay in his home another day to rest.

'Ma rey.' He smiled, shaking his head.

'Kalak yawrey, khyerang-gi kalak ma-giu.' I told him I had my own food.

'Ma rey,' he repeated.

As a last attempt I offered to pay him, but he still shook his head.

I squelched about in the mud loading my bedraggled horse and set off up the river in the rain. I spent the day mostly on foot, as it was too cold to ride. We passed villages, clusters of tiny stone houses that would have been quaint or pretty on a good day but were cloaked in wet blankets, their narrow lanes quagmires of mud and dung. I lost my gloves somewhere and the heel came off my other boot somewhere else — at least now they were even. I was looking for a place to stay and take a rest day, but we didn't find anywhere suitable and that night I slept under a bush by the river.

The next day we rounded a wide bend and found a small settlement, just a couple of houses, a little shop and a basic lodge next to a road where weary truck drivers could pass the night. I bought a few bits and pieces. I hoped to find some more gloves, but they didn't have any and I had to make do without them for the rest of the trip. In a room next door the family who ran the place had set up a little restaurant. I asked them to make me a bowl of *tukpa* and as my lunch was being prepared I was struck by a strange feeling of familiarity; had I been here in a past life? I glanced out the windows behind me at a stand of poplars and another wave of *déjà vu* washed over me. I *had* been here before, but not in a past life. I'd stopped here for lunch with the police on the way from Xianza to Namling. Finally I knew where I was.

I remembered how dejected and depressed I'd felt last time I was there. I'd been overcome with a sense of failure as I was driven out of the mountains; now I was heading back. I still felt as if I had only the slimmest chance of success, but it was better than the no chance at all I'd had last time.

My buoyant mood continued for much of the afternoon. The sun shone but it wasn't too hot and the road I was following would lead me all the way to Xianza, although I planned to head west long before I got near the place.

Chapter Nine

We had been seven days on the road since our last day off; Whitey was exhausted and so was I. We needed to rest, and late in the afternoon I found a lovely little campsite, a sheltered spot on a slope of reasonable grass, high above the road between two ancient and gnarled juniper trees. I let Whitey off to graze and managed to dry my sleeping bag in the last of the day's sun. It rained all night, however, and by morning I was back to square one, spreading everything out again to dry.

The rest of the day was fine and I passed most of it sitting by the fire making tea as Whitey grazed above my camp. For the first time since I'd set out from Lhasa I felt as if I had a moment to stop and think about something other than what was immediately happening. I thought of the pilgrimage I kept telling myself I was trying to make, how I still wanted to leave something of myself behind when, or if, I made it to Gang Rinpoche. My wish was still to 'die once', but I realised how hard it was to let that part of me perish. Even after what I'd been through two years ago it wasn't long before the good old selfish, greedy, grasping me came out of his slumber and starting running the show again. And though I'd tried to ride off and leave him, I'd greeted him like an old mate and was glad to have him back. Once again I'd allowed him to lead me wherever I wanted to go.

I'd brought the Dalai Lama's book with me again; until now the only time I'd taken it out of its cloth cover was to dry its damp pages, but finally I picked it up and started reading. I flicked it open to whatever page it happened to land at — His Holiness was talking about the preciousness of the human rebirth I had somehow found myself blessed with; I could have been reborn anywhere and in any form. Instead of sitting in the sun with a mug of hot tea, I could be writhing in pain in any one of the dozens of hells the Buddhist teachings assert exist. I could have been born a cat and spent my whole life perched on the lap of the greatest lamas but unable to understand a single word of any of their teachings.

Even as a human I could be anywhere, in a land without the freedom to practise any religion I choose, in a place where Buddhism is unheard of, in a family so poor and hungry that spending money on books by the Dalai Lama would be the last thing I'd do, or so rich and famous my life would be consumed by distractions even more powerful than those I already had and I wouldn't have a moment to think about spiritual practice.

But here I was in Tibet of all places, a Buddhist rosary around my neck, a book by the Dalai Lama in my hand and a (very) basic knowledge of the Buddha's teachings, which had been passed to me by a precious, realised lama, Khensur Thabkye Rinpoche. Like a starving man who has an enormous plate of food placed in front of him, I had to decide what I should do now. Tip it onto the floor for the dogs?

As a human who had already met Buddha's teachings, who had access to qualified Tibetan lamas and who had most of his mental faculties pretty much in order, if I chose not to take advantage of these gifts wouldn't I be wasting this opportunity? If I spent my life in pursuit of money and status, things that could provide me with food, shelter, drink and the possibility of sex, wouldn't I be no better than the animals I saw on the grasslands around me? After all, these are the only things on the mind of a dog — if they are the only things on my mind, am I no better than a dog? Have I been living like a dog most of my life already, with almost every weekend passed with wine and sweet company?

And now that I was on the great pilgrimage to a holy mountain, what was I going to do with the opportunity? Make the best of it or spend the whole time moaning about the weather? Was I going to return home a better person with a new understanding of who I was, or return with a bunch of photographs, a few souvenirs, and a couple of tall tales? Was I going to take the chance to let that part of me 'die once' or carry it with me, feeding it and making it stronger? Was I going to take the teachings of His Holiness and Khensur Thabkye Rinpoche to heart and really work to put them into action and transform my shambles of a mind, or just read and forget as soon as I closed the book? The sun was warm, I was dry and I felt safe in my little campsite. I closed the book, lay back on the grass with my hat over my face and dozed off in the sunshine.

Late the next afternoon I found myself in a freezing storm of rain and snow as I slowly led Whitey up a road to the high and barren pass of Chugu-la. It was this pass I'd crossed in the jeep with the police two years ago, the one they'd told me marked where the worlds of the *drokpa* and *po-pa* met. I finally felt I was back where I should be, back where I'd left off. The skies had punished me all day; I'd walked to try to warm up, but with the increasingly thin air and the weight of the wet *chuba* it was a struggle. I paced myself by reciting the mantra *Om mani padme hum*, one syllable for each step, but I could only say the short phrase a few times before I'd have to stop, rest and gasp for breath.

Darkness was falling by the time we reached the mass of soaked prayer flags limply flapping in the wind in a bleak expanse of high grasslands surrounded by mountains. It was a long way down the other side to where I found some camps; twice I tried to find somewhere to spend the night, but each time I asked for space on their floors the nomads waved me out. However, one old man told me there was a *dru-khang*, a guesthouse, only a few kilometres further on. We rode on into the darkness and I felt it was a small miracle when I found the place, an L-shaped row of little rooms around an open yard. The rooms were dank and dusty, mice already in residence, but after eleven hours crossing a pass of nearly five thousand metres in the rain, they looked like a five-star luxury retreat.

I unloaded my poor, tired horse and lugged my wet gear into the room; a young man fired up the yak-dung stove and warmed the place. He mixed a large bowl of *tsampa* and tea leaves which I fed Whitey before I took him down by the river and tethered him. I tried to get someone to cook me a meal, but they insisted they had nothing other than *tsampa*. I was starving, but the best I could come up with was a cup of instant noodles. As I made tea on the fire the door opened and half a dozen men invited themselves in to meet me. One was a young monk who could speak a few words of English; he was staying with another older lama at a nearby house as they had been commissioned to paint murals and decorations on the eaves of some new homes. The young novice was quiet and friendly, but the long day was fast catching up with me and I was almost nodding off into my tea.

'I'm sorry, I need to sleep. Please come and see me tomorrow.' The group slowly filed out the door. I pulled off my boots and sat in my sleeping bag to say my prayers by candlelight. As I curled up at last I felt contented and looked forward to the next day. I was in real horse country; from here I could head west towards the mountain and start making tangible progress. I hoped crossing the pass had marked a turning point in the journey and from now on the gods would look on me more kindly.

After sleeping through the night I took my time getting up in the morning and got the fire going. Walking out into the yard to take a piss I looked towards the river to where Whitey should have been, but wasn't. The young innkeeper told me he was loose further up the valley. I wasn't concerned, he'd always been well behaved and I doubted he'd go far. I went back inside and finished my tea before setting off to catch him. As I expected he wasn't far away. I gathered up his tether rope, which was still staked to the ground; he must have broken his head collar and grazed off. I fully expected we'd be on our way in an hour, but as I approached he turned and started walking away. I stood still and waited for him to stop and start eating again, but before I'd got within fifty metres he was on the move.

'Ho-sha!' I shouted; a well-trained Tibetan horse or yak will respond to this command and stand still. It turned out Whitey wasn't that well trained. He kept walking and when I tried jogging after him he began trotting. It was clear

I was going to need help catching him, so I headed back to the houses.

The Tibetans were in the middle of the busiest part of their day when I arrived and explained what had happened; they had herds of yaks to milk, calves to tend and flocks of sheep to get out to pasture. No one seemed interested in helping me except one old lady who gave me a nosebag filled with *tsampa* to try to coax him back. I thanked her and promised to return the bag and then set off to find the young monk.

'Good morning.'

'Hello, now you go?' he asked me.

'No, my horse . . .' and I used my fingers to demonstrate that he'd trotted off, *'Kuchi, nga-la rogpa nang-ro!'* Please help me!

The monk laughed, but to my relief picked up his hat and followed me out the door.

'Mi mangpo geu,' I said, we need more people.

'No, OK, OK.' And we set off up the valley.

The monk approached Whitey on the right, with me on the left in a very inadequate attempt to surround him. Whitey took one look and started walking off, not really running, but staying well out of our reach. The monk started running, Whitey started trotting. We needed more people. I followed my horse towards the river while the monk set off for another group of houses to try to get more help. Whitey would stop and graze every time I stopped, but as soon as I moved closer he would be on the move again. Half an hour later the monk was back. No one had come to help. We stood there looking at that damn horse, wondering what to do; we really needed a couple of men on horseback to have a decent chance of catching him, but it seemed there were none about.

A short time later a truck came over the hill; the monk ran towards the road, waving it down and when it stopped three men climbed out of the cab to help. The odds looked much better. We all fanned out to surround my dear horse, who was now seriously stretching my patience. The Xianza river flowed deep down the valley and I was sure this would act as a barrier for him; we could quietly herd him closer to the river and encircle him.

Naturally Whitey had other ideas. He was enjoying himself and wasn't about to let us spoil it. We edged closer; as I expected he walked to the riverbank, stopped and turned to look at us, his ears pricked. Then he turned away, walked into the river and waded across, the water halfway up his back. When he reached the other side he kept walking into the hills without looking back and was soon over a low ridge and out of sight. I'd lost my horse; I was stuck there.

The men from the truck shrugged and went on their way, leaving me and the monk standing in the middle of nowhere. I looked at my young friend, my only hope to catch Whitey again, but when he shook his head I worried he was going to tire of helping me and go back to his work. Without him there'd be no way I'd get my horse back. *'Kuchi, nga-la rogpa nang-ro,'* Please, help me, I repeated.

'OK, OK.' He pointed further up the valley, *'Drongpa yawrey, mi mangpo people,'* he said, there's a village and many people.

He told me to wait where I was and set off to get help. For the next three hours I sat by the river, scanning the hills with my binoculars to try to catch a glimpse of Whitey, but he was nowhere to be seen. Without someone on horseback, or a large group of people, it was hopeless. I'd prayed that crossing the pass marked the turning point, but again I found myself up against a brick wall. Whitey had been expensive and I hadn't got my money's worth from him yet; there seemed to be very few horses in the area and I might not be able to buy another one. But what worried me most was that I was next to a road leading straight to a town I knew was policed; it wouldn't take much for the cops in Xianza to hear about me. If I stayed there too long, I'd be caught.

Eventually the monk returned, though this time he was on the other side of the river. We yelled to each other as I tried to find out if he'd found anyone to help me, but we were too far away to communicate. However, he gestured for me to sit down and seemed confident that everything would be OK. Not long after, a Tibetan turned up on horseback, the monk pointed him to where we'd last seen Whitey go and he set off into the hills.

Another couple of nervous hours passed with no sign of Whitey or the rider and my hopes began to fade. I couldn't bring myself to accept this trip might be over just because my horse had wandered off. I kept peering through my binoculars, trying to see something. I slowly turned a hundred and eighty degrees, searching the hills and river plains until I was facing downstream. I caught sight of something moving. It was the Tibetan, leading Whitey. He must have had to chase him for kilometres downriver before catching him. I dropped to my knees in prayer, *'Tujachay Buddha!* Thank you, thank you!'

I set off to meet them and when I reached my new very best Tibetan friend, I threw my arms around his shoulders and hugged him. *'Tujachay! Tujachay!'* The man looked embarrassed, but I was almost in tears with gratitude. I took a hundred yuan note from my wallet and tried to give it to the nomad to say thanks, but he refused outright. I tried tucking the bill into the fold of his *chuba*, but he still pushed it back.

'Khyerang-la ne-kor!' he said to me, you're on a pilgrimage. I promised the young man I would offer the money to a temple on his behalf if I reached Gang Rinpoche. He smiled and went on his way. The monk had waded back across

the river and we set off towards the guesthouse as the skies darkened.

With Whitey secured with the tether rope around his neck we trudged back to the guesthouse. Black skies were sweeping up the valley and the monk was impatient to get home and avoid a drenching. Every now and then he turned back to face the clouds, curling his fingers into an open fist, holding his hand to his mouth before reciting some kind of prayer, and then blowing his breath to the storm, as if he was using a magic spell to delay its arrival. It wasn't working. I could feel the air pressure build and urged him to go on without me, knowing I was slowing him down. He hurried on and I was soon walking alone across the grasslands in the downpour.

Back at the houses I fed Whitey the nosebag of *tsampa* I'd been carrying all day and returned it to the woman. I bought a new head collar from her husband for a few yuan and made a simple set of hobbles from a piece of yak-hair rope. I took Whitey back to the river to graze and wandered over to where the monk was staying. I was deeply indebted to him; if he hadn't taken it upon himself to help me I would still be without my horse. I felt guilty I'd taken him away from his work for a whole day and tried to give him some money to make up for the lost time. He refused and instead poured me a bowl of tea, stoked up the fire and offered me a dish of rice.

I was away early the next morning, heading west across the grasslands and into a wide valley that would lead me to the next pass, Nam-ni-la. Whitey went well, walking strongly after his semi-day off and we made good time. By the end of the day we had nearly reached the top of the valley. There were a few families in their summer camps and I stopped briefly for tea before crossing the valley to camp in the lee of a hill, which gave me scant protection from the wind.

It rained on and off all night and again I hardly slept. I got up early, wanting to get out of the bag and packed up ready to leave. Thankfully Whitey was still where I'd tethered him, but when I went to bring him in to load up I realised something was very wrong.

He was sitting on the ground and when I jabbed him in the ribs with the toe of my boot he wouldn't get up. I had to boot him in the arse a few times before he staggered to his feet, and stood shaking with his back legs wobbling. I thought he might be suffering from exhaustion, but counted that out as he'd had so much energy the day before. I removed the hobbles and started leading him towards my camp. He walked a few metres and sat down, lying flat on his side with his legs stretched out. It took several attempts to make it to where I had left my stuff. I could get Whitey to his feet, but he'd only make it a few steps before his legs would give out. It was obvious he was finished; I couldn't lead the poor animal, let alone ride him. Once again I felt like I'd hit a brick wall. Tibet had thrown another obstacle in my way.

I looked around the valley; the pass wasn't much further on and I had been looking forward to crossing it and putting a barrier between myself and Xianza, but I was stuck again. I needed to get another horse, but I hadn't seen any at the camps I'd passed the previous day. I felt like giving up, but I set off leading Whitey. Every few minutes he would collapse in a heap.

'Ngay ta yakpo ma rey,' I told the old man at the first camp, my horse is not good.

'Aa.' He nodded, seeing Whitey drop to the ground.

'Nga la ta chig nyo do yo,' I want to buy a horse, I told him. *'Ta yawrey?'* Do you have a horse?

'Ta mindu.' He shook his head. The old nomad said something to his son, who went into the tent and came back with a basin of *tsampa* mixed with whey. We offered this to Whitey, but he didn't even bother sniffing it, disinterested in eating anything. A storm of heavy rain was sweeping up the valley and we retreated inside. The old guy's wife served me tea and *tsampa* while he rummaged through boxes and bags at the back of the tent. He handed me two lumps like small stones, indicating they were medicine for the horse. One was clearly a lump of mineral salt but the other was a deep reddish colour. I tasted it — sulphur.

Once the rain had passed we went outside, where the nomad broke the lumps of salt and sulphur in two and wrapped a small piece of each in a little ball of *tsampa* dough. He held them in front of Whitey's nose, hoping he might eat them. He wasn't interested, so he prised the horse's jaw open and shoved them into the back of his throat. He had to do this several times as Whitey kept spitting them out; eventually they stayed in his gob, although I don't know if he swallowed them. Next the Tibetan lifted Whitey's tail; he seemed to know what he was doing and felt along the base of the tail as if feeling for pressure points; every time he hit one particular spot Whitey would wince and try to move away.

'Sangnyi yakpo yawrey,' he said, tomorrow he'll be fine. I wasn't convinced.

It was afternoon by the time I got back to where I'd slept the night before. There was no question of going any further, so I started a fire and spent the rest of the day sitting outside in the open waiting for the next storm. Whitey spent the whole time lying on the ground. Every so often he would get up and move a few feet and then lie down again, making no attempt to graze or drink. In the evening I gave him some more of the 'medicine', mixing it with small lumps of *tsampa* and forcing my fingers into the back of his throat. I could feel his huge molars as I stuffed my hand in his mouth, knowing that if he'd decided to bite down he could have crushed my fingers. After the salt and sulphur I shoved another piece of *tsampa* inside him; this one had a couple of aspirin hidden in it. I had no idea if it would do him any good, but I decided he couldn't get much worse.

Before it got dark the old man wandered over and told me he had a friend down the valley with a horse to sell and he'd bring it the next morning. This sounded hopeful and I went to bed feeling optimistic about the next day. In the morning the horse turned up as promised with the old nomad and the younger man who owned it. He was a small brown gelding, much smaller than Whitey and quite jumpy, though I guessed he hadn't been ridden for a while and would settle down after a day or two. After much arguing we settled on a price of four thousand one hundred yuan, which was way too much, but the Tibetan wouldn't take any less. They were taking advantage of my situation; they knew Whitey was finished and I was stuck in the hills, there were no other horses around and I'd have to take whatever I could get.

Reluctantly I handed over the cash and my poor Whitey. I was sad to see him go as he'd been well behaved most of the time and had carried me over some tough terrain. Before I gave him to his new owner I prayed for his protection and health. 'All Buddhas, Bodhisattvas and Holy Beings, please protect Whitey from the sufferings, fears and dangers of this life. May he quickly recover from his illness and live long. Please bestow your blessings on his body and mind.'

I loaded up my new horse, making adjustments to the tack to fit his much smaller frame; he was a scrawny little pony and so I named him 'Scrawny'. When it was time to go I shook the men's hands and climbed into the saddle. A second later I was flat on my back. Scrawny had gone berserk, bucked like a rodeo horse and thrown me off. I was shaken but unhurt and still had the reins in my hand. I tried again, but this time I couldn't even get a foot in the stirrup. I asked his previous owner to get on, thinking he'd be a much better horseman and might be able to settle him; however, the nomad shook his head and refused. For the last few days I felt as if I'd been in a good luck/bad luck story: my horse escaped, but we'd caught him again; my horse got sick, but I'd bought another one, but it was half-wild — I'd just paid a small fortune for a horse I couldn't ride.

There was no way I was going to get the men to take him back and without a horse I'd be stuck. Even if I couldn't ride him I still needed something to carry my gear. The men told me to walk for the first day, using Scrawny as a packhorse and ride him tomorrow. I wasn't impressed, but it did make sense. It was possible he hadn't been handled for several months and after a day's walk he might calm down enough to be ridden.

I picked up the lead rope and set off towards the pass. We got to the base of the climb leading to the other side. I looked up at the mountain. I was already breathing hard and questioned whether I could make it over, so decided to have another shot at getting on Scrawny.

It was a repeat performance. I'd hardly got my leg over his back when he started bucking like crazy and threw me onto the ground. This time I landed heavily on my tailbone. I desperately hung on to the reins, knowing that if I let go he'd take off and I'd have no chance of catching him. Scrawny stood over me as I lay on the ground, my back aching from the fall. Slowly, I mentally went through all the bones in my body, checking to see if anything felt broken. To my relief I was still intact, though the pain in my lower back made getting to my feet slow and sore.

After my second dumping I was too afraid to get back on. I was out of sight of any camps, kilometres from any town, and a broken arm or leg or worse was a terrifying thought. I would have to walk into the pass. The climb was exhausting at this altitude and though I surprised myself, it was still a desperate slog to the top. Every time I felt myself tire I instinctively thought to get on and ride, and it was difficult to accept it wasn't possible. Even when I reached for my water bottle on the side of the saddle, Scrawny would pull away. I had to restrain myself from giving him a thrashing, as it would only make things worse; I could feel anger and hatred for the damn animal welling up inside, but I was determined not to let it take over. By the time we reached the little cluster of prayer flags I was cursing myself for being so foolish.

There was a small consolation that from the top of the pass I could see a large lake and I knew exactly where I was on the map. I walked Scrawny all the way down the other side and across an empty grassland south of the lake to camp by a large river. There was no one else in sight. It had been a long day and while I felt I'd managed the walk well enough, I knew I could only make it through another day or two without riding. I'd either have to find a way to ride Scrawny or look for another horse.

I tethered him out for the night, staking him to the soft ground of the river flat; somehow during the day I'd lost the hobbles. I crawled into the bag to say my prayers and write my diary. A massive orange sun slowly set behind the mountains on the other side of the valley; the dark skies were clear and the wind had gone to bed for the night. I watched Scrawny graze quietly in front of me. He slowly moved across the pasture, nibbling as he went, taking a few steps to the next green patch and feeding again before moving on. The scene was idyllic and the stresses of the day lay quiet for a few minutes, until it suddenly dawned on me that Scrawny was grazing further than his rope

A young nomad couple in their yak hair tent; they gave Ian shelter from a storm.

Small stone village in the 'lowlands'.

Ian making *tsampa* at his camp under the juniper trees.

The monk and nomad who recaptured Whitey after he had escaped.

A village tailor.

Ian in a cave where he stayed for two nights.

Child shepherdess at
Taro Tso lake.

Monlam in front of the cave at Taro Tso.

A nomad family in their tent near Rinqin Tso lake.

Ian in disguise with Monlam, about to set off towards Darchen to find the pilgrim trail around Mt Kailas.

Ian in front of Kailas.

Ian and a tired Monlam on top of Dolma-la pass, 5636 metres.

A well-dressed
Tibetan pilgrim on
top of Dolma-la.

Sunrise over Lake Manasarovar at the ruins of Cherkip Gompa monastery.

The blue of Lake Manasarovar from the roof of Gossul Gompa.

Ian at the end of the trail giving Monlam away to the lama at Langbona
Gompa.

should have allowed. He'd pulled the stake out of the ground and was loose. I sat up and reached for my boots, but it was too late. At the same moment Scrawny realised freedom was at hand. There was nothing I could do and I watched him gallop off into the darkness. Fuck!

He was gone. I'd lost my horse. It was pointless even trying to catch him as there was no way I could run after him at this altitude and I knew he would run all the way back to his home on the other side of the pass. In the morning his previous owner would find him and spend the rest of the summer laughing about the fool tourist who'd paid a fortune for his horse and then let him escape.

I lay down and pulled my sleeping bag over my head. I was stuck in the middle of nowhere without a horse and there was no one else for kilometres. It was too far for me to walk all the way back over the pass to try to find him and besides, I couldn't even bear to think about the next day. 'Fuck,' I repeated; it was all I could manage.

Tibet had won the day, and it seemed she might win the whole bloody war. I felt totally beaten and for the moment I couldn't care less. If a truck heading back to Lhasa had driven by just then I would have gladly headed home to forget the whole damn thing. *Fuck.*

The morning was clear and still. I slowly packed up, not looking forward to the day ahead, wondering what was going to happen next. I decided to set off on foot up the valley to try to find another horse. There was a road heading in that direction which I guessed must lead somewhere, although I had no idea where or how far the next village or camp might be. I piled up my riding gear, the saddle, blankets and bridle, and left them by the river, hoping they would still be there when I came back . . . if I came back. They were too heavy to carry and if I didn't find a horse I'd be forced to head back to Lhasa. If I had to do that I knew I'd give up on the idea of riding to Kailas and instead ask Tseyang to help me arrange transport and go by road while I still had time on my visa. I hated the idea, but if I couldn't buy another mount I wouldn't have a choice. I rolled up the *chuba* and slung it on my back, threw my saddlebags over my shoulder and said goodbye to my saddle.

After five minutes' walking I had to stop and rest, gasping for air. The added weight of my *chuba*, oilskin, water bottle, sleeping bag and saddlebags seemed to double the effects of the thin atmosphere. Before long the sun was high and hot. I staggered under the load and collapsed in the dirt, taking several minutes to get my breath back and then several more trying to get to my feet. My back ached from yesterday's fall and my feet were killing me in my tight boots without any heels.

I followed a track that led over some low hills; under normal conditions they wouldn't have been an obstacle, but now they seemed like an impassable barrier. I could barely make it a few metres before I'd throw off my loads and drop to the ground. It took all morning to go a couple of kilometres. If there was no one living in the area I wouldn't make it. I felt completely hopeless; my only comfort was the thought that I couldn't get any lower.

Towards the middle of the day I heard the sound of a motor coming towards me from behind. I dropped my stuff and scanned the road with my binoculars, terrified it could be a jeep full of police. To my relief it was a small trailer pulled behind a walking tractor. As it got closer it turned off the main road and started along another track. Using the little energy I had left I ran down to meet it, waving my arms. I hadn't seen any other traffic on the road all day and this might be my only chance of a lift.

'Kan an dro?' I asked. He pointed and babbled something I hoped was the name of a village. *'Drongpa yawrey?'* I asked, is there a village?

'Rey, rey.' He nodded. I threw my bags in the back and we set off. An hour later we topped another rise and a small village came into view. The driver dropped me off and continued into the hills. I had to find a horse.

Several locals stood around and one young lad invited me inside his home for tea. I was starving and when I noticed a semi-fresh leg of mutton hanging from the rafters I offered his mother ten yuan to cook me a meal. Before long she was heaping my bowl with boiled meat and rice. I asked if the family could sell me a horse. At first no one seemed to understand. I explained again what I needed and when they finally understood they shook their heads and shrugged. I sank inside, not knowing what I'd do if I didn't find another animal.

By then news of my arrival had spread and a few of the neighbours came to see me. One beautiful young village girl walked into the room with her baby in her arms. As soon as we looked at each other I felt an instant connection, as if we'd met before. I could tell she was intelligent and there was a calmness about her that relaxed me. I felt at ease, as if by her just being there everything was going to work out.

Droma sat next to me and I told her I needed to buy a horse, explaining that I'd ridden from Lhasa and my last mount had escaped the night before. Amazingly, she seemed to understand almost everything I said, even with my poor command of Tibetan, and when she spoke I knew exactly what she was saying, although I would never be able to repeat what she'd said. She said something to the young man, who spoke to his mother; she handed him a rope hanging by the door and he went outside.

'*Ta yawrey?*' I asked her, does he have a horse?

'*Rey, ta yawrey.*' Yes, he did.

While we waited for the horse to be brought in, the mother served everyone butter tea.

'*Kan an dro?*' Droma asked, where are you going?

'*Gang Rinpoche,* I'm doing *ne-kor,*' I told her.

'*Gang Rinpoche ne-kor!*' she exclaimed and gave me the thumbs up. '*Yakpo! Yakpo!*' Good, good!

Before long the horse arrived in the dirt yard. It was a small brown stallion, very small. I could tell he would only get me a week down the trail at most and the price of two thousand five hundred yuan was way too much. However, when I nervously climbed on his back the animal stood quietly and I was so relieved to find another horse, any horse, I would have paid any price. We went back inside and I counted out the notes. I got him to throw in a wooden stake and a long yak-hair rope to replace the one I'd lost and also an insurance policy in the form of a set of hobbles.

We loaded my gear onto the horse and tied it round his belly with the rope. I shook hands with the young man and then with Droma. She smiled and again I felt her aura of calm. I suddenly felt as if she had been sent by someone, or something, to help me and I'd been foolish to have worried about the situation. Of course I'd find another horse, of course I was going to be all right. The people would take care of me.

And so I set off again, my money belt considerably lighter, but at least the load I'd carried to the village was off my back and onto a horse where it should be. I felt lighter, too; perhaps the good luck of meeting Droma and buying a new horse finally marked a change in fortune. But once again I had a nagging fear bad luck would follow good and I wondered what was going to hit me next.

The little horse walked steadily behind; if my last horse had been scrawny then this one could only be 'Skinny'. Just before dark we reached the spot where I'd spent the previous night. As I looked over the ridge above the narrow river flat I was relieved to see my pile of tack. I tethered and hobbled Skinny and set up my camp before collecting dung for a fire. It was a clear, still night and as the sun faded I counted my blessings — despite all the hassle, I was in a better situation than I had been the day before. I wouldn't be able to ride Skinny for a whole day every day if he was going to last long, but at least he could carry my gear and I could ride when I needed.

It was a lovely morning and I didn't wake up until nearly nine. I loaded Skinny with no trouble but felt wary and nervous as I climbed onto his back, half-expecting him to go crazy and throw me off. Of course he didn't and we were soon on our way. I stopped at Droma's village and was taken in for tea by the same lad. I asked about Droma but was told she'd taken her yaks out to pasture. We carried on up the wide valley towards another lake; the weather was good for most of the day — cloudy, cool and comfortable — but the afternoon brought heavy showers of cold rain. I walked for much of the day, but whenever I felt worn out I could take a relative break in the saddle and we made good time.

I was passing another tiny village as a storm hit and was taken in by a family and given tea and *tsampa*. The people were kind and I showed them my maps and photos as I waited for the rain to pass. However, the door to the little dwelling opened after a few minutes and another villager stepped inside. He made me nervous straightaway; unlike the other *drokpa* he wasn't wearing a *chuba*, just a nylon jacket. He seemed out of place and I wondered if he was some kind of petty official like the one I'd met in the village of the Bonpo *gompa* two years before. The kind of person who might report me. I smiled and greeted him. He smiled back and looked at me the way any other curious local would, but I didn't relax. He asked me where I'd come from by horse and I told him I'd been in Xianza.

'*Xianza nyin-ma katseu dey pa?*' he asked me, how many days were you in Xianza?

'*Sum,*' I told him, three, '*Xianza nga trogpo yawrey.*' I have a friend in Xianza.

'*Khyerang-la trogpo ming karey-rey?*' What's your friend's name?

'Wang Ling.' The first Chinese-sounding syllables that sprang to mind. '*Gyanak korsung-wa yin.*' He's a Chinese policeman.

'*Aa, rey.*' He nodded.

I hoped that if he believed I'd just spent three days in Xianza with a Chinese cop he wouldn't think it worthwhile reporting me, if that was his duty or intention. He did seem to accept the story and didn't ask anything else, but by then the rain had passed and I was anxious to be on my way. I didn't feel right there. I was sure there were no telephones in the village, or anywhere in the valley, but I had seen a couple of trucks and Xianza could probably be reached in half a day by road. I was probably being paranoid, but I preferred to think of it as caution; whatever, it put me on edge and I was glad to ride away.

We reached the lake late in the afternoon and rounded its southern end on a stony road below a high range of mountains. At about seven I reached another village and the whole town turned out to meet me. *'Tsong khang yawrey?'* I asked, hoping to be able to stock up on supplies, is there a shop? I was taken into a yard to a small shed; an old man unlocked the door and showed me into the valley's only retail outlet. There was almost nothing for sale — crap Chinese socks and T-shirts, torch batteries that were probably already flat, poorly made army surplus sneakers, a few bottles of Chinese beer and sacks of wool. I bought some lollies, most of which I immediately gave away to the kids in the crowd.

Among the people of the village one young girl stood out. She was in her late teens and dressed in modern jeans and a sweatshirt, her feet in colourful trainers. She could speak a few words of English and we ended up going to her home for tea and bread. Half the village crowded in with us and the girl told me she was a student at a Chinese university in Lhasa, home for the summer vacation. All the other girls were dressed in traditional long skirts and high-necked shirts, grimy aprons around their waists, their hair in long plaits threaded with lumps of coral and heavy beads of amber and turquoise around their necks.

The situation struck me as an example of what was happening to Tibet's nomadic youth. Every family was expected to send one of their children to school, and if they could afford it, or if their fees were paid by the Chinese government, on to university. This girl had a fashionable haircut and despite having been born in the heart of the Tibetan plateau she wouldn't have looked out of place in any city in China. It was obvious that when she returned to her village she hadn't wanted to dress as her sisters did.

I wondered what her future would bring. Would she marry a village boy or someone from the city? Would her children grow up next to her lake or on the streets of Lhasa? As the Chinese continue to pour more money into Tibet, will more of her younger brothers and sisters be enticed away to be educated and seduced by the promises of jobs and wealth? Will the villages in these isolated valleys of Tibet slowly lose their children until there aren't enough to sustain them any more and they fall into abandoned ruins?

It was starting to get dark so I asked the girl if I could stay the night in the village. The girl's parents didn't seem to be around and I tried to say that of course I didn't expect to stay in her home with her; however, this didn't make it through the translation and understandably she looked rather disturbed. There were heads shaking all around and I gave up trying to ask again. The girl gave me some bread and I set off again across a high plain, heading towards the hills and the next pass.

An hour later I camped alone next to a stream below the base of the pass. Two huge black crows hopped from rock to rock along the riverbank, screeching to each other. All through this area I'd seen several species of birds — seagulls, terns, long-necked geese, Siberian cranes, kestrels and eagles. The birds called to each other in strange, eerie tones that sounded like the voices of small children yelling as they played.

After a very wet and cold night it was hard to get up, but we were away by ten the next day. I passed a single tent after an hour; the family were busy with their yaks but the father sent his son into the tent to bring me a kettle of tea and I carried on into the pass. The trail was rough and too steep for little Skinny to carry me so I walked to the top. It was another tough climb, but the weather had cleared and there was enough wind to keep me cool. Skinny walked well and gave me no trouble; he was a friendly little fellow and well behaved. After we crossed the pass I felt safer and I relaxed further when we turned into a narrow, empty valley. There was a road on one side of the river, but it was very rough, difficult even for a jeep, I thought, and I didn't see anyone else for the rest of the day.

That night I camped alone by the river and in the morning headed deeper into the hills. Again I didn't see anyone; the only sign of nomads in the area were small groups of bull yaks left out to graze until they were needed in the next breeding season. The road we followed steadily became fainter, though I could see tyre tracks in the mud so I supposed it must lead to a pass.

At midday the road led me round a sharp bend in the valley, where I found a large green canvas tent. As I climbed out of the saddle two teenaged Chinese boys came out to greet me.

'Ni hau,' I greeted them, and they showed me inside.

A middle-aged Chinese man sat on a wide sleeping platform at the back of the tent, surrounded by playing cards; I must have interrupted them in the middle of a game. They were well equipped with a small diesel generator, a radio, piles of quilts and blankets, cooking pots and woks, but what caught my eye was a wooden bench laid out with stocks of cabbages, mushrooms and sweet peppers. Real food!

I showed the three men my photos; they were friendly but seemed shy and I was at even more of a loss to communicate with them than I was with the Tibetans. I couldn't speak any Chinese except for the most basic phrases and none of them could speak Tibetan. However, the thought of a well-cooked meal made me eager to communicate despite the lack of any common language. I pointed to the vegetables and the woks and mimed someone cooking, then opened my wallet and took out ten yuan to show I'd pay. One of the young chaps immediately began chopping, while the other fired up their stove. The older man poured me Chinese tea and gave me a steamed bun.

While my lunch was cooking I tried to ask the men what they were doing in the middle of nowhere. One of the boys pointed upstream to another canvas shelter set into the bank. Diesel drums in front indicated heavy machinery inside and an excavated hillside further on told me they were looking for precious metals. I showed them the bracelet on my wrist and asked if they were hunting for silver. The older man shook his head and curled up his lip to show me a capped tooth — they were gold miners.

Soon I was scoffing down a great bowl of spicy vegetables while the men went back to their card game. I guessed they would spend the summer looking for gold; there was no work that day it seemed, perhaps it was a day off or maybe their machinery had broken down or run out of fuel. The road I had followed ended at the camp and I imagined they were kept in supplies by a truck once a week. They seemed happy to be there; perhaps they were from poor parts of China and grateful to have some kind of employment. When I left they gave me a couple more steamed buns and when I handed them the ten yuan they laughed and refused. As soon as I was out of sight of their camp I broke one of the buns into pieces and fed it to Skinny.

During the afternoon we headed into the pass called Nari-la; there was no road, no trail, nothing, and I wasn't even sure I was going the right way. All the walking I'd done in the last few days was taking its toll and I had to ride some of the way. Poor little Skinny was also becoming worn out; he was slow and becoming slower as he tired and I was already thinking of trading him in as soon as I got the chance.

At about three in the afternoon we made it to the top of the pass and stopped to rest next to a small *lhabtsi* with a couple of faded prayer flags; it didn't look as if anyone came this way much. It was steep down the other side, but when we reached the river in the next valley I found several families camped there. I stopped for tea and asked about horses, but none were offered. By evening I was at the bottom of the valley where two rivers met and flowed into the mountains. I set Skinny out for the night and walked over to my neighbours in a tent not far away. I asked if they could give me some dry dung to make a fire. I only needed a few pieces but they generously filled my bag and the old woman even offered to lend me a cooking pot.

Back at my camp I collected rocks to make a fireplace. I piled the chips of yak dung inside the small circle of stones. The wind was blowing and I had to lie on the ground with a saddle blanket over me to have enough shelter to light a small piece of dung. I only needed to get the first bit lit to get the fire going; as long as the dung was completely dry it would smoulder like a cigarette, one piece would set another alight and if there was enough breeze

I would soon have a blazing bed of embers on which I'd sit my little tin teapot. It was a lovely evening, no clouds at all and the sky was soon bright with stars. I sat next to my tiny fire with the *chuba* wrapped around me and said my prayers as I waited for the next cup to boil. Evenings like this were my favourite time; the struggle and stress of the day was over, I felt safe and optimistic about the day to come. A shooting star flashed briefly in the sky and I made a wish that I would reach Gang Rinpoche. Making it to the mountain and delivering my lama's ashes were still paramount in my mind, but I knew that even to be where I was now, sitting by a fire in the nomadic heart of Tibet, free with my horse, a map and compass as my guide, a river as my road and the stars for a tent, was a great blessing in itself.

In the morning we set off into the narrow valley, and had to cross the river twice as cliffs that dropped straight into the flow blocked our way. It was deep and fast, and as Skinny waded into the rising water I was terrified he'd be swept off his feet. I had to work hard to keep him under control and guide him through the best way I could see. Skinny may have been small but he had a big heart — he was as brave and tough as any Tibetan horse I owned and we made both crossings safely.

By evening we were camped on a grassy flat high above the river. The river was too big and fast even to consider crossing and I wasn't sure I was on the 'right' side. I could see the valley would shrink further as we travelled down and there was a good chance I would run into a dead end and have to turn back. The next day I went on foot, as it was too rugged to ride. Before long we were picking our way around boulders and scrub in a slender gorge as the river roared past. There was no sign that anyone ever came this way.

As we rounded every twist in the gorge I hoped the valley would widen and the way become easier, but instead it just got tougher, rockier and slower. Finally we came to a massive rock outcrop that jutted into the river and completely blocked our way. I left Skinny to graze and went ahead to try to scout a way past. There was no way we could go round the rock, the river was much too deep and turning back would mean a whole day's ride back up the valley over the same difficult terrain. Our only chance was to climb over it.

I scrambled up the steep slope. There wasn't even a goat track, just a mass of boulders and patches of loose dirt. If we came this way Skinny would have to both climb over large rocks and squeeze between them where there was barely enough space for me to get through. Some of the ground was unstable, there were places where it had already fallen away and the slope gave way to cliffs that dropped straight onto rocks or the river below. A fall here could be fatal for either one of us and even a lesser injury would still mean disaster.

I sat on a rock wondering what to do. There was no question of trying just to see what happened — once we started I knew it would be impossible to turn Skinny round and go back, there wasn't room. I hated the thought of putting my little pony across such an obstacle but I hated the idea of turning back even more. I climbed back down and gathered up Skinny's lead rope. 'Come on, boy, let's give it a go. Just take it slowly and we'll make it OK.' I rubbed his ears, patted him on the neck and we set off.

We slowly edged our way across the slope. I would only walk a couple of steps and then pull Skinny along behind me, trying to pick a way where he would at least have some footing. At times I'd stop and move loose rocks on the ground so he wouldn't have to step on them and thus perhaps save him from a stumble that could have pushed us over the edge. I was terrified of injuring my horse and Skinny was well aware of the danger; sometimes he would pull against me and refuse to take another step. I'd rub his ears and try to comfort him. 'Come on, Skinny, you can do it!' And my brave little mate would put his trust in me and follow.

We were almost across; there was only one more patch where the mountainside had completely fallen away above a steep drop of several metres, after that we would be on a more gentle slope of grass and scrub. I hopped across, testing the ground as I went; it seemed stable enough and I pulled Skinny behind me. Then he fell. I heard a crash and turned round to see his frightened little face and his front legs, scrambling for a hold, disappear from sight. 'Skinny!'

He fell six metres onto the rocks below. He was directly below me and I couldn't even see him. I climbed across the rest of the slope and slid down the bank, dreading what I might find — a horse dying in agony with broken legs — I'd be stuck in the middle of nowhere with no one to help me. For a moment I had an awful thought: what if he was injured beyond help and I had to destroy him? Of course I didn't have a gun, how would I do it? Cut his throat with my dull knife? I couldn't bear to think about it.

I found him standing by the river. As I approached he pulled back and tried to turn around, obviously shaken by the fall. 'Good boy, it's all right, boy, good boy.' I tried to soothe him and he stood still as I picked up his rope. I stroked his neck and crouched beside him to check his legs; he was standing on all four, which was a reassuring sign. I ran my hands up and down his legs, feeling for anything that didn't seem right. He had a graze on one hind leg but it didn't seem to bother him, otherwise he was unhurt.

'Oh, Buddhas! *Tujachay!* Thank you, thank you, thank you!'

We stood there for several minutes to give us time to calm down. Skinny recovered much sooner than I did and started nibbling on the grass; my legs felt like jelly and it was some time before I felt able to carry on.

We walked on for another hour and at last the valley opened out and the going became easier. We stopped on a gentle grassy slope and I unloaded the saddlebags and left Skinny to graze while I started a fire. I sat in the sun with my warm mug in my hand, watching eagles circle high over the peaks above me. Skinny ate for a while and then sat on the grass right beside me as if he wanted to join in the picnic. I broke off a piece of my *tsampa* and fed it to him and rubbed his ears. He shook his head happily and let me lean my back against him; he'd forgiven me. I'd only had him for five days but I felt he'd done enough; he was tired and couldn't go much further. I promised I'd trade him first chance I got. I admired the little horse immensely for his courage and despite his limitations I would always think of him as one of my better horses.

By evening we had come to a small open plain surrounded by mountains; there were a couple of camps on my side of the river and a village on the other side. Through my binoculars I could see several horses grazing and I knew that if I could cross I'd have a good chance of buying one of them. However, the river was deep and slow and I hadn't seen anywhere to ford it.

I stopped at one of the tents and was met by a young man called Sonam. His elderly mother served me tea and a bowl of rice while her son smoked and played a six-stringed guitar-like instrument that he told me was called a *dram-ge*. I pointed down the river and asked if there was a road heading that way. He told me there was no road, no villages and no people. I knew I'd have to cross the river here and find another horse. I asked him if there was a place to cross to get to the village and he pointed back upstream and told me there was a bridge. I'd passed the bridge earlier; it was a rickety little swing-bridge some twenty metres long made from wire and a few frail planks. Not for the faint-hearted. I knew I could manage it, but there was no way I could get Skinny across. However, Sonam insisted we could both get across and we set off back upstream with his younger brother.

We made it to the bridge, unloaded Skinny and ferried my saddlebags and riding gear across the river. The bridge swung violently as I inched my way over, but the two Tibetans just laughed and skipped ahead. I waited on the far side while they went back and led Skinny downstream a short distance. The younger lad took off his shoes, rolled up his trousers and led the horse as deeply into the water as he could. Then he dropped the lead rope, gave him a shove forward and whacked him on the rump. Skinny stood there for a moment then tried to turn round. The two brothers shouted and waved their arms to chase him further into the river. He took a few steps into deeper water and the Tibetans splashed stones into the river behind him. Skinny seemed to understand what he was supposed to be doing and obediently waded into the flow, the water nearly over his back, and crossed to the other side where I was waiting.

We loaded up again and set off towards the village, which Sonam told me was called Yuba. We arrived just before dark so I unloaded Skinny and put him out for the night above the village; he'd done so well that day and I hoped it would be his last. Back in Sonam's house I told the men who had come to see me that I needed to buy a new horse. There seemed to be some interest and I was hopeful I'd get another animal the next day.

After tea and *tsampa* the next morning the men who had horses to sell waited outside with their steeds. I finally found myself in a buying situation where I had the upper hand; with more than one person offering a horse for sale I would be in a much better position to bargain. Of the four horses I was shown one was smaller than Skinny and not worth bothering with, another was bigger but looked half-emaciated, but the other two were fairly good mounts. I asked the men how much they wanted for them and even their starting prices were reasonable. Before deciding I saddled both horses for a test ride. One was very skittish and I had trouble controlling it; although it was better than the other horse I refused it, remembering what had happened with Scrawny.

The horse I chose was a brown gelding, in good condition, big enough and well behaved. We settled quickly on a price of two thousand yuan, which I thought was very fair. My new horse was an odd fellow; he had shoes on three of his hooves and was blind in one eye, so I named him One Eye. I loaded up and handed Skinny over to his new owner. I was sad to say goodbye to the little horse, but before I left I snapped a few hairs from his tail to leave at Gang Rinpoche in the hope he would receive the benefits from the blessing of the rest of the journey.

I shook Sonam's hand, grateful to have met him, and set off into the hills on a high trail towards the next pass. One Eye went well, but I still had to walk over the steeper parts of the path; he walked close behind and often when I stopped to catch my breath he would walk into me, thumping his head in the middle of my back. With his blind eye I think he couldn't see I had stopped.

The pass was one of the toughest yet, very steep on a trail of loose stones and I could feel I was at a much higher altitude. Despite the struggle I was keen to make it to the top. I always felt a sort of optimistic expectation when I climbed a pass, hoping to find something good on the other side, a beautiful lake that would give me an exact location on my map and tell me I'd travelled further than I'd thought, a monastery I hadn't expected to see, a village with a well-stocked store, or perhaps a new and exotic group of locals.

Chapter Ten

This time, however, the only thing I found was a freezing front of rain. Down in the next valley I found a river I could follow west to its source and as the rain continued I took shelter with a family in their tent. The father was reluctant to let me inside and grudgingly gave me a couple of bowls of watery tea. Their yak-hair tent was full of holes and leaked like a sieve. They looked as miserable as I felt in the cold, damp tent and I couldn't understand how they could stand to live out there. The old mother was more kindly, though, and gave me a warm bowl of delicious milk straight from the yak.

As soon as the rain eased off slightly I kept going. It rained most of the day, which forced me to walk much of the time in an effort to keep warm. Later in the afternoon I came to another house and stopped outside the yard. I called out a greeting over the wall and eventually two women came out, an old mother and someone who I guessed was her daughter. I was desperate to get inside and out of the rain, but the women were on their own and wouldn't let me past the front gate. They brought me a kettle of tea and offered me *tsampa*, but I wasn't hungry, all I wanted to do was get out of the atrocious weather. I begged to be allowed in, but they were unmoved and I had no choice but to carry on. One Eye was going well on his first day on the trail, but I was exhausted. My legs and feet were so sore I could hardly walk properly and my back still ached from my fall. At night it was too painful for me to turn over properly and lifting anything would send me into such agony I'd nearly cry out. I needed to rest.

Late in the afternoon I entered a narrower part of the valley; clouds hung low, shrouding the bare peaks. Massive rock formations rose from the valley floor and the mountainsides were studded with colossal spires of rock, like gigantic teeth. In another place it would probably be on a list of scenic wonders, but here in Tibet it was hidden in a valley, there wasn't even a road leading to it. I started looking for a campsite or somewhere to stay. I knew the rain would continue all night and dearly wanted to be under some sort of roof.

As evening set in I found a cave. It had a low roof, but it was deep enough to be able to get right inside and keep my stuff out of the rain. There was an overhang in front, under which I could make a fire out of the weather and in another smaller hollow around the corner I found a pile of dry dung. There was a small area of fairly good grazing below the cave and a crystal-clear stream a short walk away. It was perfect! I unloaded One Eye, happy with how well he'd done on his first day and lugged my gear into the cave. Most of my stuff was still wet and while I hoped the next day would be fine enough to dry everything out I knew it wouldn't be a complete disaster if the rain continued. The floor of the cave was dusty, loose dirt mixed with sheep dung, but it was far better than sleeping in the rain. Under the overhang I gathered rocks and made myself a kitchen with a floor of stones to keep everything out of the dirt. I made tea and instant noodles for dinner, wrote my journal, said my prayers and crawled into my sleeping bag. As I lay down to sleep I wondered when someone in my family had last slept in a cave.

The next day was mostly overcast with frequent showers, although the sun did come out long enough for me to get my gear mostly dry. One Eye grazed contentedly and apart from a few trips to the stream to collect water and shave I spent most of the day beside the fire, drinking tea and reading the Dalai Lama's book. I felt very ascetic, sitting in a cave in Tibet studying the Buddha's teachings having renounced my homeland. There was even a clump of nettles growing nearby which reminded me of Milarepa, the Tibetan sage who lived in a cave at Kailas on nothing but nettle soup, so much so his skin is said to have turned green.

However, as I read it became clearer that what was more important was how the practitioner behaved after he left his cave. The idea of prayers, meditation and listening to teachings is like recharging a battery, but the whole point of recharging a battery is to put it to use. Even if I spent the rest of the year sitting in my little cave studying and meditating on Buddha's teachings and then reverted to my usual self-centred, grasping me as soon as I left, I would have done nothing but waste time and drink tea.

It's easy to develop compassion, patience and tolerance sitting in front of a beautiful statue in a temple or listening to an inspired teaching by a realised lama, but it's bloody hard to keep that feeling going when the teaching is over and you're back in the real world again. There were times when I'd sat listening to Khensur Thabkye Rinpoche expounding the Buddha's thought with wonderful clarity, charm and wit, so much so I was really moved. The idea to hold all sentient beings as dearly as one would love their own mother would well up inside me and I felt sure I could do it; I felt I could interact with anyone as if I was meeting my best friend. The ideals he taught often struck me as simple common sense, as if they'd always been part of me but I just didn't know it, as if I was seeing my own face in a mirror for the first time.

Then the lesson would end; it would be late, I'd be tired and have to drive home through the city. By the time I'd reached the end of the street most of what I'd learnt had been left behind at the front door of Rinpoche's Buddhist centre. Some idiot would cut me off at a roundabout, I'd blast the horn and swear. I'd be in a hurry to make it home to watch the late news but the driver in the car in front of me would be slow to move off when the lights changed. 'Bloody hurry up! It's green!'

And even here in Tibet I was tested every day. People turned me away when I asked for food and shelter. 'Bloody nomads! I only want to get out of the fuckin' rain! I'm not going to hurt you!' My horse was slow and misbehaved. 'Would you walk a bit faster, damn you!' or 'Stand still while I'm trying to load you!'

The real test was not how deeply I could meditate or how long I could stay in retreat in a cave eating nettles, the real test was whether it made a difference when I crawled out into the sunlight where I would be in contact with others. I finished my tea and looked around to check on One Eye. He was hobbled but wandering off around the side of the hill and out of sight. I'd have to leave my comfortable possie and bring him back. 'Bloody horse!'

That night I was woken from the depths of sleep by One Eye screaming. I sat bolt upright, hitting my head on the roof of the cave. The high-pitched, blood-curdling squeal continued and I scrambled to find my torch and crawl out of the cave, thinking he must be being torn to pieces by wolves or a leopard. I scanned the pasture below the cave with the dim light of the torch, trying to find him. There was another equally monstrous shriek, but the voice was different; it was another horse.

Finally I spotted One Eye. A nomad's grazing horse had wandered by during the night and finding an outsider in his valley had come to investigate. The two animals were standing side by side, shoving each other, trying to bite and kick each other. One Eye was at a disadvantage with his feet hobbled, so I picked up stones and hurled them at his rival to even things up. 'Fuck off!' After a few minutes' swearing and another dozen mostly poorly aimed rocks, the horses gave up their shoving and the local wandered off. I crawled back to bed and slept until daylight.

I was away by ten the next day and we headed on up the valley towards the next pass, La-war la. We carried on making good time and by late afternoon we were nearing the pass where the valley had widened into an open barren plain. There seemed to be three or four ways out of the valley, but I chose the most directly western route. The pass was low and an easy climb; I was able to ride most of the way without putting too much strain on One Eye.

We crossed over into another high valley surrounded by bare rock. The place was almost completely devoid of vegetation, so desolate and dry I felt as if I was riding across the surface of the moon. The only sign of life came from a solitary *khang*, the wild Tibetan ass. Further down, the valley turned into an enormous canyon with fantastic walls of rock. High caves and tiny streams sprung almost from the tops of the ridges then vanished back into the stone before they reached the valley floor.

In the evening the wind howled up the canyon, wearing me out and finishing me off for the day. We made it down into a grassy valley and camped up just after seven. There was no one else in sight, but I wasn't alone. On the ridge above my camp I watched several large antelope with my binoculars, magnificent beasts almost the size of a small Tibetan horse, with massive straight, black horns, which angled slightly forward. They were proud animals, wild and as free as any creature could be and they looked down from the safety of the ridge on us lesser beings with disdain.

It was a beautiful evening and the wind died as One Eye grazed next to the small stream. During the day he'd lost the shoe from his front left foot, but I hoped I'd be able to have it replaced somewhere. I made tea and *tsampa* and checked my maps. From where I was, or at least where I thought I was, I could head down the valley and out of the mountains until I met a river marked as the Ta Kuo Tsangpo, then follow that north to a large lake, Tangra Yumco. Once I made it to the lake I would have cut a sizeable chunk out of the journey.

It was a dry night and I slept well, with my head out of the bag; the half-moon was so bright it illuminated the valley, and the walls of the distant canyon on the other side seemed to glow. The morning was frosty and cold but we set off early and headed down onto an open plain. Every so often I'd pass a little cluster of three or four whitewashed houses. I stopped at one for tea and stocked up on supplies of *tsampa*, butter and *chura*, even managing to get a lump of fresh mutton, all for ten yuan.

I woke to light rain the next morning but got up thinking it would soon ease off. It didn't; in fact, before I even got a chance to get dressed the drizzle turned to a heavy downpour. I crawled back into the bag and lay there for the next two hours, cold and wet, waiting for it to stop. When it finally eased off I managed to get the fire going; a mug of tea cheered me out of my misery and we set off into more rain. It was a month since I'd set out from Yangbajian, but the day was going to turn out to be anything but a happy anniversary.

One Eye was slow, which frustrated me in such unpleasant conditions. I tried not to lose my temper, but as the day wore on it became harder to resist giving him a thrashing. We came to a small river, which should have been an easy crossing, but for some reason One Eye kept shying as I tried to drive him into the water. It took several attempts to get him to cross and when he finally did he stumbled on every rock, almost throwing me into the river. Whether he couldn't see them or he was just plain stupid I didn't know. When we eventually made it to the other bank I realised he was limping. I climbed off and found the shoe on his right foot was loose and hanging on with two nails. There was no way I could repair it, so I had to prise the thing off with my knife.

As we carried on the sun made its only appearance of the day, and it was a cameo role at that. I hoped the weather was starting to turn for the better, but an hour later another front of freezing heavy rain arrived. We tried to keep going, but before long the rain was falling so hard I had no choice but to let One Eye turn his rump into the wind and we sat in the middle of the valley, hoping to wait it out but all the time getting wetter and colder.

This wasn't a passing shower. I could see no breaks in the sky; the rain had taken up residence for the day. There was no one in the area and no shelter. Twice lightning cracked so close to us I could almost feel it and the thunder was deafening. Soon I was so cold and depressed I was nearly in tears. As the rain continued without a break, I eventually climbed off One Eye's back and started walking through the storm. After an hour we rounded a bend and found a small town, not marked on my map. We crossed the river on a bridge of wooden logs and I was soon standing a couple of hundred metres away from the first buildings. There was no one in sight, everyone was sheltering indoors. I walked One Eye to the edge of town and stopped beside the meagre shelter of a wall. I was in plain view of the main street, which had turned into a small inland sea of mud. Just a hundred metres away, jutting out from the fronts of squat buildings, I could see signs that advertised the kind of little noodle shops I'd eaten in on the first leg of the trip and stores full of useful goods and supplies. I was sorely tempted to tie One Eye to a fence and go into town. Within a few minutes I could be inside out of the rain, eating a huge meal. I could stock up on necessities, I could get my boots fixed, I could probably even find someone to reshoe One Eye; there might even be some kind of hotel, I could sleep that night in a dry room.

But on the other side of the street was a large concrete yard surrounding an official-looking four-storey building. This probably contained the offices of the local authorities and the police. I remembered my fake permit; could I perhaps use that and bluff my way through? But it was too risky, the local police might accept it and treat me like a foreign guest, but they were just as likely to recognise it as phoney and arrest me. There were probably telephones here and they would at least call Lhasa to check its validity.

I knew that if I went any further into the town this could be the last day of my ride; I'd be putting myself in grave danger of being caught by the police and this might be as far as I'd get. I stood there freezing, wet and miserable to the point of despair. I was almost beyond caring and nearly considered the risk worthwhile. Just then a gate opened in the wall only a few metres away and a young Chinese man walked out onto the street to have a piss. I pulled my hat down and stooped down behind One Eye's back. When he'd finished he dashed back inside out of the rain, leaving me alone again.

I had to leave; if I stayed there any longer someone would see me. I was already taking a chance I couldn't afford. I turned One Eye and we walked behind the back of the town slopping through mud and shit that had washed out from a stinking toilet hut. We crossed a swollen stream and headed away from the town; the rain provided cover and I was sure no one had seen us.

We carried on over low hills and the town disappeared behind us. I walked and walked and walked, my boots sloshing with every laboured step, half-full of water that had run down my soaking jeans. I was so cold and exhausted that I started to worry about hypothermia, but I was terrified that if I stopped moving I wouldn't be able to start again. At six o'clock we came to a small village where a group of women took me in and gave me tea and *tsampa*. Finally I was out of the rain and next to a fire.

I was desperate to spend the night inside; I knew it could be dangerous if I had to sleep in my bag in my soaked clothes. I was already so cold I was shivering, my hands so numb I could hardly move them and I might not survive a long night in the rain. But when I asked the women if I could stay in the village they shook their heads. I stood up to leave and walked out into the yard to collect poor One Eye. He'd had one hell of a day too and I'm sure he didn't want to go any further, but if we couldn't stay we'd have to keep walking until we found somewhere else.

Outside the yard was a young man; one of the women spoke to him and he pointed to another house a short distance away and invited me to his home. I put my hands up to the side of my face to mimic a pillow and asked if he could give me a place to sleep the night.

'Rey, rey.' He nodded.

I nearly burst into tears again, this time with gratitude.

We unloaded One Eye and set him out to graze. The young man helped me lug my sodden gear inside, where I emptied the water out of my boots and spread my stuff out to dry. The little house was cold and most of my stuff still wouldn't be dry by morning. The young man's wife served me tea and flat bread before going out to tend the yaks for the night. They had two children, a new baby and a boy of about two, who alternatively played with a cigarette lighter and a large plastic bag.

I sorted through the saddlebags to find out what was wet and in need of drying. The Dalai Lama's book was soggy around the edges so I took it out and flipped through the pages. The young man went off to help his wife, taking the kids with him and I was left alone to read. It had been a totally miserable day. I'd cursed the skies at every step and at times wished I'd never come to this wretched place. I'd suffered in the rain and couldn't bring myself to see how anything good had come from it.

But again His Holiness had an answer to my doubts. He explained that every aspect of my life, everything that happens to me and everything I do, can be viewed from a multitude of angles, some good, some bad. If I am suffering in some God-awful situation and only look at it from the negative side, then all I'll feel is suffering. All I had done that day was swear and bitch at the weather, get angry with One Eye, feel sorry for myself and sulk like a spoilt child when the Tibetans wouldn't let me stay. Because I focused on my suffering, it only made it worse — I'd suffered because of the suffering.

However, as the great lama went on to say, if I could convince my mind to look at the situation from a different angle I could perhaps see there was another side, a good side, something positive to come from the unpleasantness. If I could do this I would see some hope in what I'd been through, the suffering wouldn't be a hundred percent bad, something good could come from it, and I'd suffer less.

I suddenly realised I might have missed the whole point of the rain. Instead of making things harder it could very well have saved the entire trip. The rain had covered me with a wet coat of protection. Because of it I had been able to pass without being seen through a town that most likely had police; the rain had kept everyone inside, it would have even kept traffic off the road as it was much too muddy to drive. If it had been a fine, sunny day like the one I'd wished for, could I be sure I'd be sitting in this little house warming by the fire, safe from the authorities and still free? I would certainly have been seen by someone, that someone might have told his mate whose brother was a cop and I could very well be in custody, my passport and horse confiscated, my journey to Gang Rinpoche once again in ruins.

Although I still couldn't bring myself to do it, I felt as if I should have rejoiced in the rain, thanked the skies for pouring on me all day, and been glad of the cold, wet conditions. It did make me feel better; avoiding the cops was far more important than keeping dry, and if suffering a day in the rain got me past a potential encounter with the law, then I should try to be grateful, or at least not feel quite so depressed. That night I was given a great meal of two bowls of rice and a bowl of *tukpa*. I was absolutely stuffed and the long, hard day and warm food made me instantly sleepy. I unrolled my damp sleeping bag and slid inside. Before I slept I prayed that tomorrow would be fine — one day of such kind, helpful rain was enough.

My prayers were answered and the next day the skies were clear. I carried on down the river and found myself in open country, vast grassland valleys that quickly gave way to a dry, empty desert. I stopped in the middle of the day at an old campsite with a dry pile of dung and let One Eye off to graze. I started a fire for tea and *tsampa* and once again spread everything out in the sun; it was perfect drying weather, sunny with a good breeze. After a couple of hours we set off again and in the afternoon finally reached the Ta Kuo Tsangpo river below Tegchog Rinpoche mountain. At about five thirty I came to the first house I'd seen since morning. I rode One Eye into the little yard of the single, isolated dwelling and the man of the house came trotting out to greet me. *'Amerika! Amerika!'* he yelled, as if I was an advance party of some liberating army.

'Amerika ma rey,' I told him, I'm not American, *'Ngai pai-yul Nyu Ziyland.'* My home is in New Zealand.

He had no idea what I was talking about but it didn't dampen his enthusiasm. I was welcomed in and served tea, yoghurt with sugar and lumps of cold boiled lamb. Before I carried on I questioned my host about the way ahead and he told me there was a bridge further on, though he couldn't tell me how far. I knew I'd have to find it as the river was too big to cross on horseback and I needed to be on the other side to be able to head west. I hoped I would find it later that day or at least the next.

I set off across the flat, featureless riverplain, which was several kilometres wide; the mountains seemed impossibly distant. As I trudged along, time and distance became deceptive; I thought I'd walked an hour at least since I'd left the house, but when I checked my watch I found it was only ten minutes. With no features to give me a static perspective of space and only my wandering thoughts to mark the moments as they flowed by, I had no idea how much of either had passed.

That night I camped by the river on a grassy flat. It had been a good day compared to the last, both in weather and in my progress on the right track, but as I collected sticks from the riverbank to make a fire Tibet reminded me that in this land there is no such thing as a perfect day. A front of heavy rain drifted in and stayed all night. Another cold, wet night and a soggy morning packing up in the rain. I couldn't find it within myself to see a positive way to view the rain, other than to hope that it would wash away my bad luck.

Thankfully I soon found the bridge; I crossed to the western side of the river and slowly climbed higher onto the plain. With another smudge of negative karma washed away the weather slowly began to improve and I entered a high grassland that would take me towards Tangra Yumco. I carried on around the mountainside on a narrow trail high above the valley floor. Later the sun came out and I stopped to take a break and have another go at trying to get my stuff dry. This was now an almost daily chore that was becoming a bore and took up a lot of travelling time; however, it was essential I took every opportunity to dry my sleeping bag — after a long, hard day on the trail, crawling into a cold, wet bag was very, very unpleasant. I spread the bag and bivvy out on the ground and started making a fire from bits of scrubby roots. Ten minutes later a dark cloud silently crept over the peaks, thunder roared its laughter and the rain started falling. I madly rushed about packing my stuff up before it got wetter than it already was and just managed to get a single cup of tea before the fire was doused by the downpour. *No fuckin' breaks here!*

We plodded on, both worn out and badly in need of another day off. In the late afternoon we topped the last ridge and Tangra Yumco finally came into view. It was beautiful and the blessing of the view erased any grudge I'd been holding against Tibet that day. The massive lake stretched long from south to north and was surrounded by a guardian of mountains topped with snow; the blue of the water was stunning, like looking into the eyes of a child, deep and pure and photogenic beyond my supply of film. For the rest of the day I had to restrain myself from taking her photo as the lake moved from one depth of hue to another every time the wind blew or the skies changed.

In the evening I came to a little rocky valley along a stream flowing out of the mountains. In the bottom was a small stone village and after an hour picking our way through the rocks we reached the river; it was small but very fast and the round boulders made it a tricky crossing. Luckily I'd been spotted by a boy from the village, who came out and led me upstream until we reached a place to cross. I was fast running out of strength and it was taking an enormous effort to keep walking. Once I was on the other side the boy took me to his village, where I met the rest of his family.

'Cha tung!' his father commanded and ushered me inside for butter tea.

I told the family I needed to stock up on supplies and managed to get more *tsampa*, a couple of packets of instant noodles, some bread and a bagful of precious dung. Nightfall was close and I thanked the family and hurried on, looking for a decent campsite. The hillsides above the lake were sprinkled with rocks and huge boulders and I was hoping to find another dry cave. However, daylight was fast running out and the best I could do was a low overhang that would shelter me from the wind but nothing else. It would have to do; it was getting too dark to see and physically I was spent. I couldn't go any further.

I made a little kitchen behind a rock and managed to heat water for noodles before crawling into the bag. It rained on and off during the night, but the morning was glorious and I got up early to make the most of it. By some small miracle it didn't rain the whole day and I spent most of it lazing in the sun reading and watching the lake.

The only person I met that day was an old herdsman who wandered along the shore pushing his flock of sheep in front of him. When he saw my camp he walked up the slope and joined me by the fire. I offered him some tea, which he politely accepted and then seemed happy to sit and watch me.

He was probably from the village I'd stopped at the day before and as I looked at the old man I wondered if he'd lived his whole life by the lake. I wished I had more language to be able to question him in detail. He was almost toothless, his long hair scraggy and matted, a grubby sheepskin *chuba* tied around his waist.

Although we sat by the same fire sharing tea our lives were almost irreconcilably different and I knew I could never really imagine what it would be like to live as he had. His life was measured by seasons, the breeding cycles of sheep and yaks, the time to break in a young horse, to plant barley. He divided his year into times when the rains came and the grass was green, times when it would snow, times when it wouldn't.

For him there were no days of the week, nor even any weeks; in his tiny village it didn't matter what the day was, the yaks had to be milked, the sheep had to be pastured, life happened today as it had the day before. He didn't need to worry about paying bills, career moves, mortgages — the idea of a traffic jam would be completely alien. I doubted he would ever be woken by a ringing phone or a car alarm. I wondered if there was even a word in his language for 'urgent' or 'deadline'. In his world, tasks were started when it was time to start and things were finished when they were finished. Could he even understand the concept of stress?

I showed him my photos, trying to explain where I was from and what it was like there. He took the little world map from my hands for a closer look and held it upside down, not knowing that the world as I knew it went the other way round. The world for him was the lake, the mountains behind it and the river that roared past his house. For him the lake had always been there and it would remain for a thousand lifetimes after his was over. In his village he had everything he needed, all his family probably lived there, his parents and grandparents had been born there, his children and grandchildren would be as well. He had no need to go anywhere else; in fact, he didn't seem to need anything other than what he had. Although I would never wish to be reborn in such a harsh place, I envied him greatly for his lack of grasping.

Soon he left to catch up with his wandering sheep and I didn't see anyone else the whole day. One Eye grazed happily up and down the hillside and apart from him my only other company came from another pair of huge black crows that circled my camp, perching on boulders and screeching to me in their own language. Tibetans believe that crows bring messages from the spirits and I wondered what these two were trying to tell me.

Tangra Yumco had been my next destination after Gyaring Tso where I'd been caught last time, so I felt a great sense of satisfaction to see it at last. By some miracle it didn't rain; Tibet gave me the blessings of the day, but that night she took them back again. I wriggled into the bag after dark and the storm slithered over the mountains not long after. First came the thunder and lightning, an incredible display that lit the entire lake as far as I could see. The thunder announced the arrival of the storm and it rained most of the night, clearing before dawn. I made tea as I waited for my redampened stuff to dry spread on rocks in the sun, then set off around the southern end of the lake.

We travelled on a trail that took us high above the lake on narrow, rocky ridges where it was too steep and stony to ride. I led One Eye, my boot heels nearly worn down to the soles. The lake must have been a place of pilgrimage as there were spots on rocky outcrops draped in prayer flags and clothing lay in heaps, discarded by pilgrims as an act of renunciation. It was easy to see why the lake was viewed as an object of refuge and devotion; the blue of the water was nothing short of inspirational and again I had to resist taking her photo every few minutes.

The ground opened out on the other side and we travelled across the plain, finally turning away from the lake in the evening. We passed through a small valley and came out into another grassland where a village nestled below some hills on the other side of a small round lake. I checked the place out with my binoculars and on one side I could see what I at first thought was a large walled compound. When I looked again I could see villagers walking along the structure — it was a very long *mani* wall.

I reached the village near nightfall and was greeted by everyone. After the solitude of the lake I felt cramped in the small crowd and set off again, but just outside the village a large paddock had been fenced off, the grazing saved for the villagers' stock. The grass was too good for me not to let One Eye spend the night there, so I went back to find everyone milking the community's sheep and asked a young nun if I could spend the night in the paddock.

She spoke to one of the older men and he nodded his approval; later he wandered over to my camp and told me I had to pay five yuan for the grazing. I thought it was fair enough and gave him the money. I let One Eye out to feast on the thick grass, set up my little camp and started a small pile of dung smouldering. I wandered over to the *mani* wall, which stretched for over two hundred metres and was several metres wide, the top covered in thousands of slabs of grey slate etched with prayers. I joined a couple of old villagers and the nun and we circled the wall saying mantras. When I finished I went back into the paddock. The dung was burning now, fanned by the evening breeze and I heated water for tea. Just as I was about to enjoy a peaceful end to the day the whole village turned up to stare at me. One young smart-arse plonked himself down by the fire and proceeded to babble at me unintelligibly, pretending he could speak English.

It had been a long day and I was much too tired. I gestured to the comedian that he should leave and eventually he did, taking the village with him. However, my efforts must have offended him as he stomped over to the *mani* wall, began pulling the carved stones from the top and smashing them on the ground. I was shocked; the verses chiselled into the slabs were sacred, the words of the Buddha himself. He was hurling them to the ground and I wondered if he was mentally unbalanced. A moment later the nun intervened and he was led away by the villagers.

I was up early and we made a good start to the day. We crossed through some low hills and found ourselves on a vast grassland plain; further to the west was an expansive lake, Zhari Namco. The afternoon was very, very hot. I shed as many layers as I could, but the heat was almost unbearable, the bright sun scorching me. One Eye sweated under the thick saddle blankets, there was no breeze, no clouds, no people and no shade or relief from the blazing sun. I couldn't believe Tibet could be so hot; two years ago, when I'd frozen every day, I wouldn't have imagined I'd encounter such conditions.

The next day was cloudy and cooler, but just as dull. Zhari Namco came into view and I rode with her northern shore in the distance for the next day and a half. The immense lake was as blue as Tangra Yumco but not nearly as beautiful without the surrounding mountains; in fact, I soon began to wish I was out of the area. The grassland was barren, in places almost devoid of grass and often so stony I couldn't bring myself to ask poor One Eye to carry me. Walking was far from easy; my legs and feet ached and I was desperate to get my boots fixed. The map marked a town called Maindong not far ahead. People I'd met told me there was a monastery there by the same name and it sounded as if it was a large centre. I knew it might be the only chance for me to find a cobbler, but at the same time I decided it would be much too risky to go into town and not worth the effort just to fix my boots.

Eventually we found a river flowing from the north and I followed it away from the lake and avoided getting too near the town. I was glad to leave the lake behind, although the area was still dry and we wound our way along the river, which soon became a series of brackish ponds between huge sand dunes. In the afternoon I found another village. As I walked towards the little houses I passed a garbage pile; lying among the bones, yak skulls and dead dogs was an old pair of discarded boots. They were about the same size as mine so I pulled out my knife and cut the rubber soles off the heels.

In the village I met a group of people building a new house; they were wonderfully friendly, greeting me like an old friend and again I felt as if we'd known each other for years. They took me into a yak-hair tent and served me a meal of tea, *tsampa* and boiled sheep's guts filled with cooked blood. The bowl of entrails placed before me looked hideous, but I was beyond revulsion and dived in; it was very nutritious and I stuffed myself.

Since the little band seemed to be carpenters I asked them if they had any nails I could use to tack the rubber soles to my boots. One kind grandmother immediately began digging through old tin chests at the back of the tent and came up with a handful of little nails. She wrapped them in a piece of noodle packet and handed them to me. I was very grateful as this meant I could forget about trying to sneak into a town to get them fixed, I could do it myself with a bit of luck. I offered to pay for the nails, but as usual any money was generously refused.

We carried on heading west through the hills. The evening was tough, bleeding me of any energy I had left; again the heat was stifling. We reached another small lake, which turned out to be the home of countless millions of tiny sandflies that haunted me for the rest of the day. One Eye was drearily slow and I could feel he was nearing the end of his journey with me. I was impatient and frustrated, unsettled and unable to calm down.

We stopped next to the lake. I unloaded poor, suffering One Eye and left him to graze for the night; by now I could trust him enough just to use the hobbles and a drag rope and by morning he would only have wandered a short distance. I had a wash in the clear, slightly salty waters of the lake, dipping my cup and pouring cool water over my head; the feeling of relatively clean hands relaxed me enough to enjoy a clear evening and silent sunset.

The next day was mercifully cooler and we carried on into the hills. One Eye had been unable to drink the salt water and gulped his fill at the first fresh water we came to. Later in the morning I stopped at a house and was given tea and *tsampa* by two lovely old ladies. I stocked up on supplies and headed on into another pass. We crossed it during the middle of the day and then spent the rest of the afternoon slowly climbing the valley towards the next one.

It was a long way, too far for me to walk, which forced me to ride the slow and tired One Eye. Clouds built throughout the afternoon and the rain held off until we almost reached the pass, then it struck with a vengeance. In dramatic contrast to the previous day I was soon freezing, wearing everything I had and walking to try to keep warm.

We crossed the pass and started down the other side. In the valley below much of the ground was sodden, making it hard-going. I was hoping to find a pleasant spot to spend the next couple of nights, but the area looked unpromising. Further down I could see villages above the shore of another small lake. There was a road and as I got closer to the valley floor I saw a couple of jeeps and a bus go by. This made me nervous, but I became even more apprehensive when I came out of the valley onto a hilltop above the lake. In the distance to the north I could make out a settlement that looked large enough to be policed.

I was exhausted and desperate to find a decent campsite; if I couldn't I would have to ride the next day and we badly needed a day off. We passed an abandoned campsite where I filled my bag from an old dung pile and pushed on for one more climb into the foothills. One Eye struggled over the rocky ground; I let him stop every so often to catch his breath. Finally we couldn't go on, and found a spot several hundred feet above the lake, next to a small stream with boulders I could shelter behind.

There was a patch of very good grass and as soon as I slipped the saddle off One Eye he dropped to his knees and rolled over, rubbing his tired back. I started a fire and while I waited for the water to boil I collected rocks to build a little wall as shelter, from both the wind and unwelcome eyes. I was high above the road, its course just a faint brown pencil line across the green of the plain. There was no way anyone could see me, but I still felt nervous.

It rained most of the night and was still falling in the morning. I lay in the bag until nearly ten o'clock waiting for it to stop; my legs, back and hips ached from sleeping on the hard, cold ground. When the rain finally eased I managed to start the fire; thankfully before long the clouds began to break and the skies slowly cleared.

During the day I went through my usual round of chores, drying out all my damp gear, making repairs to my tack, having a decent wash and a shave in the freezing stream, adding in the extra task of fixing my boots. I pulled them off and stuffed a long thin slab of rock inside to act as an anvil, then used another stone as a hammer and carefully nailed the rubber heels to my worn-out boots. After a few bruised fingertips and a few choice swear words I decided I'd done a pretty good job; they would last a while and I still had enough tacks for another go later.

In the afternoon I was visited by a young shepherdess, who brought her sheep onto the mountainside from the village below. When she realised I wasn't Tibetan she watched suspiciously from a distance. I waved, hoping to show I was friendly, worried that if someone thought I was a danger or a threat they would report me to the authorities.

Eventually she wandered over and stood a few metres from my fireplace. *'Dalai Lama bar';* she asked for a Dalai Lama photo and held out her hand.

'Mindu,' I told her, I don't have any. She asked again.

'Gawn da, Dalai Lama bar mindu!' I'm sorry, I don't have any. I wished I did have one, knowing how much joy the simple gift would bring her, but she went on her way to catch up with the sheep.

I continued making tea, mixing balls of *tsampa* and sorting out my stuff.

All day I had been meaning to take out the Dalai Lama's book, but every time I would think, 'I'll just do this, and then I'll do some reading.' But as soon as I'd done whatever it was I'd find something else, *OK, I'll do that, and then I'll start reading.* I stitched on a loose button, made some more tea, added a few rocks to the shelter wall, marked my route on the map, had another cup of tea, checked on One Eye, copied something from my phrase book, cleaned out my cooking pot, turned the damp saddle blankets over in the sun, cut my fingernails, then had more tea. There never seemed to be a time when I'd done everything I had to do so that I could just sit quietly and read. Even in the middle of nowhere there was always something to distract me.

It was worse at home. Every evening I'd have good, but weak, intentions to do some study, read from one of the dharma books, say prayers or mantras, or do a bit of meditation, but again it came back to: 'I'll just do the dishes, then I'll do some mantras.' But then I'd remember I had a shirt I needed to iron, an email to send, the bathroom needed a clean, the rubbish needed to be taken out and suddenly the evening was gone. I'll do extra prayers tomorrow when I've got more time. But tomorrow had just as many distractions as today.

This putting off my practice was one of the traps I always fell into; every teacher and book on Buddhism warns of it. I put off and put off, delay and procrastinate, waiting for the time when I've finished everything else. But if I don't stop and do the practice now I never will, if I don't make the time I will never have a day when I have nothing to do but study the dharma, and as I dawdle through the years I get closer to the end of my life with every minute that passes. If I leave those books on the shelf my lifespan will run out without me having learnt a thing and then it will be too late.

Since I'd set out from Yangbajian I'd tried to bring my mind around time and again to think about the idea of 'dying once'. But so often the concept I'd felt keenly on the first leg of this ride seemed lost and unreal. I tried to think about it when I was riding through long days in empty valleys when I should have had nothing else to think about, but even there my mind was full of distractions. I'd be thinking about where I was going to live when I got back to New Zealand, the first thing I was going to eat, a new improvement to my riding gear, how to say some new phrase in Tibetan, that girl I met at a party just before I left, I wonder if she'll still be around when I get back? I *never* had nothing else to think about. I'd fill my mind with meaningless thoughts and my life with pointless activities instead of doing something that would really be of benefit.

Come on, Ian, get your shit together, open that book and start reading! There was still a good bed of hot embers in my dung fire; I shouldn't let them go to waste. *OK, I'll make another mug of tea, then I'll sit on that rock over there and read!* Two crows picking through the grass cawed out their mocking laughter.

The next morning we climbed down out of the hills and onto the plain by the lake, heading west towards the next lake on my map, Taro Tso. There were fewer people in the area, but whenever I found a house or a camp I'd ask about horses. Although there seemed to be plenty of good mounts, no one wanted to sell them. We camped that night next to a small river swollen by the rain into a rushing torrent of chocolate milk. The morning was clear and I led One Eye over to be loaded up; as usual he stood quietly as I slipped the saddle onto his back and tied the saddlebags into place. Suddenly I saw him stagger and stumble; he kept his feet, however, and stood quietly. I turned to pick up my shoulder bag and he did it again. I was very worried, I thought he was going to go the same way as Whitey, suddenly becoming sick or exhausted, leaving me stuck with no transport. I let him stand and watched him — his eyes closed, his head nodded, once, twice, then again, his legs wobbled and he stumbled before steadying himself. He was falling asleep on his feet. At least he didn't seem to be sick, but it wasn't a good sign.

We walked down into the bottom of the valley where we found the occasional small village strung along what was to turn out to be quite a busy road. I stopped at one and was taken in for tea by a young man and his mother. I asked him if he could sell me a horse and he went into great discussion with his mother about horses, prices and if he should sell me one. He told me he had a horse he'd sell for four thousand yuan. I said I'd be happy to pay that much providing it was a good horse. He still wasn't sure and sat there trying to decide whether he wanted to sell me a horse or not. I kept telling him I'd give him One Eye, who was a good horse and would be fine after a couple of weeks grazing and rest, that I'd give him the money he asked for and I'd be on my way. Eventually he seemed to come to a decision and took a rope from the rafters and set out into the valley with another young lad. While he was away I unpacked my wet sleeping bag and bivvy and draped them over the wall of the yard to dry. The family had a little shop in a shed in the corner of the yard and I bought a couple of packets of instant noodles and a small lump of mutton, then waited with the old woman and a couple of kids as One Eye dozed in the sun.

Suddenly the old woman said something and pointed out into the valley; I looked up to see her son returning, but without a horse. '*Ta kaba duk?*' I asked, where's the horse? He just shrugged and said, '*Ta tsong ma rey.*' He'd changed his mind and the deal was off. I packed up my damp bags, thanked him for wasting my time and set off again.

I asked anyone I met who might possibly have a horse to sell, but without any luck. I hated the feeling of helplessness and reliance on other people; I needed someone to sell me a good horse for a reasonable price and I was very uncomfortable with the feeling of things being out of my control.

My legs were stiff and cramped in the stirrups, One Eye couldn't get any slower or he'd stop so I climbed down and walked him. All of a sudden I heard the hum of an engine. I looked back and saw a white jeep belting along ahead of a trail of thick dust. My heart leapt but I kept walking until it got closer and did my usual act, pulling my hat down and bending down behind One Eye to pretend I was adjusting the saddle. I didn't look up but listened to the growl of the motor, expecting it to pass.

It didn't. To my horror it stopped about thirty metres from where I stood. I watched carefully from under the brim of my hat as a couple of Chinese men got out and stretched their legs while the Tibetan driver filled a plastic container with water from a stream beside the road. I heard the sound of another engine and looked down the road to see a second jeep approaching; it stopped too, then another arrived, and another until there were five white jeeps parked in front of me.

There were two or three Chinese men in each jeep, along with their Tibetan drivers. My heart was pounding so hard I thought I was going to arrest and my knees were shaking. I kept up my act but I couldn't stand there for ever without attracting attention. As I expected, one of the Chinese men started to walk towards me. There was nothing I could do; if they were police the trip would be over. I could almost feel the journey I had constructed over the last six weeks crumble and fall apart. My instinct was to jump on One Eye's back and gallop off, but One Eye wasn't up to galloping anywhere and I knew that would only make me look very suspicious and could make things worse. When the man reached me he realised I wasn't Tibetan.

'Hey!' He turned and yelled to his companions that he'd found a Westerner out in the middle of nowhere. The whole group came running down from the road to see me. I was sunk. I would just have to try to bluff my way through. I remembered the permit; this might be the time to use it, but I was still reluctant to put my head on the chopping block. One of the men could speak English and told me his party was from somewhere in mainland China and were on their way to Ali in the far west of Tibet, close to Pakistan. He was wearing a black cap emblazoned with white Chinese figures, very similar to ones I had seen the police wearing last time I'd been caught.

'Where are you going?' he asked.

'I'm going to Lunggar.' Lunggar was on the southern shore of Taro Tso. I had no intention of going anywhere near it but I didn't want to tell him I was going to Gang Rinpoche. I was dying to ask if he was a policeman and put myself out of my misery, but I was too afraid and I didn't want to do anything to arouse his suspicions. We chatted about my journey, where I'd come from by horse and so on and I smiled and tried to be as relaxed as I could.

'Are you camping?' I asked, wanting to know if they'd stay in towns or on their own in the countryside.

'What?' He didn't understand.

'Do you sleep in tents?'

'Oh no, tonight we will stay in a hotel.' This meant they must be spending time in towns, towns with police; if they weren't policemen themselves, they would be likely to meet some and they might report me or mention they'd seen me. In these remote regions it was possible they had to report to the local authorities themselves. I could imagine the conversation: 'Hey, you'll never guess what we saw this afternoon!'

I was starting to lose my nerve and wished they'd get back in their jeeps and fuck off. Then the little Chinese man who had first found me pointed to One Eye, gesturing that he wanted to get on his back. 'He wants to get on your horse,' the other man told me.

'I'm sorry, my horse is very tired and sick,' I explained. He translated this to his companion, who became upset and booted One Eye in the rump. My horse hardly seemed to notice but I felt like whipping out my long knife and gutting the bastard. I was tense and stressed, close to the edge and it wasn't going to take much to push me over. 'Don't kick my fuckin' horse, you little shit!' I raised my heavy boot to kick him back.

'No, no!' The other man intervened, sending his friend back to the jeeps. 'I'm sorry,' he explained, 'he doesn't know about horses.'

'It's all right,' I replied, remembering I was supposed to be acting happy and calm.

'Can I take your photo please?' he asked.

'Sure!' And he sent someone back to his jeep to fetch his camera.

'Smile!'

'I'm trying,' I muttered as I grimaced into the lens. *Well, at least it might make a good wanted poster.*

Someone started tooting the horn of one of the jeeps. *'Tso ba! Tso ba!'* The driver called in Chinese, let's go!

'I'm sorry, we have to go,' the man said.

'Oh, that's OK, in fact I couldn't think of anything better!'

'What?'

'Nothing, have a good trip, good luck!'

'Oh, thank you, good luck for you too!' And the group climbed back into their jeeps, waved goodbye and roared off, leaving me standing in their dust, still shaking.

We carried on up the road in the same direction. Although the jeeps were out of sight I was anything but relaxed. The valley had narrowed, with high rocky peaks on every side; there was no other way to go and nowhere to hide. If the police in Lunggar came out to find me they wouldn't have a very hard job. One Eye wasn't helping either; I kept urging him on, wanting to find a way out of the valley where I could get away from the road and hide. I was cursing the young man I'd met that morning for not selling me his horse, at least with a fresh mount I'd have a better chance of escaping.

I kept expecting to see a police jeep come flying over the hill, but we finally made it to the top of the valley. There wasn't really a pass, the valley just flowed into the next one, which opened out into another sweeping grassland. There were some small mountains in the far distance on the other side and past them I calculated I would find Taro Tso. I was still desperate to get away from the road; in fact, I wanted to get out of the area altogether — there were too many towns, too many roads and too much traffic. I was standing in the middle of the two valleys when I looked up into the steep hills above me; to the north I could see another smaller valley that appeared to lead to a pass. If I took that I could leave the road behind, which would make it much more difficult for anyone trying to find me. A tough climb into the hills wasn't what either One Eye or myself needed, but I turned my tired horse round and we set off. 'Come on, boy, I need your help on this one.'

It was a hot and rocky climb on foot but we managed it well and within a couple of hours were standing in the pass. There was no one camped in this part of the valley, no road and I was sure no one had seen us come this way. We carried on around the tops of the hills and over another ridge into a small valley. I could see part of Taro Tso in the distance, so at least I knew where I was and I finally calmed down, secure in the knowledge that no one knew I was there and that the police would need a helicopter if they wanted to find me.

We camped high in the valley. I scavenged dung from an old pile and made some relaxing tea as I watched One Eye graze. I boiled some more water and made a stew of *tsampa* in which I mixed salt and some precious pepper I'd brought with me, adding chopped-up lumps of the mutton I'd bought that morning. It was only half-cooked but under the conditions and with what was available, I thought it was a pretty fair meal. I felt pleased with myself and the way the day had turned out; the encounter with the Chinese had put me on edge and I realised again how keen I was to make it to the mountain. The promise I'd made to Khensur Thabkye Rinpoche to deliver his ashes was now even more of a motivation and I felt I would do whatever it took to avoid being caught and keep my word.

I got up well before daylight; again One Eye was nodding off on his feet as I loaded up, but we set off early across a high grassland above my camp. As we travelled across the expanse we met a small group of wild *khang*, one male and his little harem of two mares. The usually elusive animals were in full view — the stallion seemed to see One Eye as a threat and kept shadowing us from a distance, stamping his feet and snorting warnings.

On the edge of the grassland we started down into another tremendous valley. I couldn't see it from where I was, but further down to the west was another lake, Chabyer Caka. We would reach the lake in a day or two and beyond it were some serious mountains. I doubted One Eye would make it through and I was becoming desperate to replace him.

The grassland was dry and sparsely populated and I hardly saw anyone all day. While I asked everyone I met if they could sell me another horse, when evening rolled in I was still with poor old One Eye. He'd been so slow it had nearly driven me insane. I wasn't making the progress I needed, I still worried about the cops, but what concerned me most was that One Eye could expire out here and leave me trapped.

That night we camped among the rocks on an outcrop like an island on a sea of grass. There was no water so I made a single cup of tea from the water in my bottle. Further on to the west I could just make out a scattering of a few houses. I had no idea if they were occupied but that night as I said my prayers I added a line in the hope that I'd be blessed with a new horse the next day. I prayed directly to Khensur Thabkye Rinpoche. 'Oh Rinpoche, please guide me to find another horse tomorrow.'

Amazingly it didn't rain the whole night and I slept through for the first time in weeks, not waking up until nearly nine o'clock. I packed up and loaded my weary One Eye and set off towards the distant houses. 'Come on, boy, hopefully this will be your last day.'

We arrived to find the people had moved out of their homes. In summer they pack up their belongings, lock the door and shift into yak-hair tents. I wondered why they did this, as the houses were much more comfortable and even in summer there could be bitterly cold days. I guessed that after a long, hard winter with an extended family cramped into one or two small rooms they were happy to have more breathing space and freedom to move.

In front of one I met a nomad carding wool. He called into the tent and his wife brought me a kettle of butter tea and a small sack of *tsampa*. Once again as I ate and drank I told the man I was in need of another horse. He seemed interested and we talked about horses and prices; by this stage I would have paid any amount for anything I could get and as the discussion became more detailed I began to feel hopeful.

'*Ta yawrey?*' I finally asked, do you have a horse?

'*Ta mindu.*' He shook his head.

I was about to set off when the man offered to put shoes on One Eye's front feet for thirty yuan. I accepted, not knowing how long I was going to have to continue with him and thinking it might help him get through another day or two. The shoes were rough wrought iron and held on with only four big nails. Although One Eye moved all over the place and played up while the nomad did the work I thought he did a pretty good job and we set off again. Through the afternoon I was glad I had accepted, as most of the way was over very stony ground.

I kept asking everyone I found, but without hope of success. I felt as if I was going to be stuck with my unfortunate One Eye until he dropped dead, which in the state he was in, might not be too far away. At about six o'clock we came to a pair of houses on a hillside, the lake now in view further to the west. I was taken in for tea and met a portly middle-aged Tibetan man who gave me tea and the dry crust off pots of boiled milk. I could hardly bring myself to tell him I needed to buy another horse, dreading the disappointment that always seemed to follow. However, the man seemed to recognise my gloom and took it upon himself to help me.

He spoke for several minutes to a woman in the house then told me her husband had a horse to sell. The woman's home was another kilometre further on, so after tea the three of us set off together. On the way the man asked me if I had any Dalai Lama pictures. I told him I was sorry I didn't have one to give him and he nodded sadly. I explained how if the Chinese caught me with pictures of his beloved leader I'd be arrested. The man understood and as a consolation I told him that as far as I knew His Holiness was well and happy in India.

When we arrived I met the woman's husband and she went off to tend their sheep. My new friend explained about my need for a horse; the man nodded and said he'd sell me one for five thousand yuan. This was a lot, but I said I'd be happy to pay that for a good horse, which of course he insisted his horse was. I felt an instant liking for the two men; although what would pass between me and the owner of the horse was a business transaction, I could feel both men wanted to help me. I'd told them I was going to Gang Rinpoche, that I'd ridden from near Lhasa and both seemed to respect that and were keen to see me safely on my way.

Their only reservation was what I would do with the horse after I'd completed the journey; to this I promised I would give whatever horse carried me that far to a monastery in the area and I wouldn't let it fall into Chinese hands. This reassured them. It was getting late and I was told the man would send his son out onto the plain in the morning to get the horse. I decided to camp on the hillside above their home by a tiny stream and said I'd come back the next day to get the horse.

I led One Eye up the hill, unloaded and set up camp. 'Well boy, this might really be the end of it for you this time.' He just turned round, rolled in the dirt and started grazing. I doubted he would be unhappy to be left here. I felt very hopeful; the men had seemed definite. I started a fire and was making tea when I looked down the hill to see the Tibetan and his two sons heading towards my camp, leading a white horse. I wouldn't even need to wait until morning.

I grabbed my binoculars to see what condition the horse was in, dreading it would be an elderly plodder and I'd find myself no better off. However, even from a distance I could see he was a reasonable mount. The horse was a white gelding, his coat was in excellent form and he was one of the fattest horses I'd seen in Tibet. I guessed he'd been grazing on the plain for several months and while that might mean he wasn't very fit, I knew he could last a considerable time, possibly even get me to the mountain. Before making a final decision I slipped onto his back and rode him around my campsite; he was well behaved and walked without much encouragement. He was sold!

Five thousand was probably too much but I didn't mind, joking with the nomad as I handed over the money, pretending I had misunderstood and the price was five hundred, not five thousand. He asked me what I'd do with One Eye, I told him he was part of the deal and I was giving the horse to him. He shrugged as if he didn't really want my poor old horse and when they left they didn't bother taking him with them, just leaving him on the hillside. One Eye certainly wasn't concerned and I was sure he wouldn't argue with being set free. The nomad invited me to visit his home the next morning for something to eat before I continued. I said I would and set the new horse out to graze in the last moments of daylight.

I ran my hands over his smooth, strong back and breathed a deep sigh of relief. I'd be on my way in the morning on a good fresh horse. I tried to think of a name for my new travelling companion, then remembered how I'd prayed to my dead lama the night before to guide me to a new horse. My prayer had been answered, so I named him 'Monlam', which means 'prayer' in Tibetan. The horse was a blessing and in the weeks to follow he would come to embody the good qualities of all my previous horses. I would come to love him as a dear friend.

Chapter Eleven

It was a beautiful clear morning. I loaded up Monlam and walked him down to the house, where the family served me tea, *tsampa* and lumps of boiled mutton before I set off. Monlam went well, with a quick walk, and he was well behaved. Closer to the lake the land was even more barren than in the valley; sometimes we travelled for kilometres over ground bare of any vegetation, just a fine grey gravel.

Chabyer Caka was a salt lake and from the top of a ridge I could see plants and factories for farming and processing mineral salt around its lower shores. In the afternoon we crossed a wide saltpan in one corner of the lake. The landscape was dull and inhospitable and I was happy when we turned away from the lake and headed into a pass. I led Monlam into the hills; he didn't lead well and it was hard work dragging him up the trail.

He was mortally afraid of mud; perhaps he'd had a bad experience on the plain, where mud holes and bogs would have been common. He refused to walk across patches of dry mud even though they were as hard as cement. He wouldn't budge and we'd have to go around them. He'd even balk at tiny dry streambeds only a couple of feet wide and I worried what was going to happen when we had to cross a river.

We crossed the pass and I was surprised to find myself at the western end of Taro Tso; I thought we would have already passed it, but there we were. It was a beautiful lake, her waters fresh and clean. We walked down into a pretty little bay on the shores and then over a ridge, where I found the first house I'd seen all day. The people appeared to be poor but that didn't affect their hospitality; I was taken inside, where I met an ancient grandmother sitting on the floor by the fire. 'Tashidelik momo,' I greeted her as grandmother and she took my hand and touched it to her forehead.

Her son served me tea and I asked if I could buy some noodles; they didn't have any but instead gave me some rice. The man was so generous he kept trying to fill my bag to the brim but I had to insist on only taking enough for a couple of meals, any more would be too much to carry. He kept going into his storeroom and coming back with whatever they had to eat and offering it to me. I ended up topping up my *tsampa* and sugar bag and leaving with a bag of popped barley.

After a while I rode back over the ridge into the little bay. Although my horse was fresh I'd been on the trail for five days and needed to take a break. At the other end of the bay I could see what looked like an overhang at the base of a rocky cliff, which I hoped would give me some shelter. I walked across the bay gathering sticks of dry scrub for my fire as I went. When I reached my 'overhang' I was delighted to find it was a deep cave, set in the cliff face a few feet above the ground — a long, round hole high enough to sit up in and several metres deep. I crawled inside to check it wasn't inhabited by bats or badgers or anything else that might be dangerous. It was dusty, the floor littered with old feathers, but I decided it would do me as a home for a couple of nights. I unloaded Monlam and ferried all my gear into the cave before staking him out for the night. There wasn't much grass, but I figured it wouldn't do him any harm considering the shape he was in.

I made tea and *tsampa* and munched on the popped barley as the skies darkened. It was warm in the cave and I felt comfortable and safe. I slept well until about two in the morning, when I woke to the sound of rocks rattling. At first I thought it was Monlam dragging his rope over the stones, but when I crawled to the entrance and shone my torch outside he was standing perfectly still. I crawled back inside and went back to bed.

Half an hour later I was woken again; this time I realised the sound was coming from inside the cave. I lay curled up in my bag with the torch in my hand as I ran through a list of unpleasant creatures that might be living there: snakes, rats, weasels or some other creepy-crawly. There was another scuttling under the stones by the door. I shone my torch just in time to see a blurry brown flash vanish into a hole. I thought it must have been a rat, but when I sat still with the light dimly shining in the direction of the hole a little, fat, short-tailed mouse popped out.

I watched him scuttle along the side of the wall until he got to my saddlebags, where he started nibbling on the canvas. I chased him off but took a handful of the popped barley and placed it on a flat stone near my little roommate's hole. By morning it was all gone and I decided the cave was big enough for both of us and besides, he was there first.

I woke up at eight the next morning. The skies were clear and I could see Monlam grazing happily. I looked forward to my day off by the lake. I thought about getting up but before I could move I saw a jeep coming around the side of the lake, heading straight towards the cave. There was a dirt track around the lake but I hadn't expected to see anything on it. I lay back down and listened to the noise of the motor grow, barely audible above the thump of my heart. I prayed they would just think I was a passing Tibetan who had chosen to overnight in the cave. The noise grew louder but thankfully faded as they continued by without stopping. I was relieved, but the encounter put me on edge for the rest of the day and I found it hard to relax.

I let Monlam off to graze and got the fire going for tea. A couple of crows screeched from the cliff top above me as I spread my maps out and worked out I had ridden a thousand kilometres in the forty-five days since I'd set out from Yangbajian. I traced the black line across Tibet that marked my route and looked to the left of the paper, to the west of the plateau. I suddenly realised I'd come over three-quarters of the way. Using a small piece of paper to measure the twenty-five or thirty kilometres I averaged a day, I calculated that if I kept up the same pace I could arrive at Kailas in another two weeks.

I could scarcely believe it and rechecked my estimates three times. But I was right; for the first time, just for a few minutes, I allowed myself to concede I might just possibly, perhaps, maybe, conceivably make it. And then I checked myself. *It's a bloody long way yet, don't get cocky, don't think it's going to be easy, don't think you're already there, and don't get complacent!*

I didn't think there was any chance of me letting my guard down; in fact, I felt more cautious and paranoid than ever. I was terrified of being caught and expelled before reaching Kailas and now that I was getting closer the feelings were keener. I was determined to do anything I had to do to avoid capture; if I could travel the rest of the way to the mountain without seeing another soul I'd be more than happy.

But I knew that was impossible. As it was I was camped next to a road; all day I scanned the other end of the lake with my binoculars, looking for another jeep. Two trucks passed and both times I hid in the cave, praying they wouldn't stop. They didn't, but I couldn't relax the whole day. I was surprised that even though the region was scarcely populated, I would still meet people every day and see vehicles on the roads, and I knew I would have to pass settlements ahead. At any moment I could meet the wrong people and be caught.

From then on I recited a mantra to the deity Mahakala for protection almost constantly, thousands of times a day as I rode or walked. I was still sceptical as to whether mumbling a prayer would have any positive effect, but at least I was doing something, and it couldn't do any harm. And who knows, perhaps the wrathful, six-armed, monstrous deity would help me, scaring away the police and guiding me along the safest route.

I finally calmed down when it got dark. I'd spent the whole day by the fire drinking tea and cooking rice, it had been a beautiful day and Monlam had hardly moved. I crawled back into the cave and left some more of the popped barley on a flat stone for the mouse. I lit a candle, which filled the dusty little cave with a warm, cosy glow. I didn't even have to worry if it rained. In my dry sleeping bag I wrote my diary and then before I lay down to sleep I looked at the photo of my lama. Khensur Thabkye Rinpoche smiled back at me from wherever he had gone to. 'Help me, Rinpoche,' I said. 'Help me get through this last bit to the mountain, then I can leave your ashes to rest and go home.'

The next morning I was in the saddle by nine. I felt much more relaxed as soon as I started riding, thinking that if someone turned up now I could at least try to escape on Monlam. He went well and we stopped at the same little house I'd visited on the way to the lake a couple of days before. Again I was welcomed in and served tea and *tsampa*. The man's ancient mother was still in the same place on the floor by the fire.

'Khyerang-la amala lo katsay yawrey?' I asked the man how old his mother was.

'Gyay-chu gya dun.' He told me she was eighty-seven.

I wondered if she had lived all her life by Taro Tso, coming to know the lake like one of her own children, feeling its mood change and watching her own life change with it. She must have already been adult when the Chinese invaded; she would have heard of the fall of Lhasa and the flight of the Dalai Lama, probably offered tea and *tsampa* to refugees fleeing to the border. Perhaps they had begged her family to join them, having seen the atrocities dealt out by the invaders to those who refused to renounce their faith and their leaders. But she had chosen to stay and I wondered what her life had been like.

I carried on and Monlam came to his first river with me. I dreaded the battle we might have trying to get across, given his fear of mud; however, to my pleasant surprise he waded straight in and carried me to the other bank. We turned away from the lake and headed into the hills, again following a well-worn road that made me uncomfortable, but the only jeep I saw was a rusting body on bricks in the middle of nowhere.

We crossed valleys and grassy ridges as we steadily climbed higher towards the pass. For part of the afternoon we travelled on what appeared to be a very old road. It must have pre-dated wheeled vehicles, as I could see no sign that trucks or jeeps had ever been on it. Often it would just vanish into the ground, but I'd carry on and stumble across it later. The stones had been moved and the ground levelled to make a fairly good path. I wondered who had made it, why, and where it led. I tried to keep on it, but by the end of the day we'd lost it completely.

By evening we were well up the valley and I knew we couldn't be too far from the pass. However, it was too late to consider trying to cross that day so I stopped next to an old campsite. I started gathering dung but gave up as it was too wet. I was dying for some hot tea, some simple comfort at the end of a hard day, but there was no chance and before long the weather closed in, making lack of tea the least of my worries.

Saturated clouds blew up the valley, cutting me off into my own miserable, wet little hell. I hurried to set up camp before the rain burst and tried to take shelter under my piece of canvas groundsheet behind the crumbling wall of an old cattle yard. I sat there as the rain and hail pelted me, my fingers wet and frozen, the hail stinging when it struck them. After several minutes I gave up; the rain had set in for the night. I ran back to my bivvy bag and tried to set up my bed, stash the saddlebags inside, take off my boots and coat, and get into my sleeping bag before everything got too wet.

It was hopeless; within moments everything was soaked in the frigid downpour. I screamed out curse after curse at the sky, at the rain, at the ground, at myself for ever coming to this damn place. The zip on the bivvy got stuck and I struggled for several minutes to get the thing closed, all the time getting wetter. The sleeping bag was no easier to close and then I had to contend with the heavy wet hood of the bag sticking to my face. I wished I was back in my little, warm, dry cave with the friendly mouse. Gang Rinpoche may have only been a couple of weeks away, but there was no way Tibet was going to let me off with an easy ride. I lay in my wet bivvy inside my wet sleeping bag in my wet clothes, hungry, cold, sleepless and despairing, until a dismal dawn lightened the skies just enough for me to get up.

I had hoped the rain would have passed by morning and although it had mostly stopped the valley still dripped under a blanket of dense cloud. I slowly loaded up with freezing fingers, stuffing the wet bags into their covers and throwing the soggy blankets onto a shivering Monlam; with his head down and mane sodden he looked as dejected and miserable as I felt.

At nine we set off up the valley. I walked to try to get my blood moving and some warmth into my body, but it wasn't long before I felt my energy running out like the uncoiling spring of a wind-up toy, and I had to ride. A couple of hours later I felt we were nearing the top of the pass that would lead us to the other side. I could only feel this, because I couldn't see a thing as cloud completely obscured the way.

We must have reached the top; the ground levelled out but it was covered in several centimetres of fresh snow and the sod underneath was soft and boggy. I looked back down the valley the way we'd come and saw another front of falling snow closing in. I desperately scanned the land around me with my binoculars, trying to find which way I should head, but it was hopeless. In the cold and damp they fogged up and the cloud was so thick I couldn't see more than fifty metres. The snow hit, making conditions even worse; I was getting colder and started feeling weak, the altitude was like a cloak of lead which seemed to be trying to pull me into the ground. This was not a pleasant place to be. I started to feel afraid.

I couldn't ride any more. Monlam was struggling on the soft ground and I was too cold to sit still in the saddle. I climbed off his back, took the reins over his head and started walking towards what I hoped was the pass. After half an hour's slog I conceded we were going the wrong way, we were getting higher instead of lower and I retraced my steps back to the middle of the pass.

I stood in the falling snow and looked around, trying to guess which way I should go. Apart from the way I'd come any direction could lead me over the pass to the safety of the valley on the other side, but I could just as easily head straight into the mountains. I was getting close to being colder than I should be and I knew I would only have one more chance to find the way out. If I got it wrong again I would have to give up and ride back down. I checked the compass to get coordinates to find my way back, terrified I'd become disoriented with the falling snow and lack of visibility.

I was taking a great risk by pushing on; sensibility told me I should head back now but I decided to try again. I turned and looked at Monlam; he seemed smaller than when I'd bought him, as if he was being dwarfed by the enormity of the situation. He was my last lifeline; if I couldn't walk any further I would put my life in his hands, or rather on his back, and ask him to carry me out. 'OK boy, come on, little mate, we can do it!'

I took one last look around, hoping to see a break in the clouds and a sign of which way to go, but again there were no clues. Before we took the next step towards an uncertain outcome I prayed to Khensur Thabkye Rinpoche. 'Oh Rinpoche, please show us the right way to go, please guide us out of the mountains, please bestow your blessings on our bodies and minds.'

We trudged through the snow, the flurries getting heavier. For thirty minutes we struggled across the difficult ground, filled with doubt, fear and apprehension. Were we heading in the right direction or walking towards disaster? 'Oh Rinpoche, please help us, get us the hell out of this bloody place.' My prayers were becoming less eloquent and more desperate.

Suddenly I noticed there had been a change. Were we walking down? I tried to keep calm; it could just be a dip in the ground, but as I walked on the slope became steeper, then we met the headwaters of a tiny stream. We were heading down, we'd done it, we'd crossed the pass. *'Tujachay Rinpoche! Tujachay! Tujachay!'* I wept with gratitude and relief and cried out my thanks to the sky.

As we got lower the valley came into view, I could see several yak-hair tents where I knew I could get some shelter. However, the snow got heavier and the wind blew right through me; soon the snow wasn't falling, it was blowing horizontal to the ground.

I led Monlam to the nearest tent and as we approached a barking dog brought an old man to the door. He stuck his head through the opening and squinted at me through the snow. I was afraid I'd be turned away, but as I got closer he hobbled out using two sticks. We tied Monlam to a rock and I dragged my cold wet self inside next to the fire; the old man's wife was roasting *tsampa* and the fire was blazing.

'*Cha tung,*' the old nomad said, offering me tea.

I reached inside my coat and pulled out my tea bowl. I tried to hand it to the old woman but it slipped through my fingers and fell on the floor, my hands too numb to hold it. My host raked some hot embers onto the dirt floor and I held my hands over them until the circulation returned. It continued to snow heavily; it was pointless to try to carry on until it stopped and I spent a couple of hours with the old couple and their little granddaughter. I tacked another layer of rubber to the heels of my boots as my last repairs were starting to crumble and had quite an interesting conversation with the man. He was crippled, I guessed since birth, which must have meant he'd had a difficult life. I doubted he would have been able to ride a horse or climb into the mountains to herd his stock. And perhaps because of his limitations in his nomadic world he seemed to have taken a much greater interest in what was happening on the rest of the planet; he was the only nomad I met with any idea of international events.

He had a transistor radio to listen to news broadcast from Lhasa or China and seemed very concerned about the situation in Palestine. From what I could gather, things must be getting worse and he wanted to know who was fighting who, and why? At first he wanted to know if America was fighting against the Palestinians; I told him America was fighting everyone. Then he was very concerned as to whether my country was involved in the conflict and whose side we were on. I told him New Zealand wasn't fighting anyone. Perhaps he saw their struggle as being similar to that of Tibet, the wish for a free and independent homeland, feeling that human suffering of this kind was universal.

Finally the snow stopped enough for me to carry on. I said goodbye to my worldly friend and carried on down the valley. Before long the valley narrowed and became too rocky to ride. I spent the rest of the day slogging it out on foot, trying to pick my way through the rocks and scrub. It was exhausting after the ordeal we'd been through that morning, but as the day turned to evening the weather slowly started to clear and the sun came out long enough to get my sleeping bag semi-dry.

I had hoped to reach the next lake, Rinqin Tso, but the difficult ground made the going slow and we stopped at six thirty. There was no one camped in this part of the valley, probably because most of the ground was covered in rock or scrub and there was little grazing. I found one good patch of thick grass for Monlam; he'd gone well and had given me no trouble in the pass and I was very grateful.

That evening as I sat by a smouldering fire of damp scrub trying to make tea, I caught the sound of a low distant hum. I'd been hearing this faint noise for the past few weeks on quiet, still evenings and at first I'd jump inside, thinking it was the far-off sound of a jeep. Of course it wasn't, there was no road where I was camped. Then I'd think it was the wind — it wasn't, it was perfectly still. Perhaps it was the sound of the river flowing? A buzzing insect? But there were none. When I concentrated I could hear it clearly, a sound with no discernible source and coming from no particular direction, a sound that was everywhere. It was the sound of Tibet. She seems to have her own tune, as if the very ground or air hums with energy or life.

The next morning the skies were clear, though the valley was frosty until the sun rose and my sleeping bag inside the bivvy was covered in a sheet of thin ice. We carried on down the valley, still on foot, crossed a low ridge and found Rinqin Tso. The lake and the entire surrounding plains were empty. I spent several minutes scanning the landscape with my binoculars, but couldn't find any sign of anyone and for the rest of the day I didn't meet a soul.

We rode around the southern side of the lake, the sun high and hot across the near-desert terrain. Later in the afternoon we crossed an open plain of sand and mud. Monlam still refused to cross patches of dried mud, no matter how much I encouraged him. He refused to set one foot on the sand, and eventually I had to get off and lead him across. But still he was afraid and leapt over the narrow strip without having to step on it. I led him back and forth, trying to show him it was safe. Then I found a wide patch of cement-hard dry mud. I led him into the centre — again he was extremely nervous, snorting and sniffing the ground. We stopped in the middle and stood there for a while until he calmed down, then I led him round in circles, trying to prove he was completely safe.

Before long we both calmed down enough to continue and rode on until we reached a large muddy river. It was slow and wide but didn't look like too much of an obstacle. I sat on Monlam's back on top of the high riverbank, trying to scout the best way to cross. We rode down to the water's edge and started in; the water was deep but Monlam went well until we had almost reached a small island in the middle. The water was too murky to see its depth and suddenly we found ourselves in a deep hole, the water halfway up the saddle.

My boots filled with water as Monlam fought to stay on his feet; I could feel the riverbed was soft and he struggled to keep moving. I had to fight to keep him under control and moving forward; he kept trying to turn around and head back to the bank and I knew he'd lose his balance in the turn and throw me into the water. With the weight of my water-filled boots and heavy clothing I might not make it out.

He stopped altogether. 'Come on, Monlam! You've got to move!' I kicked him as hard as I could, but he hardly budged. In desperation and fear I whisked out my long knife and whipped him across the rump with the flat of the blade. This seemed to be the motivation he needed and he struggled on, carrying me to the island. There we rested for a few minutes before carrying on across the next braid of the river.

This time it wasn't as deep and we headed towards another sandbank. However, the water turned deep again after a few metres, forcing me to change direction and instead of making in to the middle of the sandbank we reached the top. That would have been fine, except that the top of the bank was being hit directly by the river's flow, which saturated the sand and tiny pebbles, making it into something akin to quicksand.

Again poor Monlam was struggling and I had to whack him hard with the flat of my knife. He mashed his hooves into the waterlogged sand, using all his strength to try to pull us both out. At any moment I expected him to collapse beneath me and throw me into the river. If I ever needed protection it was now and I rattled off the Mahakala mantra as fast as I could.

The deity must have reached down with its giant hand and dragged Monlam out, as a moment later we were standing in the middle of the strip of sand, my poor horse breathing hard. We crossed the last stretch of water without trouble and I climbed out of the saddle on the other bank. I emptied the water from my boots and wrung as much as I could get out of my socks while Monlam grazed. He'd done so well in the crossing that I instantly forgave him for his antics earlier in the day.

That night we stopped on a hillside next to a stream high above the western side of the lake, where there were some little stone houses the nomads used when they brought their stock to graze. They were locked, but I found one that was open — it was just walls and an open doorway without a roof but it was better than nothing. It would give me some shelter, although the weather looked as if it would stay fine for the night at least and I felt safe hidden inside.

I set Monlam out next to the stream and started a fire. The wind died and the skies changed to a deep shade of blue as nightfall set in; it was peaceful and quiet, the hot mug in my hand comforted me and I felt satisfied with another day survived, another river crossed, another few centimetres on the map covered. All of a sudden there was a commotion from the mountainside above my camp, howling, yapping and whining. Wolves!

I looked across at Monlam. He was standing rigid, his head high and his ears pricked as he looked towards the mountain in the direction of the haunting cries. I grabbed my binoculars and searched the mountainside, trying to spot them. I didn't think they would be hard to find — it sounded as if there were several and they didn't sound far away. I started at the tops of the peaks and worked my way back and forth across the slope as I moved my gaze down. I couldn't see a thing, so I tried again. I could hear them clearly, but still couldn't find them on the mountain.

I couldn't find the wolves because they weren't on the mountain; they were at the base of the hills just above my camp, only a few hundred metres away. I watched them for some time. They must have known we were there but didn't seem the least bit concerned, which was a relief. It was a small pack, what looked to be a mother and her four half-grown cubs. With darkness coming the mother was about to set off into the valley to hunt and the cubs had worked themselves into an excited frenzy, hoping she was going to return with food.

I watched the mother trot across the hillside away from my camp towards the lake; this was her domain, she was the dominant predator, but it seemed she was allowing me to spend the night and pass through. The cubs made their way back into the hills and I watched them for a while until it got too dark. Monlam still looked on edge, so I walked over, gave him a pat and fed him a lump of *tsampa*. 'Don't worry, boy, if the wolves come back give me a yell and I'll help you!' Before I retired to my little home I gathered a small pile of stones to hopefully see off any attackers that might prey on us during the night.

Inside my shelter I wrote my diary and said prayers before getting into my sleeping bag. I had taken off my wet socks and draped them over a rock inside the walls hopefully to dry by morning. As I lay down to sleep I could smell something that made me think a small animal had died. Perhaps a rat had crawled under one of the stones to finish its life. I sat up and flashed the torch around but couldn't see anything. Then I realised the stench was coming from my socks. I'd hardly taken them off in the last month and a half and had never bothered to wash them; as a result, they smelt like a decomposing animal.

In the morning I woke to a fantastic dawn and watched the sun rise over the lake from the comfort of my sleeping bag. I got up early with the intention of restarting the fire for tea. However, when I stood up and looked over the wall to check on Monlam, he was nowhere to be seen.

'The wolves!' Then I realised it would be pretty much impossible for a pack of wolves to bring down a horse and devour the whole thing without leaving a trace or making a sound.

I pulled my boots on over my stinking socks and walked onto the hillside. I spotted Monlam grazing a couple of kilometres back towards the direction we'd come. He'd broken his rope during the night, but he was still hobbled and hadn't gone too far. I packed up, knowing that by the time I'd caught him and come back it would be too late to give myself the luxury of tea before setting off. I walked across to catch him, but when he saw me coming he started jumping in the hobbles, trying to get away. I stood still and waited for him to calm down, terrified he'd break the hobbles and take off. If he did I'd be in serious trouble. Before long I got close enough to grab the end of his rope. 'Come on, boy, what do you think you're doing, eh? You're lucky the wolves didn't get you!'

I rode him bareback to camp; we loaded up and set off again around the side of the lake, then away from it and up a wide valley, following a road. As we neared the low pass I started to see people, which told me there was something on the other side of the pass I'd rather avoid. And when we made it to the top, as I expected, I found a small town — not much more than a cluster of houses and a couple of larger buildings, but big enough to have some kind of Chinese official stationed there. On one side I could see a couple of pool tables next to a large canvas tent; I was certain there would be a shop and restaurant inside and again the thought of a hot meal of meat and noodles was hard to resist. The risk was too great; I pulled my hat down, put my sunglasses on, wrapped a scarf round my face and carried on across the hills away from the town.

I had to pass close to some camps by the river near the settlement and even from a distance people stopped their daily routine and watched me go by. I thought that as long as I didn't meet anyone face to face, I'd be OK. If I did meet someone there would be a chance they'd report me, but I reasoned that if they didn't know for sure I was foreign I'd be safe enough. I was eager to find somewhere to stop for tea and something to eat, but we hurried on to get clear of the town.

At two in the afternoon I stopped for tea and *tsampa* with a family in their yak-hair tent; they were a jovial bunch and we shared a few simple jokes before I set off again. I hadn't gone far when I saw a white jeep go by in the distance, heading towards the village. This put me on edge again and I was eager to get some distance between Monlam and me and the road. We rode out into a vast grassland that seemed to stretch for ever. We were heading northwest towards a lake called Nangla Rinco, although I intended to turn directly west before we reached it.

From my maps I knew there was a river on the edge of the grasslands that I would have to cross and I hoped to reach it that day so I could put the crossing behind me. Every time we topped an elevation in the grassland I expected the river to come into view. I tried to kid myself that it must be 'just over that rise', but by then I knew nothing in Tibet is just over that rise. There is always another rise.

At least we were making good time. The ground was firm and easy riding without too many stones, Monlam was walking well, even crossing muddy patches without too much difficulty, and the weather was sunny but cool. I kept watching the hills on the other side of the plain, trying to judge how far away they were and when I'd reach them. But it was impossible to estimate the distance, the grassland was featureless and there was no way to get any idea of size or space. The hills could have been half an hour away, or they could have been five. I found myself anxious to get off the open expanse, I wanted to make it to somewhere.

At eight in the evening we had to stop, we still hadn't reached the river and the hills were still far away. We found another small river of cloudy water and I decided to stop for the night — it was too late to go on and I had no idea how far it was to the next water. Monlam was tired; he'd done well that day, carrying me at least forty kilometres.

It was a clear, still night; the stars were amazing and I lay in my bag looking up at the array sparkling against the dark sky. Suddenly a bright light appeared on the ridgeline of the far-off hills. At first I thought it must be the lights of a truck or a jeep. I felt safe; it was too dark for anyone to find me, but as I watched it I could see it wasn't moving. It wasn't the lights of a vehicle, it was another star that had risen above the hills, brighter than I would have believed a star could be.

In the morning I was up before dawn and started the fire for tea before setting off. Just as I was packing, two Tibetan men approached on horses; they stopped a short distance away and sat in their saddles looking at me. I tried to wave them over, preferring them to see me as harmless and friendly rather than strange and suspicious. However, they refused to come any closer, turned their horses and rode off in the direction of the village I'd passed the day before. I was unsettled even more by the probably meaningless fact that they were wearing identical caps. My paranoid, authority-phobic mind told me this must mean they were part of some kind of local militia and the caps were their uniforms. Were they about to gallop into the settlement and alert their superiors?

I kept looking over my shoulder, expecting to see a jeep coming after me over every hill as we rode west across the grassland. After only an hour we reached the river and found our way blocked. The river was a deep, sluggish flow; we made an attempt to cross but only a few metres out from the bank it was clear it was much too deep. The river would only grow if we headed downstream, so I turned Monlam and headed upriver.

For the rest of the morning we rode along the banks of the river, trying to find a place to cross. The delay annoyed me and I was keen to get off the grassland and into the relative safety of the hills. We had to cross somewhere and when I came to a point where the river looked its widest, and hopefully shallowest, I decided to give it a try. There were several camps on the opposite side and I reasoned that the nomads there would bring their stock across the river to graze them on the abundant grass of the plain. Before the actual river there was a wide expanse of boggy holes dotted with clumps of grass.

I walked on foot, leading an unwilling horse behind me. I'm sure he knew what we were in for as he could smell the mud. I dragged him after me as we tried to pick our way across the maze of muck and sod. Every time I thought we were making progress we'd run into stretches of near-still water, they weren't too deep to cross but the muddy bottoms made them impassable. For the next two hours we walked in circles. I almost gave up and tried to head back to the bank, but by then I'd lost my way completely and couldn't even retrace my steps. I trudged on, wading through pools of putrid muck to the next half-solid lump of ground, hauling poor Monlam behind me. I'd had to drag him into every wet hole and once in he'd be so eager to get out the other side he'd trash his way across, showering me with stinking mud. Before long we were both covered.

I was almost at my wits' end and starting to worry; if we took a wrong turn and went into a deep hole it could be a disaster. I was terrified Monlam would come to grief and end up sinking in a hole of mud. The expanse of bog was so wide I might not be able to get him out and there was a very real chance he could die in the swamp. I tried not to think about it and instead prayed to anyone who was listening to get us the hell out of there.

Before long the prayers seemed to be answered and further on I could see a couple of men heading towards me. They had taken off their shoes and socks so they could wade through the mud. Not far away I could see their flocks of sheep and I was grateful they had come to help me. They led me on what felt like a secret trail across the labyrinth, as if we were entering a forbidden land. I felt sorry for them, as they must spend every day on that awful landscape feeding their sheep.

However, before long we were out of the muddy hell for the time being and one of the men took me to his tent, where I met the rest of the family.

The yaks had not long been sent out to pasture and the women were cleaning up after them. They scooped up the fresh yak muck with their bare hands into great handfuls of sloppy digested grass, then they'd walk to the edge of the yard and throw the muck to splat on the ground, where it would dry and could be used as fuel.

I was shown into the tent where the rest of the men were lazing about drinking tea. One of the women took a break from her 'muck raking' and came in to serve me tea. She'd barely wiped her filthy hands on her *chuba* when she shoved her fingers into a sack of *tsampa* and offered to fill my bowl. Instead, I took the sack from her and helped myself, though I knew it probably wasn't worth worrying too much about hygiene now, I'd made it this far across Tibet without getting sick.

The family were kind and gave me a couple of packets of instant noodles and a coil of boiled sheep's guts filled with cooked blood and I set off again, riding across the rest of the plain towards the hills. I still had kilometres to cross before I reached them and again I found myself picking my way through bogs, around stagnant ponds and across brackish braids of the river. It was a great relief when we finally crossed the last patch of swamp and began climbing into the hills.

The day was already old but I wanted to push on; we had been on the trail for five days since leaving Taro Tso, and we needed a day off. I was looking for a campsite with good grazing, fresh water, shelter if possible and away from any roads. It was a steep climb into the hills and the grass grew fairly thick; I passed abandoned campsites and managed to fill up my dung sack, but there was no water in any of the valleys.

We rode on into the evening and were soon climbing into a pass. I rode halfway to the top but got off to walk, as I could feel Monlam struggling. As we neared the top I felt the usual excitement about what I might find on the other side, a small stream with a grassy meadow for Monlam, a nice little cave, perhaps, in a safe nook in the valley where no one would find us and we could rest happily. Instead, we rode into a wide-open valley with a well-worn road running up the middle and no water.

As we walked down into the valley the weather turned — great wet clouds darkened the sky. By the time we got to the bottom it was pouring down and freezing. I got off and walked to try to stay warm as we headed up a side valley around a massive rocky peak. I hoped the streambed I could see running around the base of the hill would hold water and the amount of stone made me think a dry cave might be possible.

We dragged ourselves up the other side in the rain and howling wind; it had already been an exhausting and stressful day across the bog and I felt as if I was being pushed beyond my limits. I wanted to stop somewhere, set up camp, make some tea and cook my noodles, and then go to sleep. Tibet, it seemed, had other ideas. We made it to the base of the cliffs and found the stream was dead, there was hardly any grass and as I stood in the downpour I saw a truck struggle by on the road below. We were too far away to be recognised, but it made me feel dejected. I hadn't found anywhere to stay, it was getting dark and I was desperate to stop. This wasn't the place, though, and on we plodded, right around the peak and then back down into the valley, still hoping to find somewhere.

The rain continued, I was soaked and all my gear was wet again, Monlam was dragging and suddenly it all became too much. *This isn't fair! This isn't fuckin' fair! You fuckin' country, give me a fuckin' break!*

I howled at the sky and burst into tears of frustration, misery and self-pity. Tears flowed down my already wet face and weeks of tension born from the daily struggle and the constant battle against the land, the conditions, the cold, the altitude and myself boiled over and rushed out unchecked. Dry sobs stuck in my throat, I held out my hands to the sky, my face tortured, my mouth gaping in what felt like physical pain, I'd never felt like this before and I was afraid. *What was happening to me? Was I dying once?*

Something deep inside was fighting to get out, desperate to escape and get away, but it just couldn't find its way out. I continued to cry, not even trying to stop, not caring what a sorry, pitiful, weak sight I must look, not that there was anyone to see. I felt as if I was physically breaking in two, as if my heart was tearing itself into pieces.

As darkness fell the rain eased off and I calmed down into a state of numbness. I made it back down into the valley floor, where we found a small stream; however, there was no grazing and the ground was bare dirt. 'I'm sorry, boy,' I said to Monlam. 'We have to keep going.'

And we went on into the darkness.

Soon it was too dark to see, the clouds blocking even the moon, and I had to use my torch to find my way. I could feel we had left the valley and were in a more open area, but I had no idea what was around me in the space outside the beam of my small light. I kept to the stream, frightened that if I lost my only landmark I could find myself wandering aimlessly in the darkness. I remembered descriptions I'd read about beings in the *bardo*, the intermediate state Tibetans believe we travel through between the end of one life and rebirth in the next. Some, due to their lack of positive karma, find themselves lost in the darkness and spend eons wandering about, trying to find where they are supposed to be reborn.

At ten o'clock we were still walking and when another rainstorm hit, Monlam stopped and refused to move. He'd had a gutsful too, and he wasn't going any further. He turned his rump into the rain and I crouched on the ground in front of him as scant shelter until the worst of it passed. 'Come on, boy. I promise we'll stop at the next decent spot.'

We went on for a few minutes in the dripping rain and found a strip of grass along the stream. I unloaded poor Monlam, set him out to graze and set up my damp camp. Apart from the grassy strip all around was bare dirt and mud, so I unrolled the bags two feet from the stream. It was pitch dark and impossible to discern anything more than the spot I stood on. I had no idea if I was near a road, on the edge of a cliff or metres from a warm, dry cave; in fact, I could have been camped next to a Chinese nuclear missile base and I wouldn't have known.

I felt totally beaten, but I was determined not to let Tibet win the day; I was going to make tea and have my noodles even if it took the whole bloody night. I had my sack of dung, which was still mostly dry and I gathered stones from the stream to make a fireplace. Unfortunately the wind had died — where was it when I needed it? I had to lie on the wet ground, blowing constantly on the lumps of dung to get them smouldering enough to heat the water, my eyes full of soot and smoke. Eventually the water was hot enough, I made the noodles and a single mug of lifesaving tea before dragging off my boots and crawling into my sleeping bag. I lay down to sleep at two in the morning after writing my diary by torchlight. It had been the longest day of the trip so far. I still ached inside, but I felt that by making something to eat and drink I had finished the day with a tiny triumph. The last line in my journal read: *I made tea! I beat you, Tibet! I fuckin' won! Ha!*

I woke in the morning grateful to find myself under clear skies; the rain had passed over during the night. I was in the middle of a massive open valley, the bottom of which looked to be a desolate saltpan and I was glad we hadn't gone any further. Monlam was grazing happily; there was some quite good grass along the banks of the stream and no sign of human life. Apart from my horse the only other souls about were the usual pair of black crows.

I had no desire to move. It was far from an ideal place to take a day off, out in the middle of nowhere with absolutely no shelter, but we had water, grazing and enough dry dung to see us through the day. I cleaned the worst of the mud off my gear and got most of it fairly dry. Monlam spent his day blissfully rolling on his back in patches of dry dirt and lying in the sun. I dearly wanted him to get me all the way to the mountain, which felt closer every day, so I decided to only ride for three days at a time from now on, then take a rest day, so as not to tire him out before we got there.

I checked my map again, almost refusing to believe how close the mountain was; if we continued to make the same progress we could reach it in a week. It felt unreal, too good to be true and I was sure I'd made a mistake, or that some new disaster was about to befall me. I couldn't allow myself to feel I had a chance of being successful, afraid that if I did it would be snatched away.

In the afternoon I sat by the fire with a mug of tea and tried to think about what had occurred the day before, in the storm. What had happened to me? What had I felt? Why had I felt like that? Had I lost or found anything? I felt ashamed of the way I'd behaved, how I'd been reduced to a blubbering idiot. I could imagine people at home telling me how brave I must have been to cross Tibet alone on horses, but there had been no one to see me the day before; if there had been, what would they say then?

I also felt afraid because of the way I'd cursed Tibet and how I'd felt as if I'd beaten her the previous night, as if she was a god and I'd offended her by claiming to be greater. I knew it was a dangerous way to think. If I ever thought I was better or stronger than the land I was riding over, Tibet would turn around and crush me in an instant. Coming even this far wasn't a victory over Tibet — she was allowing me to pass through.

In the morning I was woken before daylight by a few spits of rain. Nothing came of it and I drifted back to sleep for a while until I was woken by the thunder of hooves as a small herd of *khang* raced past. It was a dry morning and we rode into the bottom of the grassland and met a river, which I guessed to be the Wamo Tsangpo, and followed its flow upstream for the rest of the day. I passed dozens of houses, but none were occupied and I didn't meet anyone until later that afternoon, when I came across a group of men building more of these little dwellings. When I asked them where everyone was, they told me the people were all *drokpa* who had moved to summer pastures with their stock. I wondered if they were the people I'd met by the boggy river a couple of days earlier.

I tried to check with the men if the river flowing past us was in fact the Wamo. *'Wamo Tsangpo?'* I asked and pointed to the river.

'Hako masong.' The man shook his head, he didn't understand.

'Khyerang-la tsangpo ming karey-rey?' What's the name of your river?

'Tsangpo.' River. I thought he must have misunderstood again.

'Tsangpo ming karey-rey?' I asked again.

'Tsangpo!' He repeated, river.

'Tsangpo ming yawrey?' Does the river have a name?

'*Ming mindu.*' As far as the men here were concerned, the river had no name, it was just 'the river' and that was that.

I realised how ridiculous it was of me to expect the names on a map of Tibet made in the United States to match what local nomads called their river. Later in the day I met another group of builders who told me the river was called the Yari Tsangpo; this made more sense, as further to the west there was a large Chinese settlement called Yari. Over the next few days I would ask anyone I met what they called their river and every day I got a different answer. The river seemed to be whatever you wanted it to be.

That night I camped on the banks of the mysterious river; it was another dry evening and I made my usual dinner of tea and *tsampa*. The river was large and swift and I needed to cross it the next day. I'd been told there was a bridge at Yari, but I dearly wanted to avoid getting any closer. Even here, beside the river and hidden by some little sand hills, I was still nervous.

In the morning we found a place to cross and were soon heading away from the town across an open, stony and very windy plain. We struggled across the expanse for most of the day, finally riding into the hills in the late afternoon. I stopped at the first house I'd seen all day and was taken in by a wonderful family. I was nearly out of food and when I asked if they could sell me some they loaded me with *tsampa*, sugar, cheese, butter, three packets of noodles and a large coil of sheep's guts, enough for a feast. I tried to pay, but the father refused to take even the ten yuan note I offered, so I promised the family I would use it to make an offering on their behalf at Gang Rinpoche.

The man and his young son walked me to the top of a rise above their home and gave me good directions. He said I should follow the river up and then turn onto a smaller branch to the north, this I could then follow for the next few days. It would lead me to a pass and on the other side I would find another river that flowed onto the Barga Plain, above which Kailas sits. The river was like an expressway to the mountain and if things went as planned it would deliver me to her back door.

We shook hands and I carried on. Towards evening I came to another house; unlike most Tibetan homes it was made of concrete and painted a grubby yellow. By now anything out of the ordinary made me nervous and my paranoid imagination warned that it might be some kind of checkpoint. This was a route to the sacred mountain, which itself wasn't far from the borders of Nepal and India; perhaps the authorities controlled access to the area to stop refugees?

The valley was narrow and there was no way I could follow the river and not pass the house. I'd have to take my chances. As I approached I was seen by a couple of kids and soon the rest of the family came out. The old father shook my hand warmly, but the first thing he asked was my name. No one had done this before; perhaps he'd been told to look out for someone? I looked over the wall into the family's yard and saw a small white satellite dish. The old man told me it was for their TV, but I wondered if it was for a phone. As soon as I was gone was he going to rush inside and call his superiors in Yari?

I set off again after a few minutes and tried to tell myself to stop worrying. The old man was probably just a herdsman who'd saved enough money to build a home from concrete and buy an old TV; there was no reason why he would be some kind of warden or informer. The valley I was in was isolated and remote, there was barely a road and it seemed unlikely the Chinese would station a checkpoint there. All the same, I walked on for some time to make sure there was distance between myself and the house before stopping for the night.

In the morning we went on up the valley as it narrowed and to my relief the road disappeared. Soon we were higher and in an area that didn't look as though anyone came through much at all. The only place to ride was next to the river, as all around were hills and mountains of bare rock. We had to cross the river dozens of times, so often I lost count. We stopped in the middle of the day on a little meadow and I let Monlam graze while I had a snack of cold boiled Tibetan sausage. Inside the sheep gut casing was the animal's cooked blood, its chopped-up liver, kidneys and other organs, and lumps of cooked fat. It looked worse than it sounds, but it was high in protein and nutrition and by that stage of the trip seemed like a special treat.

When we carried on the valley eventually opened out and we reached a fairly well-constructed road. I crossed the river so that I'd be away from any traffic — as it was the only things I saw were three trucks that went by in the afternoon. They were travelling together in a little convoy and the canvas-covered backs of the trucks were full of Tibetan villagers. I guessed they were on their way back from their pilgrimage to Gang Rinpoche. I was now close enough to see people who had actually been to the mountain.

Later, I passed the only other people I saw all day, a group of Chinese men out fishing. I was still on the opposite side of the river and far enough away for them not to be able to see I wasn't Tibetan. A couple of hours later I passed their camp; they were part of a construction gang building bridges. It disappointed me that this region, which had been remote since the beginning of time, wild and untouched, was now being tamed, scarred with roads and crossed with bridges, the Chinese pushing further into the fringes of Tibet.

I wanted to make the next day a day off. Apart from the Chinese workers there seemed to be no one in the area and as evening closed in I started looking for a place to stay. Soon the valley opened out even further, offering no place to hide from the road, so I turned up a narrow side valley, hoping for better luck. I wanted to find a dry cave or a sheltering overhang, but the day was running out with no sign of either.

Eventually I chose a spot in a small valley below some crumbling cliffs; there was a good stream, decent grass for Monlam and the ground was dotted with lumps of yak dung, most of it dry due to the screaming wind that ripped down the valley. I was some distance from the road, completely hidden.

I unloaded Monlam and left him to feed, set up my camp and collected a pile of dung. There was no shelter from the wind, but at the base of the cliffs were piles of loose, flat rocks. I spent the rest of the evening building myself a drystone wall that would give me some protection from the wind. I became engrossed in what I was doing, making an elaborate kitchen area, a separate area to stash the saddle and riding gear and even built a low wall around the patch of ground I would sleep on. Of course, none of this was going to give me any shelter from the rain, but I felt I'd made myself a little home for the next two nights.

It was mostly dry that night and I slept well. I spent much of the next day by the fire, as Monlam grazed up and down the valley. It was cold, with flurries of snow all morning and light rain most of the afternoon. I huddled behind my wall with the piece of canvas over my legs, trying to keep dry. I didn't see anyone all day, which suited me fine, except for the two crows who perched on the rocks above my camp most of the day. I realised there had been two crows whenever I'd taken a rest day for as long as I could remember. Were they the same two every time? It dawned on me I might never have been as alone as I thought; perhaps the inky black birds were sent to watch over me.

I read for a while in the afternoon but the constant rain made it less enjoyable as I tried to keep the pages dry. I gave up before long and lay on the saddle blankets thinking. I was still coming to terms with the idea of dying once and now that I was only a few days from Gang Rinpoche I started to worry that I wasn't going to. I didn't feel I had made spiritual progress at all; in fact, I felt more self-centred than ever, more caught up in my own little world, more concerned with what I wanted to do than ever before.

I was starting to get anxious that I was going to finish the trip and return home without changing anything in my mind. I was worried I was losing the opportunity to make a difference and if something didn't happen, if I didn't make something happen, the moment would be gone and I'd never get another chance. My determination to reach the mountain was making me more egoistic. I was becoming increasingly attached to the idea of success, making it harder for me to let things go, to stop clinging and holding on to the illusion of what I thought was me. I still *desired* as much in Tibet as I did at home, only the object was different.

It was a very cold morning. We headed back into the main valley and started climbing. Monlam walked well after his day off; he picked up his steps and I think he could feel we were going somewhere important and he was in a hurry to get there. We rode up a long slope following the road and made it to the top of an easy pass. I stopped and added a stone to the pile.

Looking back down the road I could see a vehicle in the distance coming up the way we'd just travelled. I checked with my binoculars and felt my heart sink when I saw it was a white jeep. 'Come on, Monlam, let's go!'

I jumped back into the saddle and headed for a small hill on the other side of the road, looking for a place to hide. Monlam seemed to sense the urgency and even cantered for a while. We made it behind the hill and I dismounted and crouched on the ground. I guessed the jeep would stop at the pass for a few minutes and perhaps the passengers would walk around the cairn and head on their way. There was no need to panic, no one had seen me and no one would.

I heard the engine approach and tried to listen to find out if it was leaving again, but the wind whipped away the sound and soon I couldn't hear anything. I knew it must be at the pass or very near it and so I crept up to the top of the rise I was hiding behind to peek over and see where the jeep was. 'Oh shit!' I dropped back down again and crouched behind Monlam. The jeep had turned off the road and was heading straight past me.

I cowered under my hat with my scarf around my face, praying no one had seen me and that the jeep wouldn't stop. I decided that if it did I'd jump on Monlam and ride as fast as I could into the hills. Thankfully I didn't need to; the jeep went by and I watched it drop to the bottom of the valley, cross the river and then climb into the foothills on the other side, where it stopped at a nomad camp. The occupants got out and went into the tent.

My heart was still thumping and I didn't want to lose sight of the jeep; knowing its location was my best defence. I set off again on foot but kept a constant eye on the camp; after a short time the jeep was on the move again. It crossed a hill and then stopped at another camp, again everyone got out and went inside the tent. In all likelihood it was probably a family from town visiting nomad relatives, perhaps exchanging a sack of *tsampa* for a couple of sheep. However, I was much too paranoid to accept such a simple explanation; in my mind I saw a group of government officials on a tour of inspection, checking the herdsmen had their papers in order, making sure they were declaring their stock numbers so they could be taxed and looking for anything out of the ordinary, like me.

I was hungry and cold and wanted to stop to get something to eat. I also needed to stock up on supplies and as I entered the high valley I found several camps. I was too afraid to stop, I still believed whoever was in the jeep might be visiting every tent in the area and anyone who had met me would mention they had seen a strange rider and they'd come looking for me.

The skies were dark and it was a cold afternoon, but I rode for hours before I finally stopped with a family in a canvas tent. I had watched the road over my shoulder all day, but thankfully hadn't seen the jeep. The nomads gave me tea and a bowl of rice and I filled my *tsampa* bag. They told me the pass the valley led to was called Yume-la, that it wasn't too high but a very long way, so I hurried on. I wanted to get across the pass — the last one before Gang Rinpoche.

The afternoon was spent crossing high, windswept grasslands, as we turned away from the river that had become a string of small lakes. Monlam had found his second wind and we cut across in good time. I felt strong and finally confident I had enough left in me to make it to the mountain; the wind blew back the brim of my hat so that the falling spits of rain hit me full in the face. I leant into the gale and urged Monlam on. I glanced back over my shoulder again, still fearing the jeep but now almost exhilarated by the possibility of a brush with the law, wrapped in my rugged sheepskin cloak, a black hat on my head and a short sword on my belt, a keen steed beneath me and the ashes of a holy lama around my neck. I started to believe nothing was going to stop me. I could outride anyone, and if they caught me I'd fight them off. 'Come on, Monlam! It's time to kick arse!'

Near the top of the grassland we passed a family of pilgrims herding their yaks loaded with tents and blankets. I asked them if they had been to the mountain.

'Rey, Gang Rinpoche kora!' They had been round the mountain. A young nomad woman looked up at me as I passed, young children holding her hands on either side of her, staring wide-eyed at the passing barbarian. She was dressed in her best *chuba*, weighted with heavy turquoise, coral and amber jewellery, her hair braided to her waist. As she smiled, happiness shone from her face in the weak afternoon sun. I wondered if she always looked like that or was it because she had just circled the sacred peak? Later I met similar groups; they had the same glow and I suddenly couldn't wait to get there.

On the far side of the grassland a long narrow lake lay between two ranges, like a Scottish loch. We rode on above the side of the lake then turned towards the south, into the Gang Dise mountain range and the approach to Yume-la.

I was very high in the mountains and camped at an altitude that must have been around five and a half thousand metres.

A short way into the next valley we stopped for the night at an old campsite. There was plenty of dung, but it was all too wet to burn. I made a couple of attempts to light a fire but gave up and mixed myself a porridge of cold *tsampa*. I crawled into my sleeping bag as it got dark, wrote my journal and said my prayers. The next day I would head down the valley, expecting to make it to the Barga Plain in the afternoon or evening.

I woke up early the next morning, well before daylight and looked out from under the hood of the bag to find it had snowed heavily overnight. Everything was white; centimetres of snow covered the bag and I had to kick it off before I could get out. I struggled into my boots and stood up. Monlam stood hunched in the snow; it was very quiet and very, very cold.

Packing up with frozen fingers was a slow and painful task, but we set off not long after eight, crossed the stream to get back to the road and headed on down the valley. The skies opened and it started snowing; a freezing wind numbed my unprotected fingers. I thought the wind would work in my favour by blowing the snow clouds over the mountains as we got lower, but bank after bank of heavy wet snow blew up the valley. Within half an hour I was wet and so cold I was groaning out loud.

I could only make out a short distance ahead and had no idea how high the peaks on either side of me were. I kept hoping to round a bend and find a nomad camp or warm hut, but I soon realised there was no one living this high in the valley. I looked around the surrounding rock to see if I could spot the crows, but even they had left us. We were completely alone.

Monlam plodded along behind; it was too cold to ride, although I felt myself becoming exhausted, having not eaten anything that morning. I was wretched, my hands so cold I could barely feel my fingers and I started to think seriously about frostbite and hypothermia. But there was nothing I could do but keep walking. There was no point in stopping; I could die if I did and no one was coming to help me. The arrogance and bravado I'd felt the day before were completely gone and I felt as if I was being punished by the mountains.

Soon my groans turned to sobs; I felt the cruelty of the land and its unforgiving harshness. I had nearly reached the mountain, but I felt that this might as well be the first day of the ride, as if I had achieved nothing and was still at square one. There was a real chance I might not even see the damn mountain. This might be the last day of the trip and if the snow didn't stop and I didn't find shelter soon this might be the last day of my damn life. All the effort I'd put in might still come to nothing, just like all the effort I'd invested in the other pointless ventures of my life; in the end they would all come to nothing. 'Oh Rinpoche! Help me! Get me out of here, please just stop the snow!'

I howled my prayer into the wind in desperation and misery, already convinced no one was bothering to listen. I'd got myself here, why should I expect anyone to help me get out? I was the one who created the mass of negative karma that had me stuck in the mountains in a snowstorm, how could I now hope someone was going to take it all away? I dropped my head and let the tears fall to the snow as I stumbled on, not even looking where I was going.

Suddenly a crow shrieked from a boulder on the hillside. I looked up through my tears and saw it had stopped snowing. I looked at the mountains around me — the cloud was breaking up. Minutes later, towards the bottom of the valley I could even see a tiny patch of sky; the storm was passing. The lama had heard me. I stopped walking.

This was all too much, this couldn't be happening. I tried to deny what I could feel, what I knew, what I could see in front of my eyes. *It's just a fuckin' coincidence, Ian. Things like this don't really happen, you don't just pray and then suddenly you get it! It's just a coincidence.* I tried to rationalise, to be logical, to tell my cynical, sceptical self this wasn't real. *Think how you'd feel if someone else was telling you this, you'd never believe it in a million years. Answered prayers, it just doesn't happen.*

But it was happening and I remembered how I'd prayed to Khensur Thabkye Rinpoche before, and what had happened every time. I'd got exactly what I'd asked for. I was overcome, I couldn't go on and for a few minutes I sat on a rock and bawled my eyes out as I finally felt the relief of everything falling apart. The self I had painstakingly carved like the thin sheets of slate used for *mani* stones fell from my shoulders and shattered on the ground. I let them fall and wondered why I had insisted on carrying them for so long. As I cried I tried to find words to give meaning to the thoughts I was having. I was convinced the lama had been with me every step of the way since I met him years before and I was sure he was with me now. I felt an incredible gratitude for what he'd tried to teach me and at the same time felt utterly unworthy of his compassion. I'd turned away from what he'd tried to teach me and what I knew was right so many times, why would he choose to help me now?

Then suddenly there were no more feelings, no thoughts, and no words. Just for a few moments everything was still; the wind stopped and so did my mind. I gave up trying to name, trying to label, trying to reason, and just felt the quiet presence of the lama. Just for a few seconds there was nothing else, just a calm, abiding peace, just me and him.

Then Monlam moved and the moment was gone. I let it go, knowing there was no need to try to hold on to it, Rinpoche had been with me this far and he would stay with me till the end. I had no need to worry any more. I knew I would still face obstacles and dangers — I hadn't made it to the mountain and I could still be stopped — but I knew that as long as I asked Rinpoche for help he would be there.

I looked up at the clearing peaks towering above me. Great walls of wet black rock rose on all sides and I was struck by their magnificence, their massive and terrible beauty and suddenly I started laughing through my tears. Everything I had worried about, all that I had grasped, everything that had seemed so important now appeared so comical. I giggled like a little kid; Khensur Thabkye Rinpoche had told me a private joke and he and I were the only ones who got it. I threw my arms around Monlam's neck and hugged him; the poor startled animal probably thought I'd gone mad.

We walked on into the spreading sunshine. I felt a hundred times lighter and burst out laughing every time I thought about what had just happened. The joke Khensur Thabkye Rinpoche had shared with me was a good one and it would be funny for a long time to come. Early in the afternoon we stopped to rest and I spread my wet bags out to dry. Monlam grazed and I mixed cold *tsampa* to give myself the energy to get through the rest of the day.

As we carried on the mountains turned to hills and the hills finally gave way to open ground. At about three o'clock we came to the edge of the plain; in the far distance I could see the settlement of Barga, further to the southeast I could just make out the sacred waters of Manasarovar and to the west the dark lake Raksas Tal. To the south rose the massive peak Gurla Mandhata, at seven thousand, six hundred and eighty-three metres one of the highest in Tibet and also considered sacred. I knew these names well, I knew exactly where they lay and precisely where I'd find them, as for years now I had been staring at them on my maps, wishing that one day I'd see them for myself. Now I could.

I turned to the north and for the rest of the day I rode along the base of the hills across near-desert country towards the still-invisible Gang Rinpoche. We passed several clusters of empty houses — the people had moved to their summer camps further down the valley. The closed houses reminded me of stories I'd read about the people who lived on pilgrim trails long ago. By tradition and duty they were bound to help those who travel by offering them food and places to sleep; however, on the more popular roads the number of pilgrims asking for alms put such a strain on the families' stores they would close the shutters, blow out the lamps and pretend no one was home.

I didn't see anyone the whole day and that night I camped alone next to a stream in a little valley. Far below in the middle of the plain I could see the main road, marked in dust by the occasional passing truck or jeep as they headed towards the town of Darchen at the base of the pilgrim trail to Kailas. I was safe for now, but I knew that in the next couple of days I would have to pass the town and the checkpoints at the start of the trail. I still didn't know where they were and negotiating them would take some skill and lots of good luck, but I felt calm and quietly confident. I knew I had a pretty good backer on my side.

The next morning I was up hours before dawn; I couldn't wait to get moving, excited to be so close. I hoped I would see the mountain that day, although I knew it would still be hidden by the lower peaks. I made a fire for tea and the last of my *tsampa* before setting off up the plain. Later in the morning I came across another group of pilgrims heading back from Gang Rinpoche; they were packing up their tents but took time to serve me tea and *tukpa* and replenish my supply of *tsampa*. They told me Darchen was only a couple of hours away. At first I didn't believe them, I didn't think I would come within sight of the town until late that afternoon or evening.

Monlam and I carried on. It had been two years, four months and twenty-four days since I'd ridden away from Jigme and Dhondup in Garilang. An hour later we topped a rise and the untidy jumble of buildings that make up Darchen came into view. 'Oh my god, I'm here!'

I'd made it. I'd arrived at the end of the earth, at the centre of the universe.

Chapter Twelve

My excitement was soon tempered by the knowledge that I wasn't *quite* there; in fact, as it would turn out I still had a long way to go and a lot to get through. I rode across the desert towards Darchen and by midday I'd come as far as I dared. I could see a small stone building with a couple of jeeps parked next to it. Through my binoculars I could see people in matching bright red, and very un-Tibetan, jackets walk down to the hut, get into the jeeps and drive off.

I guessed the hut was the checkpoint at the end of the pilgrim trail around Kailas and the colourful walkers were foreign trekkers being picked up at the end of their circuit. I was as apprehensive as I was excited — I would have to get past the checkpoint and the town.

It was tempting to keep going; I could try to ride past the checkpoint and see Gang Rinpoche that day, but the fear of being caught when I was virtually there stopped me, and besides, I'd waited this long, another day wouldn't make any difference. I rode up a narrow ravine into the hills where we found a grassy slope along a dry streambed. I unloaded and left Monlam to graze while I started a fire. Further up the gulch I scraped a hole in the streambed and found enough water for a couple of mugs of tea.

The plan was to hide out in the ravine until it was nearly dark. No one knew we were there and no one could see us from the plain. I would sneak out and by the time I'd reach the checkpoint it would be dark. I'd sneak past and head towards the town; once I was past I'd try to find the start of the pilgrim trail around the mountain. I had no idea where this was, my maps weren't detailed enough to show it, but I guessed it must be the most worn trail in Tibet and it couldn't be that hard to find.

Monlam relaxed in the sun but I was nervous all day. I dreaded being caught, horrible thoughts of a run-in with the police and being sent back to Lhasa without circling the mountain haunted me through the afternoon. I was determined to do all I could to stop them becoming reality and set about getting my disguise ready. I would wear the *chuba* with my hat pulled down and my scarf around my face, I smeared the rest of my exposed skin with soot from a scorched cork mixed with sunblock.

I wrapped my nylon shoulder bag in the piece of canvas and tied it to the top of the saddle, and took my camera and binoculars off my belt and stuffed them inside the folds of my *chuba*. Anything about me that was obviously not Tibetan I hid or covered. I hoped that in the darkness no one would see I wasn't a Tibetan pilgrim. My torch and anything else I thought I might need I made sure I had handy so I wouldn't have to go digging through the saddlebags.

Monlam worried me; despite the pace he'd put on in the last few days he was becoming worn out and spent much of the afternoon sitting down. I would be relying on him to cooperate with whatever I might have to put him through during the night. If he misbehaved or wouldn't keep up or lead properly in the darkness it could mean the difference between drawing unwanted attention to myself and slipping by unnoticed.

The hours dragged by and I felt like a soldier in the trenches waiting for dawn when it would be time to go over the top. I prayed to be protected from whatever I might face during the night and chanted mantras for the rest of the afternoon. Although it was probably too late I tried to tip the scales of karma in my favour. Finally, at nine o'clock it was time to go.

I stood at Monlam's head and prayed. *All Buddhas, Bodhisattvas and Holy Beings, please protect Monlam and me from whatever tonight throws at us, please bestow your blessings on our bodies and minds. And Khensur Thabkye Rinpoche, just help us get through.*

I checked the saddle again to make sure it wasn't going to slip during the march — everything was in order. I turned Monlam round and we set off down the ravine towards the mountain. From now on until I finished the circuit I would be almost totally on foot, in the spirit of the pilgrimage, I would have to walk.

We walked onto the plain and turned towards Darchen. Night was falling quickly and by the time we reached the Zhong Chu river, which flows from the eastern side of Kailas, it was almost completely dark. There was a good moon to light our way but I would have been more secure if it had been raining, which would keep anyone who might see me inside. The river was deep and fast; I climbed on Monlam's back, afraid he was going to refuse to cross in the darkness, but he waded straight in.

Luckily we could stay at least a kilometre away from the checkpoint hut and by ten o'clock we were on a dirt road leading directly to Darchen. I kept an eye and an ear out for any traffic, but the road was deserted. We walked slowly and by eleven reached the edge of Darchen.

As we got closer dogs started barking; I could see several noisy mutts running up and down the hillside above the town. 'Shut up, you bloody mongrels!' I picked up a few stones to ward them off, but they just kept baying and didn't come any closer. I followed the road, still looking for the start of the trail and before long we crossed another stream into the town.

The outskirts of the settlement was a small tent town; pilgrims had set up their camps for the summer and several were selling goods and offering accommodation. The road led right through the canvas village. I put my head down and bent over like an old man, mumbling mantras, my *mala* in my hand. As I passed in front of the tents I could see boxes and piles of supplies, but I didn't dare enter. Suddenly, a group of Tibetans spilled laughing from one of the tents; they stood by the road chatting as a few in the group drifted to the other side of the track. I had to pass right through the group. I held my breath, my heart booming, and kept walking. A few metres on I heard a shout. 'Hey!' My insides froze, but I kept on walking. 'Hey!' I didn't know what to do. 'Hey!' And finally someone answered from the camp — the 'heys' weren't directed at me, I was still safe.

Rising into the hills above the town I could see a road cut into the steep sides of the lower slopes. I guessed this must be the start of the pilgrim trail and skirted the settlement and started climbing. I wasn't sure if this was the right way, but it looked so obvious I presumed it must be. I was dying to ask — it would have been easy to ask directions but if word spread that a foreigner had turned up with a horse the police could hear of it; even if I got through the night they'd find me on the trail in the morning.

The climb was steep but steady as we slowly wound our way into the hills. Soon the lights of Darchen were below and I began to feel out of reach for the time being. The moon shone bright on the plain and in the distance I could see it shine on the waters of Raksas Tal. On and on we went to find ourselves in a high valley. It was a warm night and I was sweating under the *chuba*; later, when we stopped, my sweat-soaked layers would cool and freeze me, but for the moment I had no choice but to keep walking.

Later I stopped and sat on a rock in the moonlight. I could feel my energy fading so I pulled out an emergency chocolate bar I'd carried all the way across Tibet. The night was beautiful, the stars were stunning and I felt thrilled to be on the threshold of Kailas. As we walked on I kept expecting the mountain to come into view around every bend in the trail. I longed to see her glowing beneath the moon, but as we continued I started to wonder if we were going the right way.

Finally I was able to make out a few lights ahead. I guessed there might be pilgrims camped at the start of the trail and thinking I might meet someone during the night I stopped at a stream and washed the worst of the soot off my face. If I turned up at someone's camp in the middle of the night with a blackened face they might think I was a wrathful demon come to steal their soul!

At midnight we came to a row of *stupa* and some long *mani* walls. In the darkness I could see a camp of several tents behind the *stupa*; I knew I must be somewhere, but I had no idea where. Against the night sky on a rocky hillock above the camp I could make out the silhouette of a *gompa;* this didn't feel right, and I knew we must be in the wrong place.

I couldn't go any further, I couldn't walk all night. I gave up for the night and led Monlam away from the trail and into a little gully where we'd be hidden. There wasn't much grass, but I let him out to graze. He'd done me proud and hadn't given me an ounce of trouble. I unrolled the bags and set up my little camp. Before I went to sleep I tried to figure out where I was. I had photocopied a couple of simple maps from a book on Kailas I'd borrowed from the library at home; they weren't designed to be used as a guide for trekkers and didn't give accurate details, but I guessed the monastery above me was Gyengtak Gompa, which meant I'd come the wrong bloody way!

I fell into an exhausted sleep for a few hours, and was woken by light rain before dawn. Clouds had drifted over the mountains and in the predawn gloom it looked as though they were staying for the day. I forced myself out of the bag, packed and loaded up and we set off before anyone in the camp had risen. I was dying to ask directions, but I kept myself in the dark, wanting as few people as possible to see me. I realised I'd missed the pilgrim trail altogether, the trail to the mountain must be beyond the town around the base of the hills. We'd have to go all the way back down, almost to the town, and start again.

The rain increased and was soon joined by snow as we trudged back towards Darchen in the melancholy grey morning. After an hour we were just above the town. If I continued I would find myself on her muddy streets, which would be busy with villagers and pilgrims. We dropped down a steep slope to the Gyengtak Chu river, crossed its flow and then started climbing into the hills. By doing this I hoped to be able to cut across above Darchen.

It was a hard climb. I was on foot all the way, with Monlam struggling behind me. Finally we came to an open flat ridge directly above the town. There were several huge, ancient *mani* walls with thousands of stones in each one, all paying homage to the virtuous qualities of the sacred mountain. I could see Darchen directly below; despite the rain there were a few people about, a group of workers heading towards a construction site on the edge of the settlement.

I tried to avoid being seen, but it was too steep to go any further across so we had to start sliding down a slope of loose stones in full view of the workers. I kept my head down and though we were at least a kilometre from them, they stopped work and watched. I would have looked very conspicuous coming the way I was — there was no trail, it was a difficult climb, why would anyone choose to go that way? I just hoped they wouldn't think enough of it to bother telling anyone. At the foot of the hill I could see a well-trodden trail I knew must be the pilgrim road to Kailas.

A few minutes later I was on it. No one had approached or called out and I felt safe enough. In fact, I was so worn out I hardly cared; the weather was awful, I was soaked, cold and hungry. For years I had dreamed of this wonderful day, the start of my *kora* around Gang Rinpoche, but for now there was no joy, no elation, my only thought was to make it through the day.

As the dirt trail climbed to a low ridge I saw a couple of jeeps go by on a road below. As they got closer I crouched behind some rocks and let them pass. I guessed they were dropping trekkers at the start of the trail and didn't worry too much. Over the ridge I entered a low grassy valley. At the head of the small plain stood a great pole, made from a single tree several metres high, known as the Tarboche, the 'Great Prayer Flagpole'. This marks the start of the trail, a trail that has been walked for thousands of years by countless hordes of the faithful and the curious, all with the good karma to have made it here.

In the middle of the valley I stopped to rest, my energy draining fast. I needed to eat. I left Monlam to rest and mixed myself a bowl of cold *tsampa*. As I ate I watched three people come over the ridge after me and carry on up the trail. They were all dressed in bright, modern gear and through my binoculars I could see they were two foreigners and their Tibetan guide — the first Westerners I'd seen in two months.

I carried on and soon arrived at the Tarboche, where thousands of prayer flags dripped in the rain as the two foreigners took photos of each other in front of the pole. Each year, usually in June during the festival of Sakadawa, which commemorates the Buddha's enlightenment, the pole is taken down and the flags replaced. The ceremony is attended by hundreds of Tibetans, but for now there was only myself, the foreigners and their guide. When they saw me they stopped and stared. I must have looked bizarre, a Westerner in Tibetan dress with his horse, a great knife on his belt, bedraggled in the rain. I said hello and made three circuits of the pole with Monlam and they went on their way over a small hill to Kang-nyi Chorten, a *stupa* that stands like a gateway to Kailas.

Above the pole was a flat ridge of bare red rock, known as the 'Buddha Platform'. Legend has it that, using magic powers, the Buddha flew here with five hundred disciples from India to give teachings. Naturally the spot is considered very auspicious and sacred and I thought it would be a good place to leave some of Khensur Thabkye Rinpoche's ashes. I left Monlam grazing near the pole and climbed onto the platform.

The wide expanse of smooth, flat rock was covered in little piles of stones placed by pilgrims. One end of the ridge was raised and I walked across to it, thinking that if the Buddha had taught here this was where he must have sat, where everyone could see and hear him. I walked to the rise and took out the tiny plastic box that had held the lama's ashes for more than two years. I found a space on a large flat boulder and opened the box. At last I was to fulfil my promise by bringing Khensur Thabkye Rinpoche's ashes here. I sprinkled a few grains on the boulder and piled smaller rocks and stones on top. 'Well, here we are, Rinpoche.' I said a short prayer, asking him to swiftly return to this life to keep teaching.

Back by the Tarboche I gathered up Monlam's lead rope and continued into the valley, past the *stupa*. Further up I could see Chukku Gompa on the cliff face opposite the mountain. It looked spectacular, half-lost in the cloud, and I would have loved to visit; however, the steep trail up the mountainside was impossible in the condition I was in, so I kept going.

In the valley below the *gompa* were a couple of stone buildings at the end of the road and I guessed one must be a checkpoint. The other was probably a shop or even a little restaurant. I was dying to get something to eat, but instead walked up the other side of the valley, past the ruins of an ancient *stupa* and on into the rain. Again the rain I saw as a curse was possibly a great blessing, as anyone who might have seen me and demanded to check my papers was probably huddled inside out of the cold and I walked past without incident.

By now there were more people; faster walking groups of Tibetan pilgrims were catching up and passing me and there were also a couple of groups of foreign trekkers. One group of Americans walked past as I rested on a rock; again, no one spoke to me, they looked and looked away as they went by, not sure what to make of me. They were all dressed in colourful trekking clothes, with equally well-dressed Tibetan guides. They carried nothing apart from their cameras as all their gear was being carried on yaks herded by Tibetan handlers. There seemed to be three or four yaks for each trekker, loaded to the gunwales with tents, folding camp chairs, cooking stoves and cylinders of gas, even barrels of purified water.

In contrast the families of Tibetans I saw had almost nothing. They were dressed in heavy *chubas,* most with cheap worn-out sneakers on their feet; anything they carried was tied to their backs in old sacks with bits of string or rope. There were a few Chinese — some carried *malas* and were obviously Buddhist while others seemed to be tourists from mainland China. They were the only ones who dared approach me and Monlam, and we had our photos taken a couple of times.

I struggled on; the rain never looked as if it was going to clear. Somewhere above me stood Gang Rinpoche and though I was now on my second day at the base of the mountain I still hadn't seen her. Later in the afternoon I met a trekking guide who could speak good English. We commiserated together about the awful weather. 'Do you think it will still be raining tomorrow?' I asked.

'Maybe, sometimes when it's like this it can rain for three or four days.'

I thought with some dread that I might walk right around the mountain and not even see her. Kailas was hiding from me, she knew I was standing at her feet and that it had taken me more than two years to get here. She knew I had prayed every day that I would see her radiant face, but when I'd arrived she'd pulled a veil over her head and sulked. Despite what I'd done I still wasn't ready to meet her face to face. I hadn't earned the right and I still had to prove myself by suffering one more day in the rain.

My objective for the day had been to reach a small monastery called Dirapuk, but as the afternoon aged into evening it was clear I wasn't going to make it. I was totally worn out, the previous night's adventures and lack of food were taking their toll. I found myself struggling against the altitude and had to rest far more often than usual. Monlam dragged behind me, which made things worse. Any pious thoughts of sacred pilgrimage were gone, all I wanted to do was find some dry shelter and stop for the night.

At last I came to a couple of canvas tents set up beside the trail as teahouses and overnight rests for pilgrims. I tied Monlam outside, threw back the door and stooped inside. The tent was full of chatting Tibetans and Chinese but fell into silence as soon as everyone saw me. I swaggered across the dirt floor and took a seat on a bench by the stove. I felt like an outlaw and an outcast, a wanted man no one had the guts to tame, too wild and dangerous to confront.

But there were no shots of whisky in this saloon. I purchased a thermos of butter tea and instant noodles. The Tibetans smiled at the stranger and the Chinese grinned nervously. Finally, with some sustenance inside I cheered up. One of the tents was furnished with carpeted benches and I asked the young man in charge if I could spend the night there for a few yuan. 'OK, OK!' he said. He'd learnt a few words of English from passing trekkers.

We unloaded Monlam and carried my wet gear inside. I spread my sleeping bag by the fire and tethered my horse for the night. There wasn't much grass, but when the young man offered Monlam an armload of straw he didn't seem interested. I spent the rest of the afternoon teaching my host some more English and he asked me to paint a sign in English on a piece of white sheet to attract passing Westerners.

He told me he was from Darchen but would spend the summer pilgrimage season below the mountain running his little shop and tent. He'd made several circuits of the mountain himself, two by making full-length prostrations on the ground. He would lay his body completely flat, stand up and take three steps to where his head had been, then lay down flat again, all the way around the mountain — the fifty-eight kilometres had taken him thirteen days. Even more astonishingly, he had made two rounds of Lake Manasarovar in the same fashion. Those had taken him twenty-four days each and he showed me the scar on his forehead, caused by touching his head to the stony ground countless thousands of times.

Later in the evening another pilgrim arrived — he was a Bonpo and would circle the mountain anticlockwise. He had already completed over a hundred *kora*; for the last several years he had spent his whole summer at the mountain. Over the next few days I would hear other similarly incredible stories. I was often asked how many *kora* I was doing and my answer of one seemed very insignificant. However, when I told the Tibetans I had ridden here from Lhasa they looked impressed. Later I walked down to the river to have a wash. I took out my little mirror and understood why no one wanted to speak to me. I looked a fright, my face still so black it looked as if I'd just done a shift down a coalmine.

It was a warm night inside the tent; I was given a couple of bowls of *tukpa* and although the young man was running a business he generously refused to allow me to pay. With a full belly I slept like a baby and when I woke in the morning the tent was full of Tibetans. They were sharing thermoses of tea and legs of cold boiled mutton before they set off on the day's walk. They must have slept out in the open, probably unable to afford to sleep inside.

When I stepped outside to check on Monlam I was thrilled to see the skies had cleared during the night — I knew that within a few hours I would see Gang Rinpoche. As it turned out, the previous day's rain was the last I would have to face — it would remain fine for the rest of the trip. It was cold, though, the sun still not above the surrounding peaks and when I went to collect Monlam he was shivering in the frost.

I loaded up and thanked the young man for his kindness and before I left he gave me a packet of noodles. We set off, energised by a good night's sleep and a decent meal and I felt the complete opposite from the day before, my spirits high. We walked for an hour; the trail was easy over hard-packed dirt and soon Dirapuk Gompa came into view on the other side of the valley. I crossed a small stream, the trail dropped around some boulders and then rounded the corner of a small hill.

Suddenly I looked up; there was Gang Rinpoche's stunning north face, a sheer cliff some fifteen hundred metres high, covered in yesterday's snow. To see it at last was staggering and I instantly burst into tears of joy and relief. 'We're here, boy! We made it! We bloody-well made it!' I hugged Monlam and then made three prostrations on the ground towards the mountain. 'Thank you, Buddhas! *Tujachay Khensur Thabkye Rinpoche! Tujachay!*'

This was surely the greatest moment of my life; everything I had done had been leading up to this day. All at once I felt that every step I had taken, every kilometre I'd ridden, every freezing night, every hungry day, all the storms I'd been through, every trial, hardship and hassle, had all been worth it. I was so grateful I had come to Tibet two years ago, so glad I had carried on every time I'd wanted to give up, and so happy I had returned this year to finish what I'd started. The reward I was receiving now was worth a thousand times more than all the pain and discomfort I'd suffered.

We walked on and came to a small village of tents — again people had set up shops and accommodation. I had some tea and noodles and bought more food, including a sack of wheat for Monlam. I didn't have any intention of going any further that day. I could have stayed in one of the tents but there was no grass and I decided to cross the valley and camp near the monastery.

I walked Monlam down to the Lha Chu river and we crossed its crystal waters. Below the slopes on the other side I found a pasture of reasonable grass. There wasn't much shelter but I guessed the skies would stay clear and I was directly opposite the mountain's face. I wanted it to be the first thing I'd see when I woke the next morning. I fed Monlam some of the wheat and left him to graze. I spread my wet gear out in the sun to dry and made tea on a fire. The rest of the morning I sat in the sun looking at Kailas; she was like a beautiful woman and I could hardly take my eyes off her.

Kailas is ancient; even for a mountain she is old, having risen from the Tethys Sea some fifty million years ago. By contrast, the nearby Himalayas are the youngest mountains on earth, a mere twenty million years old. The whiteness of the mountain's face is said to reflect light into space like a giant mirror, and the four great rivers that rise from her feet, the Indus, the Brahmaputra, Karnali and the Sutlej, flow in the four cardinal directions and have watered and fed some of the world's great civilisations.

Since the beginning of time Gang Rinpoche has drawn people to her — the Bonpo and other shaman from all over Asia, Hindus and Buddhists, seekers and runners, all trying to find something or leave something behind, the faithful and the faithless, sinners and saints. Many of Tibet's great yogis spent time here: Milarepa and his disciples who renounced every worldly distraction and came to live in solitude in caves and holes in the mountains; the great Bon masters, Shenrab Miwoche and Naro Bonchung and countless others, their names remembered by the stones and their empty retreats, all came here to channel the energy from the mountain through their own consciousnesses and achieve the highest realisations. Every peak around the mountain, every river and tiny lake, every boulder seems to be associated with a deity or protector being; at places depressions in the rocks are said to be the footprints of the Buddha himself.

In the afternoon I walked back across the valley and above the tent town to the base of the mountains. To the left of Kailas is a great heap of rubble the size of a small mountain itself, said to be associated with the deity Avalokiteshvara; to the right is another associated with Vajrapani and further up the valley is yet another, associated with Manjughosa. These three together are the patron protectors of Tibet and I decided they would be auspicious places to leave some more of Khensur Thabkye Rinpoche's ashes. As I had done on the Buddha Platform, I left a few grains in each place on top of large rocks and covered them with stones, saying a short prayer at each site. I also left some directly in front of the north face and some I sprinkled into a clean stream flowing from the mountain into the Lha Chu.

Back across the river I climbed up to the monastery. As I arrived I met a group of locals and monks who were building a row of small *stupa*. One was just about to be filled with sacred objects, rolls of printed pages from scriptures, clay figures of the Buddha, incense and *khata*. I thought it would be the perfect place to inter some more of the ashes, so with great difficulty I tried to explain to one of the monks what I wanted to do. Eventually he seemed to understand, but he had to get permission from the head lama and someone was sent to fetch him from further along the hillside, where he was mixing cement.

When Tenzin Namja arrived I took one look and felt an instant affinity for him, as I would if he had been an old friend. There was a quiet calmness around him, a gentleness, but a strength as solid as the mountain above us. He shook my hand and we touched foreheads. The monk related the request I had made; I showed the lama the little box of ashes and indicated that I wanted some of them to go inside the *stupa*. Tenzin Namja nodded and smiled and gestured for me to follow him inside the *gompa*.

The small temple was still undergoing reconstruction after being totally destroyed by the Chinese. The outside of the building was complete, but inside it was almost empty, no statues, or paintings, no lamps burning, not even an altar. Up a short flight of stairs I was shown a small cave the *gompa* had been built around. This was where Gotsangpa, one of Milarepa's disciples, had lived and meditated nearly eight hundred years ago. I followed the lama up more creaking wooden stairs to his room.

He took a seat on a bench behind a low table and I knelt on the floor. The lama pulled out a sheet of paper and I wrote Khensur Thabkye Rinpoche on the sheet and he wrote the name again in Tibetan. He folded it into a packet and I tipped a small amount of the ashes inside; it was then folded up and wrapped in a swatch of cloth, which would be placed inside the *stupa*. I felt very fortunate to have been here at the right time; the lama's ashes would be sealed for ever inside a *stupa* directly in front of the holy mountain. Before I left I gave Tenzin Namja the money I had carried with me all the way from Xianza, the money that I had tried to give to the nomad who had recaptured Whitey all those weeks ago, and some money on behalf of the family who had given me food a week earlier, as an offering to help in the reconstruction of the *gompa*.

Outside again I shook hands with the lama and he touched his head to mine once more. *'Sangnyi nga Dolma-la dro,'* I told him, tomorrow I'm going to cross Dolma-la pass.

The lama nodded and smiled; as I walked back to my camp I was filled with a sense of ease, as if his serenity had infected me. For several days I would think of Tenzin Namja often; although I would never be able to say exactly what it was about him, he left a deep impression on me. I was sure I would meet him again, somewhere.

I spent the rest of the afternoon drinking tea and eating two bowls of rather unappetising instant noodles, trying to build up my strength for the next day. Dolma-la was just over six kilometres away, but it was a further seven hundred and sixty metres higher than the nearly five thousand I was at now. I knew it could turn out to be a very tough day and I wanted to be ready.

I also knew it would be something of a day of reckoning for me, as Dolma-la was the pass where I had pledged I would 'die once'. This was where I was supposed to leave the grasping, self-centred, lying, cheating side of me behind to die in the cold of the coming winter. I had hoped I would walk down the other side of the pass a changed man, at least in a small way, but now that the day was almost upon me I felt as though I needed more time. But time had run out. I was here now and I had to keep going.

That evening, as the sun went down over the mountain I sat on a rock facing the peak and said my prayers as Monlam chomped his way through another scoop of grain. The night was cold but still and perfectly clear as Gang Rinpoche shone in the moonlight, so brightly she seemed to dim the stars. I had a terrible night; the oily noodles churned in my stomach and I spent half the night throwing up. I felt weak and exhausted — not the best way to prepare for a seven-hundred-metre climb.

I didn't get out of my sleeping bag until after eight. I gave Monlam some more wheat and started the fire, still feeling sick, but I had to get something inside me or I wouldn't have the strength to make it over the pass. After tea and *tsampa* we set off; the trail was already busy with families of Tibetans and I saw a group of Western trekkers go by in the distance. The trail rose slowly towards the pass and I paced myself by reciting *Om mani padme hum* as we went. Every few minutes I would stop to rest and look back at Kailas, her face changing every time.

After a couple of hours I came to an area strewn with discarded clothing, several layers of old *chubas*, jackets, shirts and shoes covered the ground. This was 'The Place of Death', the Silwutsel Charnel Ground named after a famous cremation ground near Bodh Gaya in India. Here people leave a personal object or item of clothing to symbolise their renunciation of worldly possessions. For the last few days I had been trying to think of what I should leave here, but anything I didn't mind leaving felt too insignificant, and I was too attached to anything that would have been worthy of abandoning.

We stopped in the middle of the ground. I snipped a few hairs from Monlam's mane and threw them into the wind, making the offering on his behalf. I cut some of my own hair and a piece from the hem of my oilskin coat, but it wasn't enough. A young Tibetan pilgrim had come up the trail behind me and stopped to rest a few metres away, watching me as if he knew something was about to happen. I whisked my long knife from my belt and sliced a cut into my hand at the base of my thumb; my offering of blood dripped onto the rock. I looked up at the Tibetan, who nodded; I had done the right thing. I smiled back and we carried on.

From there the trail climbed steeply and became rockier. We passed a small pool of brilliant blue and an hour later stood at the base of the pass. I could see the daunting climb rising above me, a narrow twisting trail disappearing into the rocks; somewhere lost at the top was Dolma-la. We set off. *Om . . . ma . . . ni . . . pad . . . me . . . hum . . . Om . . . ma . . . ni . . . pad . . . me . . . hum.* And then rest. We repeated this over and over and over, each time making just a few metres before gasping for breath. It was a tough climb, but I surprised myself with how well I managed; I had expected a 'near-death' experience, but I guess by now I was as acclimatised and as fit as I ever would be, having spent two months at altitude. Slowly the pass grew nearer and I began to enjoy the challenge of the climb. My view of Gang Rinpoche dropped behind the lower peaks; I would see her again in a few days with a new face, but for now I turned away and continued to climb.

Slowly the pass drew nearer. I topped a shoulder and was greeted by the roar of thousands upon thousands of prayer flags in the wind, the top now just a walk away. *La sososososo! Tujachay Khensur Thabkye Rinpoche! Tujachay!* It was exactly two months since I'd set out from Yangbajian, I had covered fifteen hundred kilometres with five horses and now I was here, at the top of Dolma-la pass at an altitude of over five thousand, six hundred metres.

The pass was busy; there was a group of about fifteen Italian trekkers with their guides, porters and yaks, as well as a couple of groups of Tibetans, all amused to see a Westerner with a horse struggle to the top. I also saw the Bonpo pilgrim I'd met at the tent a couple of days earlier; he was halfway through another circuit. I tied Monlam to a rock and fed him the last of the grain while I left some more of Rinpoche's ashes on a boulder on the edge of the pass. On another rock I left a few articles I brought with me; a stone from my favourite beach at home, a sketch of myself a friend had made, lucky charms from friends and a couple of photos. I tied *khata* that Tseyang and Nyima had given me to a rope of prayer flags and sat on a rock in the sun.

The trekkers and the Tibetans carried on and I was left alone with the sound of the wind howling through the flags. Monlam finished his lunch and stood dozing in the sun. He was worn out and in need of another day off. I said my prayers and dedicated the tiny amount of merit I may have created to my horses and everyone who had helped me get this far. I tried to think if I had 'died', or if I could 'die' now. I tried to imagine I was saying goodbye to the side of myself I wanted to leave behind and that when I started down the other side it would be without him. But when I looked inside I couldn't find him. I knew he was still there, but he knew what I was trying to do and remained hidden. I would just have to see if he would show himself later.

I untied Monlam and turned him round to face the trail on the other side. I stood there for a few moments, thinking I had come as far as I could and the next step would be a step towards home. I finally felt I had earned the right to go back — I could be content with what I had done and when I returned to New Zealand my memories of Tibet could rest quietly within me. I had laid the demons of regret and disappointment to rest and finished what had been left undone two years earlier. Time was getting on; it was still a long way down the other side, but I took one last look over my shoulder. And then I took my first step on the trail to home.

If I'd thought the trail up to the pass was tough, going down the other side was a killer. The far side of the pass was kilometres of loose rock and jumbled boulders, and really not suitable for a horse. A person on foot or the nimble yaks would have little trouble, but poor Monlam struggled. Often the trail cut between gaps in the boulders so tight Monlam could barely squeeze through. We passed a small green lake known as the 'Pool of Great Compassion' and the land levelled out; however, the going didn't get any easier. Now there was no trail and we had to pick our way from one boulder to the next.

I was terrified Monlam was going to put his foot in a hole and break his leg, but my dear friend did well. I'd grumbled about his behaviour before, but I had to take my hat off to him that day; he really was a very good horse, brave and hardy and the most forgiving animal I've ever met. Finally, late in the afternoon we made it to the grass of the valley floor, where I found a couple of canvas tents pitched next to the Lham Chu river.

We could have gone on, but I was in no hurry. Monlam had cuts and grazes on his poor, tired legs from the rocks and while they didn't seem to bother him, I knew I'd have to give him a day off soon. I unloaded him and left him to graze; the proprietor of the humble tents sold me a thermos of butter tea and a bowl of *tsampa* and I paid him fifteen yuan to spend the night in an empty tent next door.

The campsite was a mess, the tents filthy, the dirt floors covered in rubbish and at night they crawled with mice. Outside, hundreds of plastic instant noodle bowls lay in the dirt as they were slowly spread around the valley by the wind. There was no one to collect the rubbish and the Tibetans seem to have little idea of such things. Anything unusable is thrown out the door where it will be covered by snow in the winter, but will still be there the next summer, and the next. Slowly, the most perfect mountain is being overcome with offerings of garbage.

It was a freezing night and I had to contend with mice running up and down my sleeping bag and occasionally over my face. I was up early and after more tea and *tsampa* we carried on down the valley. A short way on I passed a pilgrim making his way along the trail in full-length prostrations. I couldn't imagine what it must have been like coming down from the pass over all the rocks.

It was another cool but perfectly clear Kailas day and we walked without stopping until we reached Zutrulpuk Gompa at about one in the afternoon. I had tea and *tsampa* in a little house below the temple before going up to the main hall to have a look inside. The temple is built around a small cave where it's said Milarepa, the greatest of all of Tibet's yogis, lived and meditated, achieving enlightenment in a single lifetime.

The story of Milarepa is an inspiration; he came from a background of evil and sorcery, destroying those who had turned his family into beggars after his father died by bringing hailstorms down on their crops. But then, overcome by remorse, he turned his mind towards virtue and vowed to use the rest of his life to become enlightened. Back then the teachings of the Buddha weren't so easy to come by — the masters who knew them would only impart their wisdom to those they thought worthy vessels for such sacred instructions. Milarepa came under the guidance of the master Marpa, who made him endure years of hardships and harsh treatment before finally accepting him as a disciple and revealing the teachings.

However, his patience paid off and he was soon gathering his own disciples. They journeyed to Kailas, where they lived alone in caves, naked except for loincloths and living on nothing but wild nettle soup.

For thousands of years before the arrival of Buddhism in Tibet, Kailas had been the domain of the Bon practitioners, but due to a prophecy from the Buddha himself, Milarepa challenged the Bon master Naro Bonchung to a series of contests of their magical powers. After hurling giant boulders at each other and stepping over vast lakes in a single stride there was still no clear winner, so Milarepa suggested a race to the top of the mountain at the first crack of dawn.

In the morning Naro Bonchung set off through the air, flying on his magic drum; it appeared Milarepa would be outdone, but as the first rays of sunlight hit the peak of the mountain the great sage joined with them and miraculously appeared on the summit. The Bonpo shaman was so shocked he fell from his magic drum, which crashed down the south face of the mountain, gouging a crevice that can still be seen today, or so the story goes.

Inside the small temple I met the friendly lama in charge and paid a few yuan for a large lamp of butter, which I lit and placed on the altar as an offering. I paid a few more yuan for a smaller lamp, which I offered inside the small cave where Milarepa is said to have spent years in meditation, which has itself been turned into a shrine where Tibetan pilgrims make prostrations to the cave and recite prayers at the entrance.

I crawled inside and sat on the floor, now covered in pink linoleum. There was just enough space for me to sit upright and in the stone ceiling I could see indentations, which are said to be the imprints of the saint's shoulders. Apparently the roof had been too low, so with his handy magic powers he used his shoulders to force the ceiling up and give himself more room. Unfortunately, he lifted a bit too far, making the cave too big, and somewhere outside above the cave is another rock with the impressions of his hands where he'd pushed it back down again.

Whatever, it was a special moment to be sitting in such an auspicious place, where one man who had truly turned his mind to the practice of the dharma had lived. I realised how lucky I was to be there, how many people would do anything to have the chance to sit where I was and would never have the opportunity. I closed my eyes, hoping some of Milarepa's powers would diffuse into me, but of course despite the trials I had been through they were still minor compared to his and I was a far from suitable vessel. However, before I left the cave I took the opportunity to say my prayers and slipped a few grains of Rinpoche's ashes into a crack in the wall.

It was hot outside and looking down the valley I could see it was only a couple of hours to the end of the trail. I'd planned to spend the night near the *gompa*, but something made me want to keep going. For the last few days I'd been surrounded by other people and I had a longing for solitude again. My circuit of the mountain was almost complete; I still had to pass the checkpoint and I wanted to get that over and done with so we could take a day off and rest.

Further on we left the pilgrim trail and crossed the Zhong Chu river on foot. We began climbing into the dry hills to keep as much distance between us and the checkpoint as we could. From here the mountain was hidden by the lower peaks and I wouldn't see her again for a couple more days when I got out onto the plain. Monlam was worn out, I was nearly beat and a hard, hot climb over the hills wasn't what we needed. However, despite having made it to the mountain and successfully round it, I was still desperate not to be caught by the authorities. I still wanted to make it to Manasarovar.

Over the hills we dropped back down onto the desert plain, found the trail we had followed in a few days earlier and walked on the rest of the afternoon, retracing our steps. It was a good feeling to be walking on the same track; the last time I'd been on it I had been struggling, now I was on my way home. However, fatigue was fast running me down; it was hard going over the sandy ground and my steps were getting shorter. I was trying to make it back to a little valley we had passed before where I'd seen very good grazing.

The grass was thick, like a rich carpet. I unloaded Monlam and he sat down, lying flat on his side in exhaustion before getting back on his tired legs to graze. He'd had a tough time around the mountain over the pass and the rocks; it must have been 'horsey hell', but now, in this quiet little valley with soft green grass, he must have felt as if he was in the Garden of Eden. My feet were killing me and I spent the rest of the day and most of the next walking around on the grass in my socks.

I made a good fire for tea and noodles and sat outside until an almost-full moon rose above the hills. I crawled into my sleeping bag and lay there warm and contented, staring up at the stars. The next day was spent resting, lazing around in the sun and watching Monlam alternate between sleeping and eating. I didn't have much to do, but all day I kept thinking of adjustments I could make to my gear, things I should buy or acquire, things I should make, until I reminded myself that there was no point.

From my little camp I planned to ride down onto the plain and on to the sacred Lake Manasarovar. I hoped to circle the lake to complete the pilgrimage and then try to get back to Lhasa. I only had about a week to go, then I would give Monlam away and start hitching back to the city. I looked across at my horse sitting contentedly on the soft grass and knew it was going to be hard to say goodbye. I walked over to him. He didn't bother getting up and I scratched him behind the ears. He loved this and cocked his head to enjoy it. 'Good boy, Monlam, only a few more days, then you'll be free.'

I read most of the afternoon and as evening fell I climbed the small hill above my camp to watch the sun go down over the mountain Gurla Mandhata. When darkness had laid its blanket over the plain I headed back to make more tea before bed. I realised I hadn't seen the crows all day. It was the first day off I'd taken in ages without their oily black presence hanging around my camp. I wondered if it had been their mission to get me round the mountain and now that it was done I was on my own. *Well, thanks, guys, whoever you were!*

I woke in the morning in darkness and lay in my bag until the sun lightened the sky, but even then the moon and stars were still bright. I loaded up a reluctant Monlam and we set off onto the plain. I walked him all the way down to the bottom of the wide valley, worried about riding him. He hadn't been ridden for five days and I didn't know if he was going to have enough strength to make it the rest of the way. But I had no choice, there wasn't much left in me either and I couldn't walk all the way.

However, Monlam seemed to have regained some of his spark and he went well. We crossed the road, then a boggy flat, after which I stopped to take a break. Looking back I was met with a stunning view of Gang Rinpoche's south face. She rose above any other peak in the range, quite separate and distinct, like a last remaining tooth in an otherwise empty gum. Her face was white except for the deep, dark scar across the surface where the Bonpo master's magic drum had carved its way.

We rode on and Raksas Tal came into view. The Tibetans call the lake Langa Tso; it's shaped like a crescent moon and embodies the forces of darkness and night, in contrast to the rounded sun of Manasarovar and its light and day. The two lakes balance each other, the good and evil, right and wrong, warm and cool; one couldn't be without the other. I could just make out a monastery on the northern corner of the lake with my binoculars. I guess it received few visitors — although Raksas Tal is also considered sacred it's not popular with pilgrims. I would have loved to have been one of the few, but it was too far.

As it was the shore was still some distance and I found my way blocked, this time by a man-made obstacle. A mesh fence stretched as far as I could see on both sides and the barrier infuriated me. I couldn't see the end or any gates in the damn thing at all and if I couldn't get past it here I would have to give up trying to reach the lake. I hated being defeated and decided there was only one thing for it. I unfolded the hacksaw on my army knife and cut a hole in the bloody thing. I knew I must be gathering a large heap of non-virtue by vandalising some nomad's fence and I was stabbed in the thumb by a piece of broken wire as instant karmic retribution. We were soon on our way again, but as it turned out we would never make it to the waters of the lake. The shores were barren and empty and the last few hundred metres were a boggy mudflat swarming with sandflies. I couldn't risk taking Monlam across, nor could I stand the flies and so we turned east and headed towards Manasarovar.

We crossed a desert of low hills covered in dry scrub and later in the afternoon the great lake came into view behind Chiu Gompa, built on a high outcrop of rock next to the lake. I stopped at the base of the hill and led Monlam up to the temples. The buildings were locked and there seemed to be no one around; however, the views were worth the climb — dramatic sweeps of the lake in one direction and Gang Rinpoche peeking above the hills in the other.

The village of Chiu lay below and we climbed back down to the small collection of mud-brick houses. On the edge of the village I met an old woman, who took me to her home. I paid her to cook me a meal of mutton and noodles and then stocked up on supplies of *tsampa* before setting off towards the lake.

Chiu is built on the banks of a dry riverbed. The river known as the Ganga Chu should flow from Manasarovar to Raksas Tal, but now all that's left are a few stagnant ponds stranded when the level of the lake dropped too low for it to flow. The Tibetans believe the state of the Ganga Chu is a barometer for the general condition of Tibet; if the waters are flowing freely, Tibet must also be doing well; if the river is dry, Tibet is in trouble. By looking at the grass and scrub growing in the bottom of the riverbed I could see the river hadn't flowed for some time. At a small cairn of stones on one bank I left a few more of Khensur Thabkye Rinpoche's ashes; perhaps leaving them there might create enough auspiciousness to make the waters flow again.

Soon Monlam and I were standing on the windswept shores of the great lake. A bright deep blue stretched before us to the mountains on the other side. The circuit of the lake is eighty-five kilometres and I guessed it would take three or four days on foot. The lake lies at four and a half thousand metres, making it one of the highest bodies of fresh water in the world. Throughout history dozens of Tibetan saints have spent time on her shores, blessing themselves in the sacred waters and seeing visions on the peaceful surface. The lake also holds special significance for Hindus and Brahmins from Nepal, who trek through the Himalayas to bathe in the freezing water, believing that immersion in the lake secures rebirth as a god in their next life.

I threw some more ash into the lake next to a *stupa* draped in prayer flags at the start of the circuit trail and set off around the shoreline, heading for the ruins of a monastery called Cherkip Gompa. The trail was easy over sand and loose pebbles, but the strong wind quickly wore us down. As Chiu dropped from view we found ourselves completely alone on the trail; although Kailas must receive thousands of pilgrims a year, far less carry on and circle the lake. Over the next few days I would meet hardly anyone.

Late in the afternoon we walked along the base of sheer cliffs hundreds of feet high. Set into the face of the cliffs were hermitages, tiny refuges so high above the ground I couldn't imagine how they were reached. I wondered if the occupants were lowered by ropes from the cliff tops. Some were ancient and no longer in use, their walls broken and fallen, but further on I found some in better condition. They could be reached by precarious stairways cut into the rock, little brick huts built on ledges with a tiny yard behind, where I could see scrub had been piled up as firewood. Monks must come here from the monasteries to spend months or even years in complete solitude, walled up in their retreats to spend endless days looking out across the lake in meditation and contemplation of Buddha's teachings. It seemed an idyllic existence, utter peace and tranquillity, but the mental strength needed to commit to such a life must be immeasurable. The hermits turn their backs on the world and lock themselves in their cells, where they battle with their own minds.

By evening we had reached the ruins of Cherkip Gompa, or rather the site where the monastery must have been. It is marked by a small *stupa* and *mani* wall, but the temples have been completely erased by the Chinese. I set up camp and watched the sun set over the lake. It was a cold night, the season was turning and autumn beginning. I was awake hours before daylight and lay in my bag waiting for it to get light enough to get up.

I restarted the fire and made tea as the sun came up over the hills at the end of the lake; it was a spectacular dawn and for some time the sun and moon shared the sky, the stars still bright. We were away before nine and carried on around the shoreline as the day warmed up. After a couple of hours the trail led away from the water and I rounded a low hill to find a small monastery, Langbona Gompa, just one small temple that was still being rebuilt. A couple of villagers took me in to meet the resident lama, a long-haired old man called Tashi Puntsog. The temple belongs to the Nyingma sect and the old man opened a small shrine room that had been set up as a temporary place of worship until the restorations are finished.

After making prostrations to the statues, Tashi Puntsog took me into his room where an old lady served me tea and *tsampa*.

'*Langbona gompa trapa katseu yawrey?*' I asked the lama how many monks there were at Langbona.

He told me there were only four monks. I heard this same answer to the same question whenever I asked it at monasteries in the area and the lama told me it was a limit set by the Chinese authorities; each temple could only have a maximum of four monks.

The Chinese government's claims that Tibet has religious freedom are a farce. They severely limit the activities of the monasteries, restricting the numbers of novices admitted to the orders and refusing to allow all the *gompa*s that were destroyed to be rebuilt. Around the lake some of the monasteries were slowly being rebuilt, but others were left as untouched ruins. Four monks is barely enough to keep a monastery's buildings maintained; it's not enough to keep an active community of practitioners engaged in serious study and religious works. The Chinese can claim the monasteries have been reopened, but they are little more than museums, alive but barely breathing.

I decided that when I'd finished the circuit of the lake I would return to Langbona and give Monlam to the lama. From here it wasn't too far to the town of Hor, where I could try to catch a ride back towards Lhasa. Before we set off again I told Tashi Puntsog I'd be back in three or four days to leave my horse with him. The lama seemed pleased by my offer and came outside with me when I left to point me in the right direction. I was told not to follow the shoreline, there was a massive plain between the *gompa* and Hor and the ground would be too boggy to cross close to the lake. I would have to walk kilometres away from it to be able to stay on solid ground.

We set off again out onto the plain; the grass grew long and thick but the sun was high and hot and for the rest of the day I baked in the heat. It was an exhausting walk across the grassland; the ground alternated from sandy desert, difficult and tiring to walk over, to areas of swamp impossible to cross. We had to keep changing direction in order to avoid these obstacles, which were soon added to by fences and slow, deep stretches of the Hor Chu river. This was the only time I rode; I was sorely tempted to stay on Monlam's back, but I knew that if I didn't walk I would break the *kora*.

I could see Hor in the distance and while I tried to avoid the town, every time I changed direction I seemed to be heading closer. The ramble of buildings never seemed to get any nearer, but eventually in the late afternoon

I crawled off the plain and found myself on the edge of town. I walked through the dusty little streets with Monlam, peeking around corners to see if there were any cops about. I didn't see any sign of the law and relaxed; along the main 'street' there were little mud-brick houses with signs in English stating 'shop' or 'restaurant', usually terribly misspelt. I realised foreigners must pass through the place on their way to or from Kailas and that apart from being dressed like a bandit and having my own horse, I wouldn't be such an oddity.

I entered one establishment, someone's home where they served meals, and was soon enjoying a bowl of *tukpa* cooked with fresh ginger. However, it was far from the fine-dining experience I had hoped for, with two noisy kids running about torturing two kittens. It was good to be inside for a while, but as soon as I'd finished I went and checked out a couple of the shops. In one I met a Tibetan man who had taught himself a bit of English and I tried to buy some toothpaste. He had none and neither did anyone else and soon I was back on the trail with Monlam, heading out of town towards the next *gompa*, Seralung.

After an hour we made it back to the shores of the lake, but the afternoon wind was blasting across the waters. Monlam was agonisingly slow and I had to drag him the rest of the day. I could barely keep walking, my feet were aching, the sole coming off one of my boots and I was so low on energy I felt as if I might collapse at any moment. Finally, in the evening we came around the last bend and found Seralung in a little valley above the lake. I struggled up the slope and tied Monlam outside.

Inside the courtyard I met a young monk who showed me inside the rebuilt temple and then took me across to a lodge the monastery ran for trekkers and pilgrims. I unloaded Monlam and put him out on the hillside for the night before dragging my stuff inside. Though I was too tired to enjoy it, my accommodation was very nice — a little room with a view over the lake to Gang Rinpoche in the distance.

I was too worn out to feel like eating, but an old woman brought me a couple of thermoses of hot water. I made a cup of tea and poured the rest of the water into a basin to soak my poor feet. The bliss of warm water on my feet for the first time in months was almost too much to bear. However, my body rejected the tea; I hadn't even finished the mug when I had to hobble outside to the yard and throw up. I realised I had walked myself into exhaustion during the day and probably mild dehydration as well. I started writing my journal, but had to stop after a few minutes; my body demanded sleep and a moment later I collapsed onto the simple bed and slept like the dead.

I was woken at half past two in the morning by the sound of splashing water. A tiny mouse had somehow got himself into my washbasin and couldn't get out. I fished him out by the scruff of the neck and went back to sleep. In the morning Monlam was nowhere to be seen; he'd broken his rope during the night and wandered off. I walked up the valley behind the *gompa*, trying to find him and spotted him on the road by the lake making his way back towards Hor. He was still hobbled and couldn't really escape.

'*Monlam la! Ho sha!*' I yelled. He looked around at me on the top of the hill and obediently stopped. I slid down the slope and caught him without trouble. 'Come on, boy, where do you think you're going?' He looked sheepish, like a little kid about to get a telling off, but I couldn't be angry; he was probably hungry and off in search of something to eat.

For most of the day we walked along the shores of the lake on soft mosses and grass. I could hardly take my eyes off the lake; Manasarovar's waters were the bluest I'd seen so far and the sight of Kailas rising in the distance made for a perfect portrait. However, I was onto my last roll of film and had to stop myself from clicking away the final frames.

During the middle of the day we caught up with a group of about twenty-five Tibetan pilgrims who had spent the night at the *gompa* and set off earlier. They'd hired a truck to carry their belongings and were making their way around the circuit on foot. The group was probably a couple of extended families — everyone was there, from little kids who skipped beside the shore to old grandmas who had to be helped along.

The group moved very slowly, just wandering along, and spent much of the time picking through piles of washed-up lake weed looking for sacred objects — egg-shaped bundles of water grass, black stones, coloured sands and dead dry fish. The fish are said to have great medicinal value. I had seen their dried bodies on the altars of the *gompa*s where they'd been offered; it is said that eating a small piece will ease the pain of childbirth. When I passed the group they had stopped by a flutter of prayer flags, where there was a small spring of fresh water. The Tibetans were making prostrations to the lake, washing in the water of the spring and collecting it in plastic bottles to take home.

By late afternoon we'd made it to Yerngo Gompa, or rather the ruins of what once must have been a grand monastery on the shores of the lake. The temple was associated with Atisha, the Indian Buddhist master who re-established Buddhism in Tibet in the eleventh century after it was destroyed by an evil king. Apart from the crumbling mud walls nothing remains and I wondered what had become of the monks who had lived there.

I hobbled Monlam and left him to graze while I set up my camp in a corner of the walls, in what once must have been part of the main hall. On the ground

I found a single faded prayer flag. I dusted it off and hung it on the wall with a couple of sticks as pins. That night I slipped a few grains of ash into a hole in the wall. As I said my prayers that night I wondered how long it had been since someone had recited prayers within these walls.

The next day was perfect, sunny and warm and the lake was calm. Monlam lazed all day and I sat by the fire reading and relaxing. I knew it would only be two more days until I reached the end of the trail at Langbona and I found myself starting to look back on what I'd done, trying to decide what it meant. Had I achieved anything apart from the physical adventure of the journey? Had anything changed inside me? Would anything be different when I returned home? What was the real meaning of pilgrimage?

I had travelled fifteen hundred kilometres since setting out from Lhasa, it had been three and a half thousand kilometres since leaving Garilang, a total of over five months on horseback across Tibet. I had used twelve horses in all, crossing more passes than I could recall, more rivers than I could count, mountains, grasslands, plains and deserts. I had pushed myself close to my physical limits and at times beyond what I could emotionally bear. Now the journey was all but over, and for what?

I flicked through the pages of the Dalai Lama's book trying to find something I hadn't read before, but I couldn't find any answers. Perhaps I'd been asking the wrong questions? Perhaps I had learnt nothing, perhaps nothing had changed, nothing had improved, perhaps I was still as I'd always been. But perhaps I had to go through all of this and come this far, three and a half thousand kilometres by horse across Tibet, just to know it? Maybe this journey had been what I'd needed to put me on the start of the real path, the path through my own mind. Now, maybe, I had found it and even though I was yet to take the first real step at least now I knew where the trail began, which is much better than wandering lost and aimless in the middle of nowhere.

I looked up across the lake to Gang Rinpoche and started laughing. I felt as though I'd been chasing my own tail all the way across Tibet, running away from something I couldn't leave behind and chasing something I always had with me. I felt as though Tibet had played a joke on me. I'd travelled the whole time with the bloody map upside down, as if for months I'd been totally lost and I'd only just realised! Whatever, it was worth it just to know this much and I was grateful. It was a warm afternoon, there was little wind and when I went to fill up my water bottle from the lake I found the water wasn't so cold after all.

I wonder what it would be like to be reborn in the god realm? According to the Hindus all I needed to do was immerse myself in the sacred waters of

Manasarovar. The vast expanse of blue quickly became more inviting with Kailas shining down, her face reflected in the pure water.

What the hell! I might as well find out! I stripped off. There was no one around and I hadn't seen anyone all day and it was the first time I'd undressed since Lhasa. I stood on the shore up to my ankles in water, looking towards the mountain. This was going to be a magical experience. How many other Westerners had done this? I felt privileged and blessed — I held out my hands to the sky and waded deeper into the lake, my eyes on sacred Gang Rinpoche and a mantra on my lips. Blissful immersion was to be mine. I threw myself forward into the lake.

'Fuck! Fuck! Fuck!' I jumped up scrambling for the shore, blood pouring from my nose, I'd dived too deeply into the shallow water and hit my stupid head on a stone on the bottom, right between my eyes! 'Oh fuck! Fuck, fuck, fuck!' I told myself to get out of the water, fearing I was going to pass out and drown. I made it to the shore as blood continued to flow, covering my face and chest, Manasarovar now receiving a fair offering from my veins as well.

I laughed, realising how ridiculous the whole situation must look. *You idiot, Ian! You fuckin' idiot!* My head ached, my knees were shaking, I had two nasty cuts on the bridge of my nose, and the blood I was drenched in must have made it look like I'd just taken part in some kind of Satanic ritual. I walked back into the water and cleaned the worst of the blood off before gathering up my stuff and staggering back to camp. It was then that the reality of what could have happened set in. I stopped laughing. It wasn't funny. I could have split my head open, I could have smashed all my teeth in, I could have knocked myself unconscious and still be lying face down in the lake a week later. I had made it all the way across Tibet pretty much unscathed but I could have died in a stupid accident. The Buddhas may have been watching over me, but I certainly wasn't making it easy for them.

I calmed down and made some tea, thankful to be sitting in the sun alive and able to enjoy it. My nose still ached; I would have to wear a sticking plaster over it for the next few days and the scars would remain for much longer. It was a perfect evening and I sat by my fire watching darkness quietly lie across the lake as the stars came out one by one. I knew I would only have a couple more nights like this and I should savour them.

In the morning we set off almost before daylight, I was so keen to get moving. We walked for an hour and reached the next monastery, Trugo Gompa. I was nervous; it was a larger settlement with its own guesthouse and I had heard there was a police checkpoint. I watched the buildings with my binoculars for a while but couldn't see any activity and sneaked behind the main courtyard to the temple. Trugo is of the Gelukpa order and overseen by a young incarnate lama called Lobzang. There seemed to be no one about until I heard a door open above me; a young monk walked onto the balcony and tipped a basin of water into a drainpipe. *'Tashidelik!'* I greeted him, but he turned and went back inside.

I climbed up the narrow stairs to the balcony and invited myself into the monk's room. There were two monks inside, and a cat. I asked for tea and the youngest novice stomped across the floor to get me a thermos. He tipped some tea into my bowl and then slammed a bag of *tsampa* on the low table in front of me before returning to his seat, where he sat with his companion, sullen and sulky. I tried to make conversation by asking how far it was to the next *gompa,* Gossul, telling them I'd come by horse from Lhasa, but they barely replied to anything I said. I had a better conversation with the cat, with whom I shared my *tsampa*.

Later in the afternoon we made it to Gossul Gompa. The most spectacular of all the temples on the lake, it is set high above the waters in the face of a cliff. We climbed a narrow trail and reached the main buildings, where I left Monlam tied to a post on a ledge. From the courtyard the views over Manasarovar were incredible, I could see almost the whole shoreline and it was amazing to think I'd walked all that way.

The temples were open, but apart from the local cat there seemed to be no one about. Eventually I found an old man living in a tiny hut cut into the rock face below the *gompa*; he took me to another similar dwelling where I met a resident monk. We had tea and *tsampa* and the men asked what had happened to my nose. I retold the story and my hosts found it hilarious, although they seemed impressed I had chosen to submerse myself in the lake.

Before long we were back on the trail, heading once again towards Chiu Gompa. We'd made better time than I'd expected, so we walked slowly for the rest of the day. By six in the evening I guessed we were only a couple of hours from the monastery. I could have pushed on and found somewhere to stay in the village, but there was no need, and besides I wanted one more night under the stars, one more night alone in the wilds with my dear horse, one more yak-dung fire with strong black tea, one more sunrise over the lake. The next day would be the last.

I hardly slept the whole night, lying in my bag staring at the stars and waiting for it to get light. One side of me couldn't wait to get up and get going, to get the last day over and done with, but the other side was apprehensive about ending the greatest adventure of my life. In just a few hours this journey would be over and I'd have to say goodbye to Monlam. Even before the sun shone its first rays over the lake I was up and lit the fire. Monlam hadn't wandered far during the night and I found him in the gloom and led him into my camp to load up for the last time. 'This is it, boy, this is the last day.'

I sat by the fire looking out over the water as the sky quickly paled into daylight. After I rinsed my mug in the lake we set off. We rounded the last headland before Chiu; here there was a rocky outcrop draped in prayer flags jutting out into the lake. I left Monlam on the shore and climbed out to the last rock to sprinkle the remains of Khensur Thabkye Rinpoche's ashes. I was relieved. By leaving his ashes at these holy places, I had finally been able to keep my promise.

We walked on and as Chiu came into sight I found a camp of trekkers on the shore a kilometre from the village. As I approached, the Nepali guides came out to greet me. They were a jovial bunch who could all speak English and were astonished to see a Westerner walk up with a horse. When I told them I'd come from Lhasa they shook their heads. I was soon sipping cups of delicious Indian *chai*, and they gave me a bowl of rice pudding with cashew nuts for breakfast and a bowl of curried *tukpa*.

On the other side of the provisions truck before a row of hikers' tents I could see their charges having breakfast on folding tables and chairs. The group were Indian Hindus on a pilgrimage to the holy lake and mountain. They all looked miserable, wrapped in scarves and blankets as they huddled in the wind. No one was speaking to anyone else, they looked as if their trip was a religious inconvenience they were duty-bound but loath to do, and all they wanted was to get home, away from the cold, the wind and the dust.

Before I set off again the guides gave me packets of cheese crackers and a lump of real cheddar. An hour later we were back below Chiu Gompa and next to the prayer flags at the end of the *kora* trail. I looked across the lake towards where we'd come from in the last few days. The pilgrimage was now complete and all I had to do was get myself back to Lhasa. For the first time in five days I climbed on Monlam and we set off into the hills towards Langbona Gompa.

It felt great to be back in the saddle, but as I expected Monlam was dead slow. He was worn out and if this hadn't been the last day I doubted whether I could have pushed him any further. I'd had it too, my legs and feet were killing me, my boots falling apart; I'd run out of toothpaste, I was almost out of film and the notebook I used for a diary was nearly full. The weather was starting to turn. I'd run out of places to go and my visa would expire in two more weeks. It was time to go back.

We rode over the hills and onto a dry plain high above the lake where the views were astounding, and soon found ourselves back at the ruins of Cherkip

Gompa. I stopped for a break and had lunch of crackers and cheese before heading on; the next time we stopped I knew it would be the end of the trail. We had to climb high over stony ground to avoid the cliffs on the shores of the lake. I pushed Monlam on, impatient to get to the end. 'Come on, boy! Nearly there!'

Finally we topped a rise and the vast sweep of the plain by the lake came into view with Hor in the far distance; just around the hills below me I knew I would find Langbona. I walked Monlam down the other side. He was stuffed and I was sure he'd given me every ounce of energy he had. I thought about all the horses I'd had before him, all the kilometres they had carried me.

I thought of the first pass I'd crossed in the snow two years ago, I thought of finding Seka Gompa in the blizzard, of being chased in the jeep when I escaped, of being trapped under Ridey in the mud, of a campsite near Siling Tso, riding into Xianza when I'd given up, trying to cross Gurum-la and being turned back, meeting the monk who'd helped me catch Whitey, falling off Scrawny, brave little Skinny, finding Monlam when I needed him, and of reaching Gang Rinpoche. I felt a mixture of what seemed to be delayed fear of all that had happened to me, and an utterly exhausted relief.

Finally the *gompa* was there; we were on a dirt road that would take us to the front door and a few minutes later I was heading towards a hitching post driven into the ground by the gate. 'There it is, boy! That's the finish!'

And then we were there. I climbed out of the saddle for the last time and hugged Monlam. 'It's done, boy, it's all over, thank you, thank you, thank you!'

I'd made it to the end.

Tashi Puntsog, the lama, and a few of the villagers working on the restoration came out to greet me. I shook hands and handed him Monlam's lead rope. He said something to a young man who ran inside the temple and came back with a white *khata*. The lama presented me with the scarf and seemed very grateful I was offering him my best friend. We took photos and then unloaded the saddle and lugged it inside the gates. I told him Monlam was to stay with the monastery, that he wasn't to be sold and he wasn't to be ridden for a month to give him time to recover. *'Rey, rey, hako!'* Tashi Puntsog nodded.

I put my arms around Monlam's neck and hugged him for the last time, turning my head away so the Tibetans wouldn't see my tears. 'Good luck, boy. Thanks for everything, you're the best bloody horse I've ever had!' I whispered a prayer in his ear, praying that the Buddhas would protect him for the rest of his life and into the next. I knew I was leaving him in a good place, the people were kind and I guessed they would hardly ever need to ride him. The grassland below the *gompa* was thick with some of the best grazing I'd seen in Tibet. He would spend the rest of his days at ease by sacred Manasarovar and in the shadow of Gang Rinpoche, his reward for carrying me so well.

Inside I was served tea and my name recorded in the monastery's ledger along with a note of my offering. I hoped I was doing something to help the rebuilding in some small way at least. Tashi Puntsog invited me to stay the night, but I wanted to get moving and when one of the men offered to give me a lift into the valley, I accepted. Outside, we tied my saddlebags to the back of an old motorbike, I shook hands with the lama and we set off. As we drove down the slope I caught my last view of Monlam. He was looking pleasantly puzzled as he realised he was free, walking without hobbles or a bridle, or even a rope down towards the stream. I knew he was happy and I looked away as the bike sped on.

Chapter Thirteen

It took me five days to get back to Lhasa. I waited by the road below Langbona for an hour and felt very odd without Monlam, almost as if part of me was missing. I got a ride to Hor, where I waited by the road the rest of the day, then all of the next, until I was finally picked up by a truck the next morning. The driver and his crew were on their way to Saga, a town two days' drive away and I paid them to take me there.

Saga was quite a big place; there were lots of Chinese and I saw several tourists on their way to or from Kailas. In one little Tibetan noodle shop I met a young guide who could speak good English. I'd heard there was a police checkpoint somewhere around Saga and he confirmed this. He told me the checkpoint was a kilometre past the town on the road towards Lhasa and that I'd have to somehow get myself past it if I wanted to avoid the authorities. Although I felt more relaxed now, I was still afraid of getting into trouble and I wanted to make it all the way back without running into the law.

After checking into a little lodge in the evening I wandered out of town along the road to do some reconnaissance. I strolled along lazily, trying to look like an ordinary tourist and was soon in sight of the hut by the road with a barrier arm set up to stop any traffic for inspection. The Yarlung Tsangpo river ran below the road and I figured I could get cover from the riverbanks. There was a military fuel depot just before the checkpoint, but it didn't look like much of a threat. Everything looked simple enough. I would get up at four in the morning, walk out of town, sneak along the riverbank where the police wouldn't be able to see me, if they were even awake at that time and I doubted they would be, get past and then wait out of sight by the road for another lift.

I didn't sleep well; I was feeling quite excited and could hardly wait to get going. Just after four I sneaked out of the lodge gates and along the dark streets. The town was almost deserted and I walked slowly, pacing myself, feeling nervous but confident I wouldn't have too much trouble. Past the town I rounded a hill and could see the lights of the checkpoint and the military base not far away. I started heading for the river to begin my stealthy avoidance of the law.

Just then the dogs started barking. I couldn't see them, but there must have been a dozen mutts between the base and the checkpoint, they were all roaring in full voice and it was obvious they weren't barking at some stray cat. 'Oh, shut up, you fuckin' animals!'

I hurried on, my saddlebags and rolled-up *chuba* on my shoulder, and made it to the river. The bank was low here and didn't give much cover, but when all the lights in the army base came on I crouched on the ground, waiting to see what would happen.

Torch lights were flashing around the walls of the base; a soldier appeared at the main gates, flicked his light around but didn't come outside. I was afraid now; if I was caught I'd be dragged off to the police and I doubted they would be sympathetic to a foreigner caught trying to sneak past a checkpoint in the middle of the night. I couldn't bear to keep still and crept on towards the police hut. Now there were torches across the hillside behind the base; the soldiers had gone outside the walls and were making a search of the hills. For some reason they must have thought the dogs were barking in that direction. Later I found out Saga is on a route used by Tibetan refugees trying to get to the border of Nepal; obviously the soldiers must have thought the dogs were barking at a dissenting Tibetan, which explained why they were so vigilant.

Now I had some cover from the riverbank and soon I was below the checkpoint. I could see it just metres away, all the lights were on but I couldn't see anyone inside. I walked on, trying to keep low, careful where I put my feet so as not to kick a stone or an old can. As it was I was so edgy my footsteps sounded deafening. Just as I started to get past, a truck came by heading into Saga; it stopped at the checkpoint and I hoped the police would blame the barking dogs on its arrival. I scurried on and was soon safely past.

I walked on a couple of kilometres as day broke and the sky became light. I relaxed, thinking I was past any trouble and safe and stopped on an open stretch of road to wait for a ride. The sun rose above the mountains and I warmed up sitting on a rock. A couple of trucks came by but they were already full and wouldn't stop when I tried to wave them down so I returned to my rock in the sun.

Suddenly I looked up as a troop of soldiers came jogging over the hill on their morning exercises. They had decided to use the river flat as a drill ground and were soon metres away doing stretches and practising unarmed combat. I kept my head down, hoping they wouldn't see I wasn't Tibetan, but it was hopeless, the whole squad stopped to stare and their drill sergeant marched over and started shouting at me in Chinese. *'Hako masong!'*

I told him I didn't understand; the young officer was Tibetan and I gave him a story that I was waiting for my jeep from Saga.

He kept shouting at me and demanded my documents. *'Passport! Passport!'* he growled; it was time to use my fake permit.

I took out my passport; he reached for it but I pushed his hands away, *'Lagpa ma rey! Mig!'* No hands, I said, only eyes! He got angry and kept growling, but I refused to put my passport in his hands.

I showed him the front page and then my Chinese visa, neither of which he could read. Then I showed him the permit written in Chinese; he ran his finger along the rows of characters but didn't seem to be able to read this very well either, and I got the feeling he was embarrassed to admit it. After a moment he grunted and stomped back to his troops. I stayed put, calmly lying in the sun with my heart galloping. I was terrified he was going to head back up the road towards Saga and get the police; surely they'd have some knowledge of English — they might see the permit was a fake and I'd find myself in serious shit.

Every cell in my body was telling me to move, but I worried that if I took off the soldiers would become more suspicious and try to stop me. For several minutes I sat where I was, but when I saw the sergeant speak to one of the men who then started heading back over the hill, it was too much. I wished I still had Monlam so I could get on and ride, but at least I wasn't going to be caught sitting on my arse. I slowly stood up, picked up my gear and started walking.

I'd hardly made it a few metres when a little minibus came over the hill. I waved it down and the Chinese driver stopped out of curiosity. The vehicle was already full with a dozen people, but they managed to squeeze me in. They were on their way to Shigatze, Tibet's second-largest centre, via the smaller town of Latze and I negotiated a price with the driver to take me there. A moment later we were on our way, the Chinese Red Army left behind me in the dust.

The driver drove almost non-stop over atrocious roads, only stopping to fix frequent punctures. The ride was an agonising ordeal as I ended up sitting in the front of the van between the driver and a passenger in a spot that wasn't really a seat; it had no back and I was sitting on a coil of steel rope. Even after two months in the saddle within a couple of hours my arse was killing me.

We stopped for dinner in Latze and then drove on to Shigatze. By the time we arrived in the city and I'd found somewhere to sleep I had been on the go for twenty-four hours. I slept for three hours, then went off in search of the bus station. I'd been in Shigatze fourteen years ago on my first visit; then it had been nothing more than a few streets, the Tibetan village and the great monastery of Tashilunpo. Now it was a sprawling city. I could have been anywhere in inland China and the monastery that once dominated the city was now kilometres away, barely visible.

An hour later I was on my way towards Lhasa in a fairly comfortable bus. Later in the afternoon we stopped at a little roadside hut near a tiny village where some Tibetans had set up a kitchen serving noodles and tea. I got a thermos of butter tea and sat outside in the sun and made my own *tsampa*.

Looking around I could see the ruins of an old fort on the hillside above and I realised I'd been there before. I'd ridden through this valley on Whitey the day after the awful night in the snow. All at once I found myself back on those first difficult days of the ride, now more than two and a half months ago, days when I'd struggled so hard just to get going and when I'd thought of giving up. I looked across to the other side of the valley to where I could remember crossing the river.

The bus carried on and we were soon climbing into Hugu-la and I could see the exact spot I'd crossed the top with Whitey in the snow. Down the other side we passed places where I had camped and then stopped at a collection of huts I had ridden past. I could see the cleft in the mountains that led to Gurum-la, which I'd unsuccessfully tried to cross. I tried to imagine seeing myself go by as I had been back then, but I couldn't quite picture it. The image seemed to be of a different person altogether and I wasn't sure if that was a good sign or not.

Soon the bus was on the main Golmud–Lhasa road and finally at six in the evening the magnificent Potala came into view as we pulled into a little yard. I skipped off the damn smoky bus, elated at last. I'd made it all the way there and all the way back without meeting one single cop; apart from the soldier I'd met at Saga I'd hadn't been challenged by the authorities, in stark contrast to two years ago.

I walked onto the street, busy with evening traffic and hailed a taxi. The young Chinese driver took me towards the Hotel Kirey. As we passed the Potala I got him to stop and asked a man on the street to take my photo, triumphant for a moment, in front of the monument. Ahead, part of the road was blocked by roadworks so I had to walk the last couple of hundred yards. I must have looked a sight in my black hat and oilskins, with my saddlebags over my shoulder and a great knife still on my belt. Again the Tibetans stared and the several tourists I passed looked away.

After checking in I dropped off most of my gear and went straight to the Jokhang Temple where I made a circuit of the Barkhor pilgrim trail and made prostrations at the main entrance to give thanks for a successful return. I spent the rest of the evening on the street buying some new clothes, as I had nothing clean to put on. It wasn't easy trying to find underwear on the streets of Lhasa at eight o'clock at night, but eventually I managed to end up with a new T-shirt and some army surplus pants and sneakers. Then it was back to the hotel for my first hot shower in over two months. I stood in the hot water groaning with bliss as I scrubbed my body from head to toe. I slipped into clean, cool, comfortable clothes and went out for dinner, a huge meal of French fries, fried rice and sweet Indian tea.

After my first decent sleep in days I managed to leave a message with Tseyang's brother that I was back in Lhasa. Later in the morning she suddenly turned up at the hotel. 'Ian! Welcome back!' And she held out her hand to shake mine. That wasn't enough for me, I threw my arms around the embarrassed girl and hugged her. It was so good to see a friendly, familiar and beautiful face again. Before lunch we went to a telephone office and I called my relieved mother to let her know I was back in the city and safe. That evening Nyima joined us for dinner and a celebratory beer, my first in months.

Everything was in such contrast to the last time I'd arrived back in Lhasa, when I'd been brought in by the police. I'd felt so dejected and broken then, and now I was so contented I couldn't stop smiling. Even Tseyang noticed the change. 'I think your journey was good for you, Ian, you seem like a different person now.'

'Thanks, I guess I am.'

I spent ten days in Lhasa. Most of the time I scheduled my day by deciding what I was going to eat in which restaurant, drinking tea and wandering round the market in the Barkhor. I met Tseyang and Nyima whenever they were free, every evening I said my prayers in front of the main doors of the Jokhang and joined the throngs of Tibetans in *kora* before heading off for dinner and a beer.

One rainy morning I visited the temples inside the Jokhang to see the sacred and famous statue of the Jowo Shakyamuni. I'd visited the temples dozens of times whenever I'd been in Lhasa and while there was a ticket office at the entrance, I'd never once been asked to buy a ticket. It seemed the monks charged tour groups or Chinese tourists but waived the fee for individual travellers. And besides, I'd been told the admission was something imposed by the Chinese authorities, who took most of the takings.

I walked straight up to the entrance but was stopped by a uniformed Tibetan guard who pointed me back towards the ticket office. I shook my head and refused; I'd never had to buy a ticket before and didn't see why I should now. The guard put up some weak resistance but I pushed past him and went inside. The queue to get into the gloomy dim main temple was very long, but standing with the friendly Tibetan pilgrims, excited with anticipation like kids on Christmas morning, made the time pass quickly and I was soon going through the main doors. However, it was here that the festive atmosphere was broken.

Inside, many of the small chapels leading up to the Jowo that had been open two months ago were now closed; pilgrims could see the statues of various saints and Buddhas inside behind ancient chain link curtains but they couldn't go in. Access to the second floor, where there were dozens more rooms, was also shut off, the doors locked and bolted. As the faithful slowly shuffled their way around the great room, half a dozen aggressive guards walked up and down the line, shouting at the frightened country folk, many of whom were probably making their first and perhaps only visit to a city, shoving strays back into place and growling at everyone to keep moving.

I saw one violent scuffle break out between a couple of guards and a group of nomads who tried to push in. People had always pushed in and jumped the queue and while they drew a few frowns and scolds it had never been a problem. The atmosphere in the Jokhang had always been one of jovial friendship as people approached the statue to pay their respects. Certainly Tibetans would never become upset over anything as minor as someone jumping the queue.

Things had changed dramatically. The guards lashed out at the poor family, one young man was knocked to the floor and kicked while another man holding a baby was shoved against a pillar, setting the infant into shrieks. On the other side of the room a Chinese tour party was being shown through; the guide lined her charges in front of one mural and shouted out an explanation of what was being shown, ruining whatever solemnity was left. I looked around at the pilgrims with me; they looked frightened and cowered their heads. For some this should have been the greatest moment of their lives, when they would see their beloved statue face to face for the first and perhaps only time. This was one of the most sacred places in Tibet, but now they looked like scared kids being shouted at by a nasty schoolmaster.

I was saddened. I loved the Jokhang and Tibetan refugees I had met at home were almost in awe when I told them how many times I'd seen the Jowo, knowing they probably never would. I'd always felt honoured and blessed to be there, but as the guards pushed another old man back into line I decided I wouldn't visit again.

During the days I spent in Lhasa I met Tibetans who would confide in me their experiences and feelings towards their Chinese masters. On the surface things looked to be peaceful; outwardly the Chinese and the Tibetans got on well with each other, they worked together or did business with each other, they were polite, even friendly. But you didn't have to scratch very hard to make it bleed; not far below the surface things were rotten.

Chinese were now taking jobs and working in areas that had once been the domain of the Tibetans. Drivers and guides, stallholders, shopkeepers and restaurant managers around the Barkhor and in the Tibetan parts of

Lhasa were now Chinese. There were now enough Chinese in Tibet so that they didn't need the Tibetans any more; they had made their own economy and community and the locals were being forced out into unemployment. Chinese claims of economic benefits were nothing but bullshit; for the most part all the benefits went to the Chinese.

In a little teahouse one day I met a young Tibetan trekking guide who could speak good English. We chatted about my trip and his job, about the warm weather in Lhasa and about how I was one of the few foreigners he'd met who liked butter tea. But it wasn't long before he started talking openly about topics that could have landed him in jail had we been overheard by the wrong ears. He told me that as a child his father had taken him to the local monastery near Shigatze to become a monk. He had taken robes and had spent eleven years with his order, studying the Buddha's teachings and serving the lamas; then one day the Chinese authorities arrived.

The young man told me there had been thirty monks at his *gompa*, but that day the Chinese had told the abbot the rules had changed; from now on the monastery would be restricted to ten monks, the others would have to give up their robes and return to their villages. The man I was sharing tea with had been one of those that had missed out. He smiled and told me he enjoyed his work, but I could tell he was bitter. And this is what the Chinese call freedom of religion.

I tried to find another side to his story; surely the Chinese must have brought some benefits with them. 'There is nothing,' he said, 'the Chinese give us nothing we really want.'

'But why do some Tibetans join the Chinese police?' I asked.

'Because their children want to eat. There are no jobs now.'

'But there must be some Tibetans who want the Chinese to be here?'

'To tell the truth, I believe there is not one Tibetan who really wants the Chinese to be in Tibet. If we really had a choice, we would all want them to go.'

That line of conversation ended there. I didn't want to push the topic further and we were soon talking about lighter subjects. Even Tseyang, who I had thought would be at least more open to the Chinese, found she couldn't really be friends with them, there was always a 'problem' between them. The problem, of course, was that the Chinese had brought her country to the brink of total destruction under Mao and his Cultural Revolution and were still quietly chipping away at what was left. Slowly pulling at the threads one by one until the whole thing would start to unravel and fall apart, until her people would be reduced to a tourist attraction in their own country.

In the Jokhang I reached the glowing statue of the Jowo Shakyamuni. On each side the pilgrims and the curious were allowed to climb a couple of greasy steps to lay *khata* on the statue's lap and touch their heads to the base before being gently guided back into line by firm but friendly monks. Just ahead of me was an old woman with a small child. She was wearing a heavy sheepskin *chuba*, her hair braided, obviously from some faraway valley, the child with a matted dusty mop of hair. She was reciting a prayer and I caught a snatch of it that I recognised.

'*Sem chen tam ched de wa dang . . .*' I'd recited the same prayer before Khensur Thabkye Rinpoche's teachings; the verse prays for the happiness of all sentient beings, that they may be released from suffering and its causes. '. . . *de wai gyu dang den par gyur chig.*'

The old lady gazed up at the radiant face of the Jowo; there were tears in her eyes. She had probably never made a pilgrimage to Kailas, she may not have met a realised lama like the one who had tried to teach me, she probably hadn't even been to formal teachings or meditated, or read a book by the Dalai Lama. I doubted she could even read her own language. But her faith was stronger than mine would ever be, she was so filled with compassion it was spilling over through her eyes. She lifted the toddler and touched his head to the base of the statue as a blessing; the child noticed the foreigner beside him and smiled. Despite the tragedy Tibet had become I thought that if he and others like him could muster the same faith as his grandmother there was still hope.

On the long flight back to New Zealand I couldn't sleep. I flicked through my diary, reading passages I'd written two years before when I'd returned with the book only half-full; now there were only a couple of blank pages. I struggled to decipher my messy scrawl written in my wet tent by candlelight, or pages filled in the last few months, days recorded on nights spent in caves or nomads' homes, but more often alone in empty valleys in the middle of nowhere. I tried to find one that could sum up the whole trip, a dramatic day when I'd thought I wasn't going to make it perhaps. A terrifying river crossing or one of my escapes?

But instead I remembered an afternoon, I couldn't even recall exactly where: I'd crossed a pass and had camped alone in a valley and had been making tea on a fire when a young shepherd girl came past driving her flock. She'd watched me for a while and then approached and asked for a Dalai Lama photo. I didn't have one but she smiled anyway. For a moment I stopped struggling with the smoky fire and looked into her face. She was barely in her teens, but she was beautiful, her eyes huge and bright and I knew she'd soon be a stunner, driving all the boys in her village mad. If she'd been anywhere else in the world she would have been talent-spotted by a model agency already.

In my hip pouch I had a small seashell, like a tiny conch, that I'd found on a beach in New Zealand. I opened my hand and offered it to her; she took it cautiously, as if I was giving her a magic stone that could do evil as well as good. When she saw the object was harmless she turned it over in her hands, smiling with an expression of loveliness and delight that could melt rock.

'Gyam-tsho,' I told her, it's from the sea.

She didn't say a word, just giggled her thanks and gave me a smile that was worth a million little shells and skipped on her way home.

I was left alone in the falling darkness. The wind had died, the sun had gone down and the stars were coming out. My horse grazed quietly next to the small stream as I drank hot tea. The next day I'd tried to find the little beauty's house or tent further down the valley, but she was nowhere to be seen. I remembered I'd ridden all day and not met anyone, except for a pair of oily black crows.